Sex in the City

Sex in the City

Paul Reynolds

PAN BOOKS

First published 2003 by Pan Books
an imprint of Pan Macmillan Ltd
Pan Macmillan, 20 New Wharf Road, London N1 9RR
Basingstoke and Oxford
Associated companies throughout the world
www.panmacmillan.com

ISBN 0 7171 3688 4

1 3 5 7 9 8 6 4 2

A CIP catalogue record for this book is available
from the British Library.

Typeset by Carole Lynch, Dublin
Printed and bound by Nørhaven Paperback A/S, Denmark

All photographs courtesy of RTÉ

Contents

Acknowledgments   vii

Introduction   ix

1. Condy the Country Pimp
   The emergence of Tom McDonnell   1

2. The Vice King of Ireland
   The jailing of Tom McDonnell   27

3. Madam Mean
   The life and death of Marie Bridgeman   48

4. The Lives and Crimes of Spoiled Brats
   *Samantha Blandford Hutton, Stephen Reginald Hutton
   and Karen Leahy's upper-class prostitution business*   72

5. Cobra: The Connoisseurs' Club
   Failed organised orgies   95

6. A Woman of Substance
   Samantha's Brazilian slave labour scam   119

7. Karen the Kidnapper
   The false imprisonment of Charlotte Godkin   141

CONTENTS

8. The Businessman
   *Brian O'Byrne, the first person in Ireland jailed
   for brothel-keeping*   170

9. The Publisher
   Mike Hogan and the In Dublin *advertisements*   192

10. The Man Who Didn't Know
    *Mike Hogan, the first person in Ireland to be convicted
    of advertising brothels*   214

11. Hooker with a Heart
    Justine Reilly and her lucrative 'Caring Agency'   237

12. Professionals, Pretenders and Part-timers
    *The brothels of Arlene Hunt, Antonella Galen, Margaret
    Helly, Teresa Behan, Eileen O'Reilly, Tonja Marshall,
    Keith Thompson and Marion Murphy*   256

13. The Policeman and The Beast
    *The brothels of Peter McCormick and Martin aka
    'The Beast' Morgan*   279

14. The Last CAB and Gladiator Targets
    *Peter McCormick's conviction and his wife Elizabeth's
    money*   298

Conclusion   315

Acknowledgments

This was a strange book to write because it involved investigating the criminal behaviour of some individuals, the financial assets of others, and the sexual preferences and behaviour of many. Sometimes it was funny, other times it was confusing, and many times it was simply sad.

It wasn't an easy book to write, but now that it's complete I believe it is important that people know what is going on. I would like to thank those who helped me on a personal and professional level: my sources without whom this book would never have been started, my family and friends without whom it would never have been finished.

It's not the sort of book you can dedicate to anyone, but those who know me know what they've done, and they also know that I am grateful.

Paul Reynolds
September 2003

Introduction

On Sunday 15 March 1925 the founder of the Legion of Mary, Frank Duff, led a march into the Monto, Dublin's infamous red-light district of the late-19th and early-20th centuries. The procession of hundreds stopped at every brothel and nailed a picture of the Sacred Heart on every door. A priest blessed each house before moving on to the next one. Duff then nailed a large crucifix on the wall of one of buildings. A statue of the Virgin Mary was put up in the area. For the next 70 years Our Lady of Monto watched over the north inner city to make sure nothing so immoral and sinful ever happened there again.

It didn't work. Prostitution is the oldest crime. It was a fact of Irish life before Frank Duff's crusade: it has remained one ever since. There have been women selling their bodies on the streets of major cities for decades. In the 1970s, however, the concept of organised sex for sale re-emerged in Ireland, with women working out of houses and flats in the cities and out of mobile 'passion wagons' in the country. The idea that certain buildings became established brothels first took root in Dublin. Certain houses and flats on Wexford Street and Mountjoy Square became firmly fixed in the minds of men as places where sex could be bought.

Most of the business, however, was conducted on the streets around Fitzwilliam Square, Burlington Road and Benburb Street.

The older and more established prostitutes, who left husbands and children at home to work nights, knew everyone and looked out for each other. They controlled the business largely without the aid of pimps.

The drugs epidemic changed all that. In the 1980s and 1990s, with the huge increase in heroin addiction particularly in the poorer areas of Dublin, the capital's prostitutes were becoming younger and more desperate. Instead of prostituting themselves to feed their families they were now prostituting themselves to feed their drug habits.

In effect, this phenomenon created a two-tiered system. On the one hand there were the young, anxious and usually homeless teenagers who were prepared to do anything for the price of the next fix. More often than not they were accompanied by another addict, an anxious and unstable man, who tended to get violent if the woman wasn't making money. He could and would attack and rob her or the punters. Prostitution was becoming a dangerous game.

At this point many of the older women either got out of the game altogether or moved into brothels. The men followed them. It was cleaner and safer there. With the emergence of the permissive society and the onset of brothel advertising, the fact that sex was now for sale became an open secret. The Government also helped.

The Criminal Law Sexual Offences Act of 1993 made soliciting an offence for both men and women. There was, therefore, less chance of a person being prosecuted in a brothel than on the street. Business boomed and the number of brothels increased dramatically. They attracted a different kind of prostitute and client. The age of the brothel-keeper was born.

Brothel-keepers were a particular type of criminal who specialised in a particular type of crime. They were not hardened or particularly dangerous people. They didn't pose a threat to society at large. They were intelligent and insidious and adept at exploiting the weakest in society. They used their brains more than their fists and they didn't have to use guns or weapons in the course of their activities.

They comprised a particular type of criminal community. They weren't competitive. There were no turf wars. They had no need for gangs of heavies. There was a huge demand for what they were selling, with more than enough business for everyone to go round. There was no hostility or begrudgery among them and they had no problem with each other's operations. There was no need for protection rackets and no violence between them; they never moved to stop someone else starting up. They all knew each other and they were all making a fortune.

The type of individuals involved in organised prostitution provides an insight into the warped mentality of the criminal underworld. Vice was seen as a 'ponce or a softie's game' and no self-respecting, tough, underworld criminal wanted to be known as a ponce or a pimp. It wasn't 'a man's game', like armed robbery, drug dealing, shootings, stabbings, contract killings and murder. The brothel-keepers were, therefore, entrepreneurs who saw a gap in the criminal market. They found they could make money without interfering with or upsetting their more violent and dangerous counterparts in organised crime.

Prostitution required a certain amount of intelligence and interpersonal skills for which the average underworld criminal is not renowned. Most would not have the ability to deal with the women and their problems. Most would have neither the wit to be able to set up such a criminal organisation nor the discipline to mind and manage it on an ongoing basis. Most wouldn't have the patience for criminal activity that is not of the short-sharp-shock variety. Most wouldn't be able subtly to avoid the attentions of the Gardaí and to deal with the customers using tact and discretion. Most operate in the underworld and would be unable to deal with people necessary to the survival of the business, such as advertisers and landlords who live in the real world.

The subversives weren't involved in prostitution either but, unlike regular criminals, not because of any lack of ability. It was their warped sense of morality that kept them away from it. Freedom fighters couldn't be involved in anything so sordid and seedy. Paramilitarism on both sides, loyalist and nationalist, has always been inextricably tied in to either the Catholic or Protestant faiths. Religion and sex don't — or at least aren't supposed to — mix. Paramilitaries would never officially sanction involvement in prostitution. Whatever about extorting money from those who operate the business, subversives wouldn't run the brothels themselves.

So with gangland criminals and subversive operatives out of the way, the brothel-keepers had a free run in this part of the criminal underworld. But they were also opportunists, damaged individuals, people with serious personal, social or sexual problems who couldn't or wouldn't do a normal day's work. Most were immature, greedy, selfish, childish and incapable of taking responsibility. They couldn't accept that their actions often had tragic consequences. They were misfits who lived by night like cats. They tended to be violent only with the women.

Some brothel-keepers found they could ingratiate themselves with the criminal underworld by providing complimentary sexual services. But they were still criminals doing a dirty job and earning dirty money. Some tried to clothe themselves in a veneer of respectability and claim that what they were doing was, or at least should be, legal and socially acceptable. These were the campaigners who claimed to be providing a necessary and desired social service. Other brothel-keepers were former prostitutes. Like abuse victims who in turn become sex offenders, those women who had themselves been exploited as prostitutes went on in turn to exploit others.

Just as not every criminal could be a brothel-keeper, not every prostitute could work in a brothel. It took a particular type of woman with discipline, patience and some style. While heroin and cocaine were the main drugs used by women on the streets, the women in brothels tended to be addicted to alcohol and, to a lesser extent, cocaine.

Brothel-keeping was illegal but that didn't stop a number of specialist individuals embarking on it as a career. It made millions for them. This criminal activity was widely known about and generally ignored until the murders of two prostitutes. The deaths of Belinda Pereira and Sinéad Kelly highlighted the vulnerability of the women, and the violent and dangerous nature of the business. No one has ever been caught or convicted for either crime.

The murder investigations did, however, give the Gardaí a valuable insight into the operation of a hitherto largely unknown dimension of the criminal underworld. They discovered how the business worked and identified the main players involved. Some had already been convicted but were still in business. By 1999 the criminal activity of the brothel-keepers could no longer be ignored, largely because of the high level of media interest and the actions of the Censorship of Publications Board. 'Operation Gladiator' was set up to put them out of business.

There are no definitive figures for the number of women currently involved in prostitution. Estimates from the charities and Health Boards put the figure at between 600 and 750 in Dublin alone. But these figures represent only those women who are known and are in touch with services. It could easily be twice or three times that amount.

The reasons why women end up as prostitutes are complex and varied: social, psychological and economic. They range from poverty and addiction to abuse and coercion. In some cases it's a question of self-esteem, a belief that it's actually something they're good at. In others it's a rationalisation of prostitution as a business transaction, at the end of which both parties are satisfied.

Much of the debate about prostitution ignores the reality of the criminal enterprise. Prostitution is essentially about the sexual exploitation of women and men for the financial gain of the operators and the gratification of customers. Prostitutes are essentially damaged people who have drifted or been forced into an illegal activity. They are used and abused. The sex industry harms people. The criminal sex industry more so. The fundamental truth is that prostitutes would not be able to operate without demand. Women would not walk the streets or hang around in brothels if men who are prepared to pay for sex didn't show up.

This book explains how the organised prostitution rackets work in this country. It does so through the lives and activities of the main people involved. It maps the origins and development of their enterprises and charts the growth of their multi-million pound businesses. It identifies the people at the top who ran the brothels, the types of women they employed and the individuals who supported their criminal operations. It shows why some women take what is almost always a drastic step. The men and women on both sides of prostitution come from every social class and all walks of life. Wealthy middle- and upper-class professionals such as doctors, lawyers, businessmen and priests have all paid to have sex with prostitutes in brothels, in their offices or in their own homes.

And it's not just sex with women and men they seek. There is a disturbing demand in Irish society for sex with young teenagers and children. The extent of interest in paedophile material is clear from the scale of the Garda 'Operation Amethyst', which is investigating those suspected of downloading child pornography from the Internet. It arose out of 'Operation Landslide', the US investigation into the Internet child porn king, Thomas Reedy. Child pornography and child prostitution are lucrative, international, criminal enterprises.

Those charged here include a judge, a choirmaster, a teacher and a lecturer. Those convicted so far include the TV chef, Tim Allen, and the former Progressive Democrats councillor, Alan Robinson. Those found guilty were shown to have been part of a paedophile network of over 250,000 people in more than 60 countries. They subscribed to an Internet child pornography business that was grossing up to $1.4 million a month. They were paying to see pictures of children abused and raped — and therefore paying people to abuse and rape them.

In 1997 an Eastern Health Board study found that 57 boys and girls were working as prostitutes. A 14-year-old child prostitute was found in one Dublin brothel. Hundreds of men paid to have sex with her. Two members of the Garda Síochána approached brothels and prostitutes in 1999 and 2001 — while they were serving in the force — looking for sex with children. Kieran O'Halloran, who had himself been raped as a teenager, and Gerard Lynch were both caught and sent to prison. The link between the vice trade, prostitution and paedophilia cannot be ignored.

This book outlines the changes in society that allowed such a lucrative criminal activity to take root and grow. It highlights Irish society's ambivalence and prudery, its uneasiness with sex in general and sex crime in particular. It reflects an unwillingness at many levels to face up to and tackle a problem which has flourished here for centuries and continues to flourish here because it has been ignored. The entrepreneurial spirit of those criminals behind the brothel business in the 1990s was not out of step with the Ireland of the Celtic Tiger.

Prostitution is big business. It is estimated to be worth at least €10 billion a year worldwide, £750 million sterling a year in Britain. There are no definitive figures for Ireland but based on these figures and the amounts that brothels-keepers alone earn, it must be worth at least a tenth of that here. Very few of the women involved see much of that money. Most are as poor and as destitute 'on the game' as they are off it and have very little to show at the end of it all. The happy hooker with a big heart and a fat wallet is a fantasy promoted by men who use women, whether as customers, pimps, promoters or apologists for the sex industry. Those who survive it do so by treating it for what it is — a cruel, ruthless, impersonal, damaging and dangerous business.

This book is an exploration in an accessible form of a shady subculture. It is an attempt to shine a light into a criminal underworld which most people know little about. It is not a moral crusade and it does not propose to sit in judgment of any of the individuals involved. In most cases the courts have already done that.

1 Condy the Country Pimp

Tom McDonnell felt aggrieved. He was in the back of an unmarked Garda car on his way to Store Street Station. He'd been through this drill before: the raid, the arrest, the questions — but ultimately the release back to business. He'd even been charged and convicted previously but he only had to make a donation to a women's refuge. He'd been ordered to pay £4,500 and do eleven days community service.

McDonnell had been in this business for twenty years. Along with the Gardaí, there were others who caused him problems by interfering with him. Rival criminals wanted to take over his operation. Paramilitary organisations leaned on him for protection money. Tom McDonnell had come through it all. He'd been threatened, chased, attacked, shot at, and shot and wounded but he was still in business. He was still very much alive.

This morning's arrest was just another occupational hazard, albeit an irritating one. It had disrupted his business. He was a bit upset. He had bills to pay. 'Why are you trying to close me down?' he complained to John McMahon, the detective inspector who was in the car with him. 'I owe CAB £1.8m. I'm trying to make a few bob to pay it back and you are trying to close me down.'

McDonnell then reminded McMahon that they had met before in Store Street during the Belinda Pereira murder enquiry. Belinda Pereira was a London-based prostitute of Malaysian origin who was found dead in a flat at Mellor Court in Dublin city centre on 29 December 1996. She came to Ireland to work over Christmas. She was alone in a foreign country and she was vulnerable. She was beaten and strangled to death. The prime suspects for her murder are two pimps from Monaghan but there's not enough evidence to bring a prosecution against them. McDonnell asked McMahon if the killers had ever been caught. McMahon told him they hadn't been.

The Gardaí had kept McDonnell under surveillance for months but he continued to protest all the way to Store Street. 'I run a good place,' he said. 'I have a fellow in there keeping an eye on the girls at night.' Tom had seen the 1994 Dublin-registered van from which the Gardaí used to watch the brothel. He knew they were on to him and he told them this in no uncertain fashion. 'So if you knew,' McMahon said to him, 'why didn't you shut the place?' 'I knew you wouldn't shoot me,' he replied.

'Operation Gladiator' had begun. It was set up on 17 August 1999 after the Garda Commissioner, Pat Byrne, ordered an investigation into prostitution. The targets were not the women or their customers, but the people at the top, the people who organised, controlled and profited from prostitution. The investigation was based at the headquarters of the National Bureau of Criminal Investigation in Dublin.

Gladiator was billed as a nation-wide clampdown but in reality it was confined to the capital. Its first target was one of the longest established, richest and most successful brothel-keepers in the country. Tom McDonnell had made millions from prostitution; numerous attempts to close him down or put him in jail had failed. This was the first time a dedicated team had been set up to go after him and others like him.

Thomas 'Milking Parlour' McDonnell was born in the little village of Cooraclare, near Kilrush in West Clare on 29 January 1952. He grew up in a place called Pigs Elbow with his sister Mary, his mother Eileen (*née* Lillis) and his father Tom senior. His father was the fireman at the local creamery and Tom junior inherited his nickname from his father's occupation. He went to the national school in Cooraclare and as a teenager he worked for a time in the timber mills in Kilrush before moving to England in 1971.

At nineteen years of age Tom had ambitions to become a long-distance lorry driver but got a job in London as a builder's labourer. There he saw and experienced a thriving and vibrant vice scene. He spent his money on prostitutes and visited brothels. He saw how much money was to be made in the sex industry and how easy it was to make it. But Tom didn't learn all the tricks of his trade in London and he didn't — as they say in West Clare — 'lick it off the stone' either. The business was already in Tom's blood: he'd inherited it from his father who knew all about abusing women and children.

Tom McDonnell senior was involved during the early 1980s in the running of what the locals referred to as the 'West Clare passion wagon'. The mobile brothel consisted of a Hiace van with a mattress in the back. It serviced customers on the Loop Head Peninsula passing through towns like Kilkee, Carrigaholt and Kilbaha. Tom was likened to an A.I. man — but for farmers rather than their animals. He ran the van in conjunction with a local criminal gang and, while the farmers were otherwise occupied, the gang robbed their houses. It was difficult for customers to report the crimes because they couldn't say where they were when their homes were being burgled!

However, the Gardaí heard about the scam and began an investigation. One of the gang was arrested and charged. Twenty-seven-year-old Anthony Kelly from Kilrush had convictions already for common assault and stealing the cover off a lorry. On 9 February 1984 he was convicted of living off immoral earnings and sentenced to nine months in Cork Prison. Tom senior was never charged but his role in the affair gained him the new nickname — 'Condy'. This was the name given in Clare to a small, agile, virile horse renowned throughout the county for siring sturdy foals. Tom McDonnell senior was said to have a similar prowess.

In later years Condy's son provided prostitutes for his father. Tom junior arrived down for one of his father's birthday parties in a fleet of helicopters, with a jazz band and a couple of women. On another occasion he arrived in Cooraclare in a white suit and took his father away. A group of local people watched the old man, dressed in his best suit and carrying an overnight bag, take off in the helicopter. The talk was that he was going to Dublin to help Tom 'interview' prospective female employees. 'Isn't that the best yet,' one of the local women remarked, 'old Condy up in a helicopter.' 'Well,' replied one of the wags, 'he's been up on everything else.'

Eileen Lillis, Tom's mother, is remembered in West Clare as a decent woman from a decent family. This is in marked contrast to her husband who is bitterly remembered by certain adults today for his cruelty to them as children. Some of them swam in the Cooraclare River at Poll na gCapall and remember Tom holding their heads under the water and telling them it was the only way they'd learn to swim. In the mornings before they went to school, children were sent to the creamery with tin cans to collect sour milk for baking bread. Tom would humiliate them if there was an audience. 'Tom was up on a platform,' one man recalls. 'He could pour it in without spilling a drop but if the farmers were watching he'd pour it all over you and you'd go to school with the smell of sour milk all over your clothes for the day.'

Tom McDonnell senior was unfaithful during his marriage. When Eileen died, the local people believed that he would marry his mistress, 'Mrs Mac'. But 'Old Condy' took up with her daughter instead. Tom junior wasn't very pleased when his father started going out with a woman so much younger than himself. He had rebuilt his home for him, an old blacksmith's house in the village, and he wasn't happy to see Elizabeth McNamara move into it. However, his father ignored him and there was nothing Tom junior could do about it.

But Tom senior was also a suspected paedophile and when that scandal broke his son couldn't ignore it. On 3 September 1999 the first of three women went to the Gardaí and complained that Tom had abused her as a child. He had offered her sweets, took her to a shed behind the creamery and molested her until she cried. She was four years old. The abuse continued until she was eleven. 'Every time I came down the road to the village,' she said, 'Thomas McDonnell was waiting for me. He could appear out of anywhere.'

Tom did an egg run and took the child with him for spins in the car. His wife was a friend of the child's mother and Tom was trusted. In classic paedophile fashion it was a parental trust that he was to breach again and again. The child's grandmother, however, noticed she was distressed after one such journey and she never went in the car with him again. But the abuse continued in a neighbour's shed in the fields behind her home and in his own home while his wife was ill. Tom molested the girl in front of the fire while Eileen Lillis lay dying in the bedroom.

The national school was near the creamery and Tom waited and watched the children coming home. It may have looked like a game when he ran after them and grabbed them but it was frightening when he brought them inside. When it was finally brought to the attention of one girl's father, he remembered McDonnell doing the same to young girls in the 1950s. 'I remember Tom McDonnell putting young girls into the creamery where he worked and locking the doors behind them,' he told the Gardaí. 'I didn't know what was happening. I was only a young lad.'

The allegations were investigated and it was established that there was substance to them. The Director of Public Prosecutions directed that Tom McDonnell senior be prosecuted for child abuse. He was arrested and brought before Ennis District Court on 24 charges of indecently assaulting one of the children between 1976 and 1981. The charges were so serious that the judge refused to accept jurisdiction and Tom was sent forward for trial to the Circuit Court on 5 May 1998.

The following year he was again arrested, charged and sent forward to the Circuit Court. This time he faced twenty more counts of abusing the two other children during the 1970s and 1980s. It emerged subsequently that he had also abused at least ten more women in the area when they were children. They hadn't made complaints to the Gardaí. One of them was fourteen when he trapped her in the creamery tank but she managed to escape before he raped her. Another was the daughter of a man who took in the McDonnell family when a storm blew the roof off their house. Tom and Eileen and the two children, Tom junior and Mary, stayed with the family for six weeks. 'That's how he repaid us,' the man said bitterly, 'by abusing my daughter.'

On 26 June 1999 Tom senior was arraigned on ten sample charges; he pleaded not guilty. The victims couldn't remember the precise dates on which the abuse took place and some witnesses were too frightened to turn up to give evidence. The case against McDonnell collapsed and the judge directed he be found not guilty. However, he still faced the 24 charges of abusing the first girl so he adapted the tactic used by many others to avoid a criminal trial — he applied to the High Court for a judicial review.

Many convicted paedophiles have first applied to the High and the Supreme Courts to have prosecutions for child abuse against them stopped, claiming, for example, that the offences alleged are so long ago they wouldn't be able to get a fair trial. Most of these cases fail and in Tom senior's case it was seen as a delaying tactic. In the meantime the girl's father got a call from Tom McDonnell junior. He asked to meet him and offered him money to drop the charges. No figure was mentioned but Tom insisted the girl should be compensated. 'I told him I wouldn't be having any of his brothel-keeping money,' the girl's father said. 'I told him I want your father behind bars and your brothel-keeping money won't keep him out.'

The man made a complaint to his local Garda station about the approach. A week later he got a call from the detectives in charge of the case. They told him that Tom McDonnell junior would never contact him again and he didn't. In the meantime the case trundled on. There were submissions put forward about Tom's age, memory and health. Twenty-three years had passed between the date of the last alleged offence and the date he was charged. Tom senior said he could not locate witnesses. There were numerous adjournments and at least two postponements. One was because there was no judge available even though the family and the Gardaí had travelled to Dublin from Clare. 'We waited two years after first reporting McDonnell,' one of the parents said, 'and that was the closest we got to nailing the bastard. The legal system failed us.'

Neither the family nor their daughter, his victim, ever had the satisfaction of facing their accuser and calling him to account. The public never found out whether or not Tom senior abused the children. He was neither acquitted nor convicted. He died in October 2000 before the court proceedings ended. He was still living with Elizabeth McNamara but, thinking she was off with another man, he went out to look for her and had a heart attack at the wheel. The car crashed into a ditch near Kilrush and Thomas McDonnell senior died later in hospital. He was 73 years old.

Tom junior came back to Clare to bury his father and then booted Elizabeth McNamara out of the house. 'I was going anyway,' she said. 'I'd take no notice of him. I wouldn't want to stay there.' On 17 October 2000 the 24 child abuse charges against Tom senior were formally struck out. His victims are still not at peace. 'She'll never be OK,' one man says of his 30-year-old daughter. 'She has no confidence or no self-esteem. She's now living in England. She's hanging in there but she's not great. He really destroyed her life.'

Tom junior's life of sexual exploitation began when he returned to Ireland. He used both the building and the brothel skills he learned in England. He refurbished old houses and set up shop in Capel Street selling sex trinkets and pornographic magazines. A violent man, he was sentenced to two years in prison on 24 June 1983 for assault. It was his first conviction in the Dublin Circuit Court and his first appearance before a judge in seven years. His previous crimes had been of a minor nature and were dealt with at district court level. In just over a year between April 1975 and May 1976 he was convicted of assault, breaking and entering, larceny and being drunk and disorderly, but the most he ever got was six months in Mountjoy.

By the mid-1980s Tom McDonnell was a serious criminal with serious connections. His first brothel was in the shop in Capel Street. He set up 'Eureka' in 1984. The business prospered, Tom expanded; he was at one time running five brothels simultaneously, including one near O'Connell Street in property owned by a politician's son. In July 1988 he rented a house in South William Street and set up 'The New Mayfair Studio'. He put in a telephone and the brothel was advertised in *In Dublin* with a contact landline number.

The following year he rented a house off Lad Lane in Dublin and for the next seven years ran 'The New Imperial' brothel from there. It was advertised in *Dublin Diary* as well as *In Dublin*, again with a landline telephone number. The landlord found out that Tom was using his property as a brothel but when he tried to evict him, Tom sent a 'heavy' around. The landlord was warned to stay away and he did until Tom moved out in May 1996. In the late 1980s–early 1990s he was earning thousands every week from the men who went to his brothels.

Tom ordered some of the women who worked for him to have sex with his criminal associates. 'He made us service his friends for free,' one of them said. 'Some of them are big-time criminals, I won't tell you who they are. Tom used to say that he would get them to make us disappear if we ever talked to the papers or the police.'

From early on Tom signalled his intention to modernise Ireland's fledgling prostitution industry. He was the first criminal to bring the selling of sex out of the back alleys of Benburb Street and Leeson Street and run it as a professional commercial business. He operated a system that was a testament to his organisational skills and kept himself, his clients and his prostitutes in business. It was a blueprint for organised prostitution in Ireland and was subsequently copied by every major brothel-keeper in the country.

In October 1989 Tom bought a place in Richmond Hill in Rathmines in Dublin in the name of Anthony McDonnell. It was a single-storey terraced house with a basement and Tom set about customising it into a brothel. He locked up the basement and created three rooms or cubicles on the ground floor. In each room he installed a shower in the corner. The furniture consisted of a table, a chair, a couch and a television. There were two mirrors over each couch. Each one was the length of the couch. One was on the wall beside the couch, the other hung parallel from the ceiling directly above it. Star-crossed lovers could watch themselves in action from all angles.

All the televisions were connected to a video recorder which played pornographic movies, no doubt to encourage, arouse or even educate the clients. The kitchen at the back of the house was Tom's office. The movies were played out to the rooms from the video machine there. There was also a stereo system in the kitchen which piped music throughout the house. Tom was clearly conscious of the need to create mood and atmosphere. The lighting was suitably dim and red, or in the language of the business, 'subdued'. Tom supplied the clients with towels that were collected and laundered every week by a professional cleaning company. He had an account with Celtic Linen under the name of Pleasant Place and the van driver was paid in cash or by cheque on delivery.

Security was designed with discretion in mind. Tom was keenly aware of the need to protect the women, scrutinise the punters and keep out the Gardaí. He put a halogen light in the tree in the front garden. It came on when anyone approached. He also put a video camera in the tree and trained it on the path. The black-and-white monitor was kept in the kitchen so anyone inside could see what was happening outside by glancing at the screen.

He also installed a double door system. The first door was left closed but unlocked and on the latch. The sign on it said 'push'. The second door had two locks, one of which was a deadbolt. To get through this you had to press the intercom and ask to come in. Both doors had spyholes. The person inside could see out but couldn't be seen. Tom called it the 'New Pleasure Palace'. It was functional but sophisticated and operated with great success for four months before the Gardaí took an interest in it. The neighbours complained after they got tired of punters calling in, mistaking their homes for the brothel.

The 'New Pleasure Palace' was first raided on 24 February 1990. The Gardaí found whips, leather lingerie, handcuffs, pornographic videos, used condoms, tissues, cash and semen-stained towels. They also found evidence of Tom's *modus operandi*, rosters for the women's shifts and receipt sheets for the income. Tom made sure he made the most money from the business: his prostitutes charged £25 and gave him £15 of it. He wasn't arrested but agreed to be interviewed by the Gardaí a week later. It didn't bother him. If the raid was a warning, he didn't care. He stayed in business and they had to go after him a second time. They set up a surveillance operation and raided the brothel again a month later.

The second search, on 6 April, was akin to a pantomime. Eight Gardaí, all big men, including a photographer from the Technical Bureau, arrived at the first door and pushed it in. Seven waited at the side while one stood in front of the peep-hole posing as a customer. When one of the women, Angela, opened the door wearing only a black slip and tights, the search party rushed in.

Angela ran — bare breasts exposed — to the back of the house, with some of the Gardaí in hot pursuit. Another Garda opened the first door on the left and a 20-year-old woman ran out past him leaving behind a naked man in a very compromising position on the couch. Three Gardaí including the photographer then crowded into that room. Detective Sergeant William Hogan immediately snapped a photograph of the man before he could hide his embarrassment or get dressed.

'He was completely naked and was lying on his side. He had a penile erection,' Detective Garda George Trennier observed. 'I asked him the reason for him being there and why he was naked. He indicated that he was getting treatment for a football injury. I noticed he had what seemed to be a seminal discharge on the end of his penis. I brought this to his notice and he made no reply.' In the meantime three other men managed to get away.

The Gardaí searched the brothel for nearly two hours. They found more evidence of sexual activity — condoms, lubricating cream, tissues, towels and four more pornographic videos. Tom had replaced the five they seized the first time round. 'There was no story format attached to the tapes,' the inspector in charge, Edward Rock, said. 'They contained nothing other than explicit scenes of sexual activity.'

The interviews with Tom and the two women working in the brothel that night yielded little. 'There's no sex going on in the place,' Tom told the Gardaí. 'Can you account for the traces of semen we found on the towels we seized on 6 April?' Eddie Rock asked him. 'No comment,' he replied. The videos he said were only 'fantasy things'. He said he knew nothing about the handcuffs and he wouldn't comment on the whips. 'You are writing these,' he complained as the Gardaí took notes of what he said. 'I won't sign anything.' And he didn't.

Angela from the inner city didn't make a statement to the Gardaí, while Patricia from Kilbarrack claimed she was hired as a masseur after she answered an advertisement in the *Dublin Diary*. She said she was paid a basic wage of £100 a week. She was, however, more worried about potential publicity than the criminal consequences of her arrest. 'What's going to happen to the photographs?' she asked. 'Will they be given to the *Sunday World*? My mother knows what I'm doing but I don't want it in the *Sunday World*.'

In spite of lack of co-operation and the absence of admissions, the Director of Public Prosecutions decided there was still enough evidence to move against Tom McDonnell. He was charged with keeping a brothel between 24 February and 6 April 1990 contrary to Section 13(1)(a) of the Criminal Law Amendment Act 1935. As he was arrested and led away he threw the keys of the brothel to one of the women and said 'Keep her going.' He was brought to court and remanded to Mountjoy Jail. He wasn't there for long before he was released on bail, and it was over a year before the case came up for trial.

On 27 June 1991 Tom pleaded guilty to one of the charges and was given a four-month suspended sentence. He was also bound to the peace for a year and a half, told to do 100 hours community service and ordered to pay £4,500 to a Women's Aid refuge. It was Tom's first conviction for brothel-keeping but it didn't deter him. He walked out of court and went straight back to his booming business. He sold the house in Rathmines and moved on. He later followed a similar pattern with the 'New Fantasy Club' on Upper Stephen's Street. It opened in 1994 but was raided in February 1996 so three months later he closed it and moved on.

Tom was making so much money in the 1990s that he didn't know what to do with it. He lost money after investing in a pornographic magazine in 1991 but continued to spend like it was going out of fashion. He returned to the old homestead a wealthy and extravagant man. He knocked down old Condy's house in West Clare and built a brand new bungalow on the site. He bought a mobile home and put it in the garden for his father and mistress to live in while the building work was carried out. He put in the best furniture and fittings and then bought Condy a new car, a Volvo. He hired helicopters from Ciaran Haughey's company Celtic Helicopters to fly him down and back. He boasted that he once shared a helicopter with the Formula One boss Eddie Jordan. The helicopters landed in the field behind Tubridy's pub in Cooraclare. When the bungalow was finished he put in a helipad on land at the back.

In 1993 he bought his own helicopter, a Bell 206B Jet Ranger, the most common single-engine helicopter in Ireland and the most popular among businessmen. It could only carry up to five people so he continued to hire other choppers to ferry his friends and some of the women who worked for him from Dublin to Clare. Locals remember them flying over the fields and arriving in convoy like a scene from the movie *Apocalypse Now*. Tom partied in the pubs of West Clare and bought drink for anyone who wanted it. His proud father partied with the farmers while abusing their children behind their backs. The local boy had made good.

Tom's arrogance, extravagance and willingness to flaunt his considerable wealth did not go unnoticed. It wasn't only the Gardaí and people of West Clare who were watching. Dangerous criminals began to take an unhealthy interest in his affairs: unhealthy, that is, for Tom. Michael Travers told him he'd burn his brothels down but didn't get a chance to. He was shot dead in Darndale, on Dublin's northside, on 12 July 1992. P.J. Judge, the man known as 'The Psycho', also saw how easily Tom was making money and he decided to move into prostitution. But Judge didn't want to go to all that bother of setting up his own network of brothels and women, so he decided to adapt a practice common in business — the hostile take-over.

P.J.'s methods were far more bloody and brutal than those of the stock market. He informed McDonnell that he was quite simply taking over his operation. McDonnell was terrified but felt he had no option but to resist — and that raised Judge's ire. A few weeks later Tom was drinking in Clarke's pub in Camden Street when a man walked in, sat down beside him and produced a semi-automatic pistol. 'P.J. Judge says you have to hand over your whole operation,' he told him, 'or else!'

Tom stayed silent for a minute. Suddenly he leaped to his feet and turned the table of drinks over on the gunman. He headed out the pub door at speed with the hitman scrambling after him. Witnesses said he fired at least one shot at Tom but missed. Tom got away with his life. He also held on to his business because, like Michael Travers, P.J. Judge didn't live long enough either to damage it or take it over. He was shot twice in the back of the head in the car-park of the Royal Oak pub in Finglas in the early hours of 8 December 1996, just as he was about to start his car. It was the same year that one of Tom's longest-serving employees went to work for him — Liz stayed with him for nearly five years.

Liz was a 35-year-old married woman who lived with her husband and three children in Tallaght. In 1995 the business that they had struggled with for years finally collapsed. The couple were broke. They lost their house. They separated and Liz, with two young children and pregnant with their third, was forced to move to a hostel for homeless women. The Haven House on Morning Star Avenue was no place for children.

Just days before her third child was born, Dublin Corporation offered her a house in West Dublin. She left the hostel, gave birth to a baby boy and gradually she and her husband got back together. Times were still hard. 'It was still very tough financially,' she remembers, 'I never had any money to spare and I had three children.' They struggled on for another few months but they couldn't make ends meet so the following year, 1996, Liz became a prostitute.

It was unbearable poverty that pushed Liz towards prostitution but it was the publicity surrounding it that made her finally decide to cross the line. She said she made her decision 'after reading the papers, especially papers like the *Sunday World* who had big articles about it and the big money that was supposed to be made'. In August she bought a copy of *In Dublin* magazine, saw the 'staff required' advertisement for the Mayfair and the New Mayfair, and rang the number. 'I thought about it for a long while whether or not I'd ring but because I'd so little money one day I phoned the number. A girl on the phone told me to come in that day and start at half four.'

Liz's first job was in the New Mayfair Studio on South William Street. The women working there told her how it operated. The woman brought the punter to a room, went back to the sitting room, wrote the details in the book and put £20 in a box. This was the house money or booking fee and it went straight into Tom McDonnell's pocket. Then the woman went back to the room and offered the punter his choice of sexual service — £25 for hand relief, £35 for oral sex and £40 for full sex.

'In those days what happened was that when a client called to the door he paid £20 for "a booking fee",' she said. 'When you finished you'd get the money from the client depending on the service provided.' But Tom McDonnell always got his £20 for every customer and he always got his money first, the minute a customer walked in the door. 'All the house money went to Tom McDonnell,' Clare, another woman at the brothel, said. 'I often saw him taking the cash from the box in South William Street.'

From day one Liz knew that Tom McDonnell was running the place. She was quickly introduced to his unique style of assessing women to determine whether or not he would allow them prostitute themselves in his brothels. He didn't interview them — he simply had sex with them, whether they liked it or not. Indeed their feelings about it were irrelevant. If he didn't like it, they didn't get the job. 'He would have been my second or third client and it was always his decision to keep the girls or not,' Liz said. 'He decided only when he had been with the girl himself.'

Rape or sexual abuse is about power — not sex. McDonnell's sexual abuse of the women had more to do with control than pleasure. He was letting them know that if they worked for him, they belonged to him. He was reminding them of their own vulnerability. He was showing them he could do what he liked with them; that what was theirs was his, no matter who they were or who else they were with, whether they had boyfriends, girlfriends, husbands or children. It was a definitive statement made in the most direct and invasive fashion that left some of them subjugated and humiliated — but all in no doubt as to who was in charge. It wasn't only Tom McDonnell's clients who were sleazy.

Four women worked in the brothel. McDonnell's management style at that time was very much hands-on. He sat in South William Street each evening. Up to 30 men called in every day. If someone rang up looking for a job they were told to come in. 'We'd meet them and if they were half decent, we'd tell them to start on the next free shift,' Liz said. 'Then he (Tom) would come in as a customer and then he'd be with them and he'd decide if they stay or go. We were always short for staff so we were hoping they'd stay.' Tom didn't let on who he was and he certainly didn't pay but the women always found out they'd been with the boss. There was a price to be paid for working for McDonnell.

One day in December 1996 he handed Liz a set of keys and told her she was moving. He had transferred The New Imperial brothel from the rented house off Lad Lane to the new house he had bought at Grattan Street, just down the road from Holles Street Maternity Hospital. Liz went to work there with two Spanish prostitutes, Lydia and Clara. They operated the same system as South William Street and charged the same prices for the same range of services. McDonnell owned the house and lived there. 'In those days when you'd arrive in the mornings McDonnell would be in bed,' Liz said.

Tom employed a large number of the capital's prostitutes. More than 30 women worked in Grattan Street between December 1996 and February 2000. Some lasted only a day, others like Liz were in it for years. Business varied and that determined the women's work patterns. 'Sometimes you'd work every third day and sometimes you could be working thirteen days in a row,' she said. But while Tom always got paid, some clients had discovered a way to beat the system and leave the women short. They walked in, paid the £20 house money and, once sexually satisfied, left without paying the rest. This was the woman's £40. 'McDonnell would get his money but we wouldn't,' Clara said.

For years the women wrote these off as bad debts or occupational hazards. However, one Australian prostitute with international experience was used to dealing with what she called 'these kinds of stiffs'. She changed the system in Grattan Street in 1998. She streamlined the charges to a set fee for all sexual acts. She also introduced a time limit and simplified the collection system so that all the women got paid in advance. The flat rate was the same no matter what they did and the money was handed over before they did anything.

'We'd charge £60 for the half hour,' Liz said. 'The £60 would be taken from the client when he first came in. The £20 "booking in fee" still went to McDonnell but we were guaranteed £40 for ourselves.' The women wrote on time sheets their own names and the times the client came and went. The sheets were kept on a clipboard in the sitting room and each day began with a blank one.

Tom collected his money at the end of each shift. If for some reason he didn't show up, it was wrapped in the time sheet which was sellotaped and left in the teapot for him. McDonnell didn't need to be an accountant to make sure the woman weren't on the take. He only had to make sure he had £20 for each woman's name on the sheet. 'Nobody ever left the premises with money belonging to Tom McDonnell,' Lydia said.

Grattan Street was advertised in *In Dublin* as a massage parlour and health studio. Readers were invited to 'visit our New Luxury Studio for that Professional Touch and Personal Service'. They were informed that 'all facilities (were) catered for'. It wasn't particularly difficult to figure out what that meant. Most of the clients first found out about the brothels in the magazine. The rest heard about them from friends who'd been there. It wasn't difficult to find the brothels either. Addresses and phone numbers were given in the advertisements.

Grattan Street was a two-storey house with a steel-plated door. There was a camera hidden in the red alarm box on the wall outside which monitored the entrance. Another one inside covered the hall. There was also a spyhole on the front door and an intercom beside it. The television monitors were in the sitting room. The punters were on video from the time they walked up and rang the doorbell until they got into a bedroom. The system was only used in real time. It did not record customers and Tom didn't make any tapes. The women sat in the sitting room watching the customers call. If they were suspicious of any of them they didn't have to let them in. In fact few were turned away. The main reason for a refusal was a lack of money and an unwillingness by the women to negotiate a price. Most of these customers arrived back with the cash ten or fifteen minutes later after a trip to the nearest bank machine. There was a post box just inside the main door. It was always locked. Tom was the only one with a key. He collected the letters, and paid the ESB and telephone bills.

There were five bedrooms in the house but only four were in use — two of the three upstairs and the two downstairs. The fifth was Tom's bedroom. It was off limits to all. The customer was taken to one of the four rooms, although only one of them had a bed in it. In keeping with the massage parlour front, each had a shower, a chair and a padded bench. There was also massage oil, a box of tissues and talcum powder — either lavender or primrose depending on which room you got. In two of the rooms there were white coats hanging on the back of the doors. Tom kept a whip and a PVC skirt in his room. It wasn't clear whether they were for business or personal use.

All the women had keys for the door and gate at the front. In the morning the first woman in opened up and took the first customer. The second woman in took the second customer and so on through the shift. The woman brought the man to a room, told him to have a shower and lie on the bench. In the meantime she went back to the sitting room, filled in the sheet and put £20 of the £60 in the milk carton on the mantelpiece. After six clients, the £120 was put into the silver teapot, which was kept in the press by the video monitor. McDonnell didn't want large amounts of his cash left out in the open. The brothel was robbed a few times and he could hardly claim on insurance or call the Gardaí.

'We'd then go back to the client and give him a massage for a few minutes and then we would provide a sexual service that would include hand relief, oral sex or full sexual intercourse,' Liz said. 'On average there would be about 20 to 30 clients a day.' The women would provide the condoms and the men were told to wear them no matter what form of sexual activity they paid for. When it was over, the man took a second shower while the woman left the room to dispose of the condom. She then came back and escorted him out. The women always let the customers in, escorted them to a room, had sex with them and showed them out.

Some days were hectic, especially if there weren't enough women to meet the demand. A woman could leave one man to shower and get dressed after sex, to go to have sex with a second man. She could then leave him to shower and get dressed, let a third man in, put him in a room, take his money, and go back to the first man. She'd let him out, making sure the coast was clear, put away the third man's house money and sign the sheet. Then she'd let the second man out and go to have sex with the third. The women tried to ensure that clients never saw anyone else in the brothel but it wasn't always possible as some were left waiting until a woman was free.

McDonnell dictated how many women worked each shift. It was usually two in the morning and three in the evening. The women could, however, decide amongst themselves who worked when. McDonnell didn't care as long as he had enough staff. On busy days or during holiday time he increased the number of women per shift and worked them longer hours, not closing until midnight.

During Christmas week 2001, he put three women on the morning and four on the evening shifts. He closed Christmas Day and St Stephen's Day, but he had six women working on Christmas Eve. He also opened late which in reality meant he was selling sex in the early hours of Christmas morning. It's the most expensive time of the year and most of the women needed the money, especially those with children. Liz worked a double shift two days before Christmas and another on Christmas Eve.

McDonnell insisted that his brothels were kept clean but he didn't do much of the cleaning himself. He wasn't shy about ordering the women to do it either and he didn't pay them extra for it. 'McDonnell would come in regularly to check all the rooms to make sure they were tidied,' Liz said. 'If they weren't he'd give out to whoever was there and tell them to tidy up the place. All the girls worked to keep the (place) tidy.'

He also arranged external security particularly after the robberies. He paid a man who worked nearby to keep an eye on the place. He gave him a walkie-talkie and kept the other one in the brothel. This man tipped off the women when he saw anything suspicious outside. He was also there to warn them if he saw the Gardaí coming to raid the place. 'I have nothing to say about him,' Tom said. 'He just sits in with the girls a couple of nights and sometimes puts out the bin bags.' He collected his wages at the brothel every week.

The women had to do the shopping and pay for the basic food and cleaning products out of their own money. Each of them contributed £10 to the 'needs money' kitty to buy tea, coffee, soap, firelighters and coal (there was no heating in Grattan Street). A written record of the kitty was kept on a piece of paper over the fireplace. Each woman's name and the amount she paid was on it. 'When things started to run out we'd put up a sign,' Liz said, 'and each girl would pay something out of their own money.'

Because every client was told to have at least one if not two showers per visit, the brothel went through at least two hundred towels a week. At first the soiled ones were taken away in a van and clean ones delivered. Then McDonnell started delivering them in his wine BMW 730 to Shirley's launderette in Rathmines.

He dropped in black bags full of soiled towels and came back with clean ones. But after a while he gave it up and the women had to do that job too. 'With wet towels in plastic bags the smell would get bad and some of us would leave the towels up just to get rid of the smell,' Lydia said.

Tom never paid any of the women extra money for the additional work but they did recoup the cost of the towels from the house money. They made sure, however, to pin the receipt to the roster sheet so McDonnell could check it. The two women with cars took it in turn to bring the bags to the launderette. McDonnell never thanked them for it. 'I honestly don't get a penny extra for it, not a penny, not petrol expenses, nothing,' Liz said. McDonnell was mean to his staff and mean with his money although for Christmas 1998 he brought twelve of them out for a meal to the Trocadero restaurant, much like the staff of any small business.

Liz's husband Bill often helped her with the extra work. He carried bags of towels, coal and firelighters into the cold brothel as he dropped her off to work in the morning. 'The only reason he did that was because I asked him to,' she said. 'The previous day McDonnell told me to do the towels as Lo (another prostitute) was down the country but I hadn't done them the previous evening because I hadn't time and (Bill) did them for me.'

It is difficult to see how a man could drive his wife and the mother of his three children in to work as a prostitute and then help carry fuel in to warm up the brothel so hundreds of other men could have sex with her. In fact Bill often stayed around and had a cup of tea and a chat with McDonnell. It was as if it was a regular business, that he was her boss and that this was the most natural and normal thing in the world.

But while the prostitution business was not normal, it was lucrative. The women were making an average of £200 a day. With five women working for him and each handing him at least £100, McDonnell always received double their earnings. 'I'd get maybe five clients a day', Liz said, 'but McDonnell would get between £500 and £600 a day just for being the boss.' In fact McDonnell was earning around £1,000 a day from the brothels at Grattan Street and South William Street. He was also running another brothel in the basement of a house in North Frederick Street. 'Misty's' was only open for four months, between July and November 1997.

The brothels may have operated under exotic names like 'The New Fantasy Club', 'The New Pleasure Palace' and 'The New Mayfair' but in reality they were seedy, dark, dingy dumps. At one stage they were so busy that condoms and massage oils were delivered in industrial-size quantities. 'About a year ago a load of oil came,' Liz said. 'It came in a big van so there's loads of that stuff.' But activity on this scale did not go unnoticed and in June 1998 a property company took McDonnell to the Dublin Circuit Civil Court. They wanted him out of South William Street and the brothel closed down. This time Tom couldn't send a heavy to see the judge.

Linden Ltd suspected McDonnell was using their property as a brothel after one of its directors saw the *In Dublin* advertisements offering top-class staff for 'your personal attention'. It said it provided massage in a relaxed atmosphere and 'everything a man's heart desires'. The company knew what all this meant and it hired Insight Investigations to produce the evidence to evict McDonnell. A private detective taped phone calls to the brothel and then followed up with a visit. He and a colleague were offered 'the attentions of women' and for £120 an hour they could avail of a range of sexual services.

The company was worried that such illegal activity on their property could leave it open to prosecution. One of its directors,

Dermot Coyne, pointed out that running a brothel there was, not surprisingly, in breach of the letting agreement between Linden Ltd and Tom McDonnell. Coyne said he found out that Tom was continuing to live off prostitution since his 1991 conviction and had ignored requests to stop running the brothel on Linden's property. He also ignored the notice of forfeiture of the lease that was served on him.

Judge Yvonne Murphy granted Linden Ltd an order allowing them to re-possess their property but Tom tried to delay the eviction and sought a stay of execution. The judge said she would consider this if, for the duration of the stay, Tom gave the court an undertaking not to carry out anything illegal on the premises. Not surprisingly, Tom wouldn't make such a promise and the order was granted. Linden got its property back but the civil action failed to close him down, as did a criminal action later that year.

In September 1998 McDonnell was charged with running two of his brothels although the prosecution failed on a technicality. The Gardaí learned from the case that statements from clients as well as the women were needed to secure a conviction. Tom McDonnell was back in business but the authorities weren't finished with him yet. The Gardaí in Kilrush had received a number of complaints from people in Cooraclare about the helicopters flying in low and frightening their animals. One local breeder, Maurice Breen, complained bitterly about the effect the engine noise had on his horses. He believed McDonnell was doing it on purpose. When uniformed Gardaí approached him about it, McDonnell told the sergeant to 'fuck off!' There was only one detective in Kilrush but even so Superintendent Gerry Kelly set up a team of local Gardaí to investigate Tom's activities.

As part of the inquiry the West Clare Gardaí travelled to Dublin to interview Tom. When he saw them he laughed. He had no respect for them. He viewed them as 'local yokels', and treated them with contempt. It was a huge mistake. He underestimated them. They were polite and friendly and they charmed the information out of him. Tom boasted freely. He told them about all the bank accounts, money, houses and cars he had. They were the fools. He was making millions. They played along with him, remembered it all, put it in a file and handed it over to the Criminal Assets Bureau. It was the beginning of a major financial headache for Tom McDonnell that would ultimately see him landed with a bill for £1.9 million.

2 The Vice King of Ireland

Tom McDonnell liked to gloat. He portrayed himself as the successful entrepreneur, the likeable rogue, the country-boy-made-good who was well able to hold his own in the big city. Tom now felt invincible. The Gardaí couldn't put him away. He had walked free from court twice and was still in business. He even bragged to the Gardaí about how well he was doing. He was selling something everyone wanted. He was making a fortune and it appeared no-one could stop him. He could do what he liked. Liz said, 'He used to boast that he was the Vice King of Ireland.'

Tom scaled down his operation during the prosecution proceedings of 1998. He closed The New Mayfair in South William Street and reduced the level of business being conducted at his home in Grattan Street. He also reduced the number of prostitutes working there to just one because he got legal advice that he could not be charged with brothel-keeping if only one woman was working in the house. But he didn't lie low for long. No sooner was the case against him lost than it was business as usual. In three months he had six women working for him again.

One of the most notorious figures in the criminal underworld had already failed to take over his business. Now it was the turn of the subversives to try to get a piece of the action. A financier with underworld connections was helping Tom to hide his money in bank accounts in the Isle of Man. However, he disclosed Tom's financial secrets to a major criminal who had connections with the INLA in West Dublin and he told the subversives about McDonnell's money. The paramilitary organisation presented Tom with a bill for its own house money.

The INLA told McDonnell he'd have to pay them off but, as with P.J. Judge three years before, he refused to give them anything. But this time it was different. On the evening of 3 October 1999 he was kidnapped at gunpoint outside the Irish House pub in Harold's Cross. He was bundled into a car and driven to a house in Clondalkin where he was beaten and shot twice as a warning. The INLA had 'winged him,' shooting him once each in the leg and shoulder. Neighbours found him and called an ambulance. He spent the next three weeks in hospital. The brothel continued to operate albeit with only one woman, an Asian, Mia, working there.

Armed detectives guarded Tom in Tallaght Hospital. Old Condy came to see him and presented himself as a deeply religious and respectable gent from the country. One of the Gardaí felt sorry for him but his colleagues laughed at him when he told them all about this fine man from Clare he'd met in the hospital, up to see 'his blackguard of a son'. When they told him that the father was worse than the son, he realised then he'd been had.

During his stay in hospital Tom offered to sponsor the Under-14 Camogie team with which one of the Gardaí minding him was involved. Not surprisingly the Garda refused. But that was all McDonnell offered to do for the Gardaí. He wouldn't help them with their investigation, nor would he say who shot him or why. Detectives believe he got the message, though, and paid off the INLA after he was released from hospital.

The shooting frightened Tom. He went back to business but changed his routine. He was now more conscious of his own personal safety. He no longer slept every night in his room in the Grattan Street brothel. He left his clothes there and he'd wash and shave there when he came back at different times during the day. But now he moved around a lot. He stayed in a variety of hotels, B&Bs, apartments and guesthouses and could arrive in Grattan Street at any time to collect his money.

He was unpredictable at the best of times, but when he drank he got sloppy and careless and often let down his guard. One night he even fell into a 'honey trap' on Baggot Street. He was staggering home when a woman approached him pretending to be a prostitute. She coaxed him down a lane where a man was waiting. Tom of all people fell for the ruse and was attacked and robbed. Needless to say he never reported the crime.

It was the stench of the towels in the brothel that alerted Liz to the fact that something was wrong. 'I was away on holidays when Tom got shot,' she said. 'When I came back the towels were mounting up and they were smelling and rotten.' Liz and one of the other girls brought them to the laundry 'just to stop the pong'. When Tom came back, he continued to let them pile up and she continued to get them cleaned. 'I don't think he actually asked me to do it,' she said.

Tom had other more important matters on his mind, matters of life and death, in particular his own life and death. For a while he stopped personally running the brothel from the brothel. Instead he controlled the operation by phone, ringing in ten or fifteen times a day. 'When he'd ring he'd say how many's in, that's why he'd ring,' Liz said. Tom wasn't happy if business wasn't good. 'Jesus, it's very quiet, Jesus!' he'd complain. Gradually he made his way back to doing the towel run again but only the odd time. His main reason for calling in person to the brothels was to collect the cash.

Not surprisingly no one was ever arrested or questioned in connection with the shooting. Tom refused to co-operate with the investigation and refused to say anything to the Gardaí about it. He wouldn't discuss it or offer an opinion as to why he was shot. Without some help from the victim and main witness, the investigation couldn't go anywhere. However, by this time Tom was himself the subject of two investigations.

The investigation into Operation Gladiator's number one target had been up and running since September 1999. The detectives on surveillance outside 'The Imperial Trading Company' had taken statements from four men who admitted going in and paying for sex. With Tom hospitalised in October it was scaled down until November when three more men were interviewed. The real work to put Tom McDonnell out of business began two months later.

The first of February 2001 was the busiest day for the surveillance team. Six Gardaí working in pairs couldn't keep up with the volume of men coming and going from Grattan Street. Eight men came and went at lunchtime between 12.40 and 1.35 p.m., another seven between 4 p.m. and 5 p.m. Tom McDonnell let himself in with his keys at 3.44 p.m. and stayed until 6.20 p.m. There was also a shift change. The day crew of three women left at 5.45 p.m., ten minutes after the night shift of two arrived with their shopping. In all, nineteen men came and went between

12.40 p.m. and 5.39 p.m. Six detectives working flat out only managed to stop and take statements from ten of them.

The system was basic but effective. One team watched the brothel and noted the men, their descriptions and the times they went in and came out. Those two detectives then radioed the description on to one of the other two 'floating' teams who stopped and interviewed the men individually after they left. Each time, the Gardaí identified themselves and told the men they were investigating the brothel, not their activities. Once they had been told they had not committed an offence, most punters co-operated and told the detectives what had happened inside 24A Grattan Street.

Paul told them he got undressed and had sex on the chair. David got to choose between Edele and Lynn. Richard popped in at 1.30 p.m. and when they couldn't fit him in there and then he made an appointment and arrived back half an hour later. Arthur had to wait five minutes until Mia was finished with another man. He was rewarded when she dressed up in the nurse's outfit and offered him a choice of positions. 'I then had sexual intercourse with the girl from behind,' he crowed. John also had to wait five minutes but was short of cash and had to make do with what he could get. 'I gave her £40. She told me that I could get a blow job with a condom for that.'

There were also the hard-luck stories. Jim said it was his first visit and that he went there because he was lonely and frustrated. He had, he said, separated from his wife. 'I told her I didn't want full sexual intercourse but I just wanted hand relief,' he told the Gardaí. Declan left the brothel disappointed because he'd been unable to perform. When the Gardaí stopped him, he became very nervous. He said he visited the brothel for medical reasons. He suffered from erectile dysfunction and was anxious to get away from the police because he said he wanted to go to his doctor.

'I am on a prescription for Viagra,' he told the Gardaí. 'I saw only one girl. She brought me to a room downstairs. I stripped and the girl gave me a massage using oils. I couldn't get aroused so I left after a half hour.' The woman took pity on him and didn't charge him for her time or efforts. 'The girl only charged me £20. That was the entrance or house fee. She didn't charge me anything else because I couldn't get aroused.'

The team spent six more days on surveillance. On Thursday 2 February thirteen men dropped in between 1 p.m. and 6 p.m. The next day was twice as busy. Twenty-four men called in the seven hours between 10.45 a.m and 5.45 p.m. Nineteen were admitted immediately, five were refused, but three of them were let in later when they called a second or third time having made an appointment or stumped up with the cash. There was the usual shift change between 4 p.m. and 5 p.m. Saturday 4 February was just as busy with 21 clients in seven and three quarter hours. In those three days and only during the limited time the brothel was under surveillance, Tom made £1,320 in cash. In reality he probably made more than double that amount.

Three days later the team began their final stint. In less than four hours on Tuesday 7 February they saw eighteen men call in. The next day there were ten callers between 1 p.m. and 5 p.m. and on Thursday twenty men called between 4 and 8 p.m. That shift was notable for the fastest client, the man that was in and out in fourteen minutes. During those six days the six detectives watched hundreds of men of all types, ages, dress-code, appearance, build and social standing. They came from the city and country, in taxis and BMWs, on bicycles and on foot. From the man in the suit to the man in the grubby raincoat they had all sorts of physical, personal and emotional problems. In all, the Gardaí stopped and took statements from 32 men and that was more than enough to move in and close down Tom's brothel.

Tom knew the Gardaí were watching him. His security man with the walkie-talkies had told him. For a time he took comfort from their presence. They had stopped and spoken to him a few times after he was shot. He knew that even though they were trying to put him out of business he was safe as long as they were around. He saw their red van parked outside and he knew they followed him to the launderette from time to time. But he also knew they wouldn't wait and watch forever so it was time for him to move again.

Tom's brothels were not tied to any particular location or business district. McDonnell's was like a franchise. His brothels 'The New Mayfair', 'The New Imperial', or 'The New Fantasy Club' were his brand, his trademark, which represented sex, the product he sold. The business was portable, versatile, lightweight and flexible. He dealt in a non-tangible and transitory product. The business card for the Imperial Trading Company, that is the Grattan Street brothel, had a drawing of a nun on a motorbike on it. South William Street or Mayfair Enterprises was represented by a clown.

Tom was not rooted to any major investment in any one location. His criminal assets were very substantial but his business assets consisted of Tom himself, the women he employed and his system of doing business. All these were easily transferable. His system worked the same way wherever it was located. The actual building itself was not important. Tom could close up shop immediately and quickly set himself up again in a new location. And it didn't matter to him whether he rented or owned the property. Once discovered or harassed to the point where he felt he had to move on, he either walked away from the lease or sold the house and bought another one.

One detective compared McDonnell's brothels to weeds. Like weeds you could kill them in one place but they would quickly sprout up again somewhere else. Like weeds they could replicate similarly and simultaneously in a number of locations. And like weeds they were difficult to eradicate. The Gardaí couldn't produce what he sold — sex — as an exhibit in court. Tom had been busted so often he learned not to wait for the raid before moving on. He realised if he got out before the Gardaí went in they'd have nothing and would have to start all over again.

In the first week in February 2000 he had a batch of new 'nun on a motorbike' business cards printed up announcing that the Imperial Trading Company was relocating. The landline number for Grattan Street on the old cards was replaced by his personal '086' mobile number on the new ones. The women handed them out to the men as they were leaving. If they rang Tom in a few days they'd find out where the brothel had gone. He left them in Grattan Street for a few days but, fearing a raid was imminent, he took them away in case the Gardaí found them.

But he made his plans too late. The Gardaí also knew he knew about them and decided to move before he did. They had enough to go on and at 4 p.m. on 9 February at the Dublin District Court Judge James Scally issued Detective Sergeant Mark Kavanagh with a warrant to search the place. The warrant was executed two days later.

That morning Liz arrived to open the brothel just before 10.20 a.m. Her husband Bill arrived fifteen minutes later with four black bags of towels, coal and briquettes. Lynne, in her trademark suede coat, also arrived for work. Tom appeared ten minutes later with two more black bags. Just before 11 a.m. Bill came back in with four more bags of towels and had a quick cup of tea with Tom and Liz before he left. Tom took two sheets of paper with money sellotaped in them out of the teapot. He pocketed the cash and burned the sheets. The first knock on the door that morning was from Kevin, the first customer, at 11.10 a.m. The second ten minutes later was from the Gardaí.

Liz answered in a red bra and short skirt. 'Hello, Liz,' Detective Inspector John McMahon said. 'Why are you dressed like that?' 'I don't know,' she replied and led him and Mark Kavanagh into the sitting room where Tom was sitting with his mug of tea. He had a black steel hammer which he carried since he was shot. He also kept a claw hammer in the car. The two detectives greeted Tom by name and showed him and Liz the search warrant. Neither of them was interested in reading it.

Two other detectives, Seán Cullen and Ciaran Barry, went upstairs but the bedrooms were empty. They went downstairs past the stairway to the bedroom at the end of the hall and walked in on Lynne and Kevin Bridgeman. Marie Bridgeman's schizophrenic son was putting his clothes on. Lynne was wearing a silk slip and there was a condom in foil under the large padded bench. Kevin's mother also ran brothels around Dublin. He wasn't a bit bothered by the Gardaí but he was suffering from a mental illness.

'I've been here seven or eight times over the past four months,' he told them. 'Most of the time I use different girls. I went to the door and pressed the bell and the bird you found me with answered the door. I was looking for another bird because I had a ride with this one before and I was looking for a busty bird — you know, variety is the spice of life. Anyway she said she was the only one here so I said alright so she brought me into a room at the back.'

He continued, 'I had a bit of a shower because I was too hot. I was undressed and on the bed and she was giving me a bit of a massage. I thought I was going to have sex with her because that's what usually happens. Then she heard the knocking on the door. She put on her slip and opened the door because just before you came in she was massaging me topless. She opened the door straight away when you knocked on the door.'

Five minutes later the intercom rang. Detective Sergeant Seán Cullen opened the door and in walked Gary looking for action. 'I had £60 in my pocket,' he said, 'and my intention was to have sexual intercourse with any of the girls working here at the time.' He left after he made a statement. Liz handed over her keys and business card to the Gardaí. Lynne took the two £20 notes she got from Kevin Bridgeman from the top of her handbag and gave them to Garda Ursula Hannon. She also took off and handed over her slip and shoes. She refused to answer any questions. She simply asked to leave, put on her suede coat and walked out the door. Lynne knew her rights. She couldn't be detained. With just one man in the house she knew she hadn't committed an offence and there wasn't any evidence of her having done so.

Tom had an interesting and innocent story for the Gardaí. He told them he had lived in the house for the last three years, that Liz had come to visit him and they were having a cup of tea. 'My aunt owns it,' he explained. 'I just live here. That's all I use, the bed-room. I use the upstairs toilet. I don't use the kitchen or sitting room.' There was, however, an intercom from his upstairs bedroom to the sitting room downstairs. John McMahon spoke on it from the bedroom to Mark Kavanagh downstairs in the sitting room. 'Why,' he asked Tom, 'is there an intercom phone in your bedroom and the sitting room in the brothel?' 'I don't know,' Tom replied.

John McMahon asked to search his car and Tom handed him the keys of the red/wine BMW. He found two diaries, Imperial Trading Company business cards, four job sheet forms, a mobile phone in the glove compartment and two envelopes in the boot. One was marked '*In Dublin* money' but was empty. The other contained £200 and had 'Teapot Tom McDonnell' written on it.

There was also a letter about irishescortagencies.com, a piece of a roster, a cane stick, three leather straps, seven copies of *In Dublin*, a copy of *Dublin* magazine and an application from a woman in Ballymun flats looking for a job.

Tom was arrested under Section 11 of the Criminal Law (Sexual Offences) Act 1993. Mark Kavanagh explained to him in plain language that it was 'for keeping, managing or being concerned or assisting in the management of a brothel at Grattan Street'. He handed over his two mobile phones and was driven to Store Street station. There he was booked in and handed a notice of his rights for which he wouldn't sign.

He was then taken to the cell and searched. When he was asked if he had any money on him, he took a wad of cash out of his trouser pocket. He told McMahon there was £450 in it, but the detective counted £500. 'I asked him why he didn't know how much money was in it but he made no reply,' McMahon later said. He was also asked whether he had anything else on him and he took another £2,000 from his other trouser pocket. 'It was to pay my solicitor,' he said.

Two of the team stayed on searching the house. They found the usual paraphernalia associated with brothels — boxes of Durex, wash bags with sponges, business cards, tubes of KY Jelly and 22 bags of towels. They also took away two 2-way radios and chargers, the camera, the monitors, nearly 400 blank *In Dublin* A5-size sheets, rosters and the silver teapot. Kevin was the only customer listed on Friday's time sheet.

In Tom's bedroom they found more business cards for the Imperial, The New Imperial and Mayfair Enterprises. There were more copies of *In Dublin*, and Claire Murphy's name was written on the wall. She was the woman in charge of the magazine's adult advertisement section. Tom also had her number in his diary.

There was a caller I.D. system on the landline phone in the back room downstairs. It gave an indication of the volume of business the brothel was doing. Between 10.22 a.m. and 5.42 p.m., 83 calls were listed as having been made to the line. There were more if calls waiting were included.

Tom was questioned three times throughout the day. The first interview lasted an hour and fifteen minutes. His answers to every question were direct and unhelpful — 'I don't know' or 'nothing to say'. It came to an abrupt halt when he asked for a solicitor.

An hour and a half later Tom had developed a strategy to deal with the questioning. He was prepared to talk about anything that would not incriminate him but he wouldn't comment when the evidence of brothel-keeping was put to him. He admitted paying all the bills in Grattan Street and having the phone transferred there on 1 May 1996 from the house he rented in Lad Lane. That was where The New Imperial brothel was before but Tom wouldn't admit that.

He said he lived in Grattan Street and no part of the house was rented. He spun a yarn about the money that was found being used as a cash deposit for an apartment in Wexford. He accepted ownership of a Visa credit card, 'Yes, my signature is on the back,' he said. He did admit that six unpaid parking tickets stuck up on the sitting room wall were for his van which he regularly parked illegally outside. He didn't, however, know why they were there.

But the cracks began to emerge in Tom's strategy, as it became increasingly more difficult for him to ignore or deny the blindingly obvious. His inability to put forward explanations as each piece of incriminating evidence was put to him gradually eroded his credibility. He had 'nothing to say' about the names, ages, hair colour, vital statistics and mobile numbers of the girls found in his diary. He had nothing to say about the £2,500 cash. He refused to talk about the business cards, the rosters or the £20 house money found in the milk carton. He wouldn't explain what the women were doing in his home and why so many men were calling in at all hours of the day and night.

Then he began to trip himself up. He had nothing to say when the Imperial business card with the phone number was shown to him but when he was asked his landline number he rattled it off. It was the same number as the one on the card. When he was shown and asked about the '086' mobile, he replied 'that's my phone, it's an up-and-go phone. It's the relocation phone'. When he was shown the £30 receipt from Shirley's where he had the towels for the brothel cleaned, he admitted, 'it's a receipt for the laundry in Rathmines.'

But it was the contradictions and the few admissions in the third interview along with all the corroborating evidence that damned him. He had been fingerprinted, photographed and had his period of detention extended for a further six hours. When he was asked if he intended to open up his brothel again he replied,

'I do not, I'm finished with it.'

'Will you be living there?'

'I will but the front gate will be locked.'

'Where will the girls who were working there today go after this?'

'Your guess is as good as mine.'

'Can you tell us about the girls that work in your brothel?'

'I have nothing to say about the girls.'

Tom was released at 8.30 p.m. that Friday night and went to a party. He met Liz there and was in great form. He thought he had done well and believed he'd gotten away again. He also had a plan. The next day he called to Liz's house and told her to say nothing to the Gardaí. He explained that they'd be all right and told her to meet him at a solicitor's office at 9.45 a.m. on Monday morning.

His defence against any charge of prostitution was that there was only one female with a man when Grattan Street was searched and therefore it could not constitute a brothel. He had the women who worked for him well drilled in what to say when the Gardaí raided. The other woman, Lynne, had stuck to the plan. But Liz was different. She may have been waiting for a client when the Gardaí arrived but she was arrested because she was a suspect for assisting in the management of the brothel. Technically she did this when she helped out with the towels, rosters and general operation of Grattan Street even though she was used by McDonnell and got no extra money for it. Unlike Lynne, she could be prosecuted.

Liz thought about her situation and rang Garda Mary Sharkey on Sunday night. She asked could she come and see her in Store Street. 'I thought I'd talk to you instead of a solicitor,' she said. Liz had made up her mind to co-operate. She went into Store Street with her sister and made a statement. When Tom heard what she had done, he was furious and made a number of desperate attempts to get her to change her mind. He called out to her house and phoned her a couple of times that week urging her to call to a solicitor. He only backed off after the Gardaí warned him that if he didn't stop he could be accused of interfering with a potential witness. Liz was never prosecuted. The DPP decided there wasn't enough evidence against her and she didn't have to give evidence against Tom in court.

In parallel with the Gladiator investigation, the Criminal Assets Bureau had also carried out their own inquiries into Tom's multi-million pound prostitution racket. Detectives from Clare had built up a substantial file on his activities and CAB was able to use it as a base to go after his money. Ironically, one of the first criminal gangs targeted by CAB was also from West Clare, the same part of the country as Tom. The Bureau sent them a demand for £1.2m. It was to look for a lot more from Tom.

Tom didn't work, pay tax or PRSI. But he wasn't on the dole either and he didn't claim social welfare payments so it was clear that he was living off the proceeds of crime. He bought his first house on Kinvara Road in Cabra in Dublin in June 1987 for £31,250. He registered it in his own name and took out a mortgage of £20,000 with the AIB in Capel Street, the bank beside his first brothel. He made so much money in 'Eureka' that in less than two years, May 1989, he had the mortgage paid off. He sold the house in February 1993 for £49,000, making over £17,000 on the deal and put all the money into an AIB account in Grafton Street.

Tom was a valued customer at AIB and four months after he had cleared his first loan in 1989, the bank gave him another £50,000 to buy his second property. The house, Richmond Hill in Rathmines, cost him £62,000 but he could afford it because he had the extra £12,000 in cash. He turned it into 'The New Pleasure Palace' but put it back on the market when it was raided the following year. It sold for £77,000 and Tom made a profit of £15,000.

As part of the deal he took the buyer's house at Rugby Villas in Ranelagh which was valued at £47,500. The buyer paid Tom the balance of £29,500 with a bank draft and cash. Tom used that money to pay off some of the £50,000 he owed AIB and registered his latest property in his aunt's name. On 14 June 1996 he sold the house at Rugby Villas for £72,000 thereby making another £25,000 profit on it in four years.

Two months later Tom sold another house he owned at Upper Stephen Street for £70,000. He bought it for £40,000 just two years before and had turned it into the 'New Fantasy' brothel. He made so much money there that he repaid the £30,000 AIB mortgage on it in less than a year. Again following a Garda raid, he put the house up for sale on 30 May 1996 and lodged the money he got into an AIB account in the Isle of Man.

At the same time he bought another house at Grattan Street for £60,000 and another £10,000 in cash. He had already successfully registered one property in his aunt's name and he tried to do the same with this one. It didn't work, however. Seventy-two-year-old Agnes Whelan left Clare in 1943, married and went to live in England. She was a sister of Old Condy, Tom's father. CAB officers went to London and spoke to her about her property portfolio in Dublin. It was clear after the interview that her nephew was the beneficial owner of the new house in Grattan Street that he also turned into a brothel.

In the nine years, therefore, between 1987 and 1996 Tom bought six houses in Dublin and turned three of them into brothels. CAB only found out about one of them in Chester Road in Ranelagh when he told them about it. He made £140,000 when he sold it. He also rented another four properties which he also converted into brothels. This gave him a total of seven different brothels in Dublin. He also spent £35,000 demolishing and rebuilding the family home to a very high standard for his father at Cooraclare in West Clare. He only had to borrow £16,000 from the AIB to complete the work.

But his most extravagant and expensive purchase had to be the Bell 206B Jet Ranger Helicopter which he bought on 7 October 1993. He paid £164,278.37 for it through a series of domestic and overseas transactions. He took £99,000 from his Ranelagh AIB account, another £47,618.38 from his Cabra AIB account and borrowed another £17,500. The AIB gave him the extra money when he told them he was buying a helicopter. The total bank draft was then transferred to an account in the Isle of Man and made payable to Darwen Enterprises Ltd. The company is resident in the Isle of Man and managed in trust by AIB there. The Criminal Assets Bureau believes Tom owns it.

Tom registered the helicopter in his own name at his address in Rugby Villas and kept it in a hanger at Celtic Helicopters. He said it was for his own personal use but there are indications that he also offered it for hire. It cost nearly £100,000 a year to run with insurance, maintenance, fuel and other operating charges. Three years later Darwen sold it to an Irish company, Stanelle International, for £150,000. Along with the helicopter Tom owned a Fiat goods van, an Audi 80, a BMW and a Mercedes C180 which he bought at Ballsbridge Motors for £23,500. He paid for it in cash, punts and sterling, and along with a trade-in he handed over a cheque for £10,000 drawn on an Isle of Man account.

Tom McDonnell also had at least fifteen current, deposit, loan and Visa accounts. Fourteen were with the AIB and one loan account was with Anglo-Irish Bank. In nine years he lodged nearly £600,000 to these accounts. He put over £280,000 in his deposit accounts and managed to save £66,000 in one of those accounts in just sixteen months. He also put over £107,000 through his Visa account and repaid over £210,000 in loans. CAB also found evidence that he was operating two accounts in separate banks in the Isle of Man — one in the AIB in Douglas, the other in the Anglo-Irish Bank in Douglas. The Director of Public Prosecutions wrote to the Attorney General in the Isle of Man seeking help investigating the money trail. It subsequently emerged that Tom also had sums of £100,000 and £62,000 in Scottish Provident.

Prostitution had made Tom McDonnell a very rich man. Needless to say he didn't tell the taxman about all the money he was earning. As part of its investigation, CAB raided his two brothels at Grattan Street and South William Street, and arrested and questioned him. He claimed they were health and fitness studios but there was, of course, no gym equipment or training facilities in either house. On 1 April 1998 the legally anonymous Revenue Bureau Officer delivered his damning report on Tom's financial affairs.

He concluded: 'It is clear that Thomas McDonnell has been involved over the course of the last twenty years in the operation of a series of massage parlours and furthermore he has attempted to conceal the extent to which he has benefited by such activity through the use of offshore accounts. It is strongly suspected that McDonnell has channelled the proceeds of his illegal activities i.e. the operation of brothels in Dublin, to these accounts over the last number of years. It is also believed that the proceeds of certain property transactions, including the sale of his helicopter, have been placed in these offshore accounts to defeat the Revenue Commissioners, to whom Mr McDonnell would owe a very substantial debt. In my judgment he has a very significant tax liability and is a suitable case for assessment.'

It took Taxes Bureau Officer 5 just seven weeks to work out the figures. It was based on estimates because Tom didn't make any tax returns, nor did he keep any books, records or accounts of his brothel earnings. The only paperwork the Bureau Officer had to work from were the roster records of client numbers, details, times of operation and amounts charged for sex. It was, to say the least, a unique and original basis for such a landmark tax assessment.

On 18 May, Officer 4 handed over the tax demands for eight tax years to the Gardaí at CAB. It was their job to serve them on Tom. The amounts owed ranged from £78,771.27 tax plus 115 months' interest of £112,642.90 for 1988/89 to £129,166.40 plus nineteen months' interest of £29,708.27 for 1996/97. The highest amount of tax owed for one year was £129,405.10 for 1995/96, while the highest interest bill was £141,493.47 for 1990/91. The total bill was £1,753,302.05 but by the time CAB secured a High Court judgment against him eight months later the figure had risen to almost £1.9m (£1,831,502.10) plus costs. Tom was also charged on 26 July 1999 with seventeen tax offences including failing to make returns and knowingly making false returns. The brothel-keeping and the tax cases against him were both finally dealt with together on 19 March 2002.

Tom was calm and relaxed as he sat waiting in the Dublin Circuit Criminal Court for proceedings to begin. Dressed in a blue shirt, dark jacket and trousers, he sat on the bench chatting to his lawyer and nodding over to the reporters on the press bench. It had taken the Director of Public Prosecutions almost six months to agree with the Gardaí that McDonnell had a criminal case to answer on the brothel charges and he first appeared in the District Court on 16 August 2000. Today, nineteen months later he had finally pleaded guilty to the prostitution and tax offences and was only waiting around to be sentenced.

Tom faced fines of up to £10,000 and five years in prison on each of six brothel-keeping and tax evasion charges but he didn't think he was going to jail. He expected to be playing cat and mouse again with the photographers who had been chasing him around the courts for over a year in an ultimately futile attempt to get a decent picture of him. But CAB Officer 4 didn't do him any favours when he gave his evidence against him. 'The way Mr McDonnell has structured his affairs,' he said, 'there is great difficulty registering a judgment against him. He has property beneficially owned by him in his relations' and other individuals' names to make himself judgment-proof. We're not recovering the full amount or anything close to it. We didn't find him co-operative.'

He also told the court that Tom didn't tell them when he sold his properties and didn't pay any capital gains tax. The Revenue

Commissioners lost at least £7,000 on Rugby Villas and £10,500 on the sale of Stephen Street. In July 2001 Tom signed an agreement to pay back £75,000 within six months. Eight months later he still hadn't paid a penny. The £1.88m tax bill may seem a lot but it included interest calculated only at the lower statutory rate and with no penalties. So far, the Revenue Commissioners only had £197,000 but they hoped to make another £440,000 from the sale of the houses on Grattan Street and Chester Road. However, CAB Officer 4 said he thought, in all, they would only get about a third of the money they were owed.

Tom got one of the best criminal lawyers in the country to defend him. Barry White, who has since been made a High Court judge, complimented the Gardaí on the quality of their work. 'This was a very thorough investigation,' he said. 'Mr McDonnell was picked up by the ankles, had his pockets turned out and everything was shaken out of him by the Bureau.' He pleaded for leniency because he said McDonnell had co-operated and, because of the nature of his business, it was perhaps self-evident why he didn't make legitimate tax returns.

But the judge decided to send him to jail. McDonnell's jaw dropped when Judge Kevin Haugh told him a custodial sentence was inevitable. He couldn't control his latest, thriving, sophisticated prostitution venture from behind the bars of a prison cell. He had expanded into cyber space since his arrest and advertised on the Internet. He was now running two brothels in exclusive parts of Dublin — one in a basement across the road from the Bank of Ireland in Baggot Street, another across the road from RTÉ, in Donnybrook. The next day his new girlfriend, an English woman in her mid-40s, took them over.

'He was caught in 1991 and given a chance but he chose not to mend his ways,' Judge Haugh said. 'This health studio business is a euphemism for prostitution. The avoidance of tax was on a very large scale. He kept his assets in relatives' names. I don't know if the Revenue got him for all he earned but they will only get one third of the full liability. It's a very substantial shortfall.' He sent Tom to prison for eighteen months and fined him a total of £12,000. He also told him if he didn't pay the fine he'd do an extra six months.

Tom also consented to the High Court judgment against him for £1.9m on the day he was sent to prison. It meant that while he accepted the figures in the tax assessments he wouldn't necessarily be able to pay it all back. CAB sold three of his houses, seized any money it could from his accounts and took over £700,000 from him. But the agreement he made with the Bureau means that if it finds he has any more assets that it believes are the proceeds of crime, it can take them too. Tom McDonnell served his sentence and was released from the Midlands Prison in May 2003.

Liz was relieved when it was all over. 'I'm glad I told you about my involvement in Tom McDonnell's business,' she told the Gardaí. 'I have no personal grievance with Tom. At the end of the day I was in dire straits before I started working in South William Street and Grattan Street. I did get back on my feet and I was able to provide a bit better for my children. It's not my choice of work, a working girl, but I was desperate when I started. I always wanted to get out of the business and I'm glad now that I am.'

3 Madam Mean

Marie Bridgeman didn't deserve to die the way she did. The petite, soft-spoken, chatty and good-humoured 56-year-old was beaten and kicked to death around midnight in the small Co. Meath estate where she lived. Almost two years after her conviction for running brothels, she had managed to create the impression she had given up the vice game and was surviving only on state benefits.

The reality, however, was very different. She may have been claiming the deserted wives' allowance from an address in Glasnevin but she was also back in business running two brothels in Dublin and Drogheda. She was living with her son Kevin in the house of her other son, Paul, in the Old Mill in Ratoath. He fled the country after he was charged with possession of cocaine for supply. He's still at large and didn't come home for his mother's funeral.

The Criminal Assets Bureau had already taken the money Marie got from the sale of her house in Santry. It was also after the proceeds of her son's crimes but it didn't take his house. CAB is reluctant to seize homes and put families out on the street. On Wednesday evening, 22 January 2003, Marie Bridgeman took the bus to Ratoath and walked the short dark distance to the Old Mill estate. That night she was attacked and beaten out of the house and into the street. She collapsed in a neighbour's garden and died from her injuries.

Marie Bridgeman was one of the best-known brothel-keepers in the country. Born Marie Keane on 25 April 1946, she grew up in Finglas and married a neighbour, Kevin Bridgeman. By the time she was 21 she had two baby boys, Kevin and Paul. But the marriage didn't work out and five years later the couple separated. An 'à la carte' Catholic Marie claimed the Pope had granted her an annulment. However, the break-up affected her deeply and changed her life. She always said it was the reason why she went into prostitution. 'I got into this to look after my two sons,' she said. ' I was just separated and was struggling for money. I did it for my family.'

There were psychiatric and criminal problems with her sons. The eldest Kevin was diagnosed a schizophrenic. Marie looked after him up to the time of her death and then he was admitted to the Central Mental Hospital. Her other son Paul was in trouble from the time he was a child. He has five convictions and served time in St Patrick's Institution and Mountjoy Jail. He was convicted of assault and being a passenger in a stolen car when he was seventeen but his most serious offence was when he was caught and convicted for possession of a firearm. He was sentenced to five years in prison on 6 July 1991 with the last three suspended. Like his father he, too, married a woman from Finglas. Marie said her daughter-in-law didn't approve of what she did and they never got on 'because of what I am'.

Marie Bridgeman first worked as a prostitute before she started running brothels in Dublin. She went by the name of Angela King. 'I worked as a prostitute from 1985,' she said. 'I worked for various people.' Gardaí believe she's more likely to have started before the mid-1980s. The two main brothel-keepers in Dublin at that time were Tom McDonnell and Marion Murphy. It wasn't unusual for them to hire women, like Marie Bridgeman, who were approaching 40 and older. The majority of the city's prostitutes were poor middle-aged women with families to feed. Dublin was in the throes of its first heroin epidemic but at that time young drug addicts hadn't begun to take to the streets to feed their habits.

Marie worked intermittently for at least seven years as a prostitute before she decided to set up on her own. She established her first brothel on Wexford Street and called it 'Rosebuds'. With rent, furnishings and utility bills it cost her £1,500 to start up so she continued to take clients herself. 'I had two or three girls there as well as myself and then as time went on I didn't bother working myself,' she said.

The women rotated clients and wrote the details in the roster book — their own name under N, the time in under T, R or N for a regular or new customer and £20 under F which was the house money or fee for the operator. The brothel was a financial success. Marie was earning around £800 a week in cash so she took early retirement and went into management full-time. She sold the corporation house in Cappagh Avenue in Finglas that she lived in and moved out to a bungalow in the new suburb of Clonsilla.

Marie couldn't be precise about how much she paid for her new house in Cherryfield Court. 'I think it was around, I really can't remember but I would have put down around £10k towards it plus some money from Cappagh Avenue,' she said. 'I had a mortgage for the rest from the Irish Nationwide.' In fact the mortgage was from the Irish Permanent and was for £25,000. She took it out on 7 July 1995 and had it cleared by 10 June 1996. Marie had learned there was a lot more to be made managing brothels than working in them and it was no surprise to her that she was able to pay back £25,000 in eleven months. She even stated on the mortgage application form that her business was 'Tiffany's Health and Beauty'. 'We never called them brothels, we called them health studios but, yeah, I was always working in that business,' she said.

Tiffany's was her second and most productive brothel. She closed Rosebuds and reopened under the new name at a new address on the same street. Tiffany's was ten houses away from Rosebuds on the other side of Wexford Street. There was a shop on the ground floor and Marie rented the second and third floors of the building — three bedrooms, a sitting room and a storage room. The punter walked in the door between two shops on the street and down a hall to another door. He rang the bell and went up the stairs and in.

Marie described the layout: 'When you went up the stairs there was a room to the left, which was a sitting room for the girls. There was a waiting room on the right. Then you went up the stairs and there were two massage rooms and another room up over them and toilets.' She gave the landlord an address on North Circular Road and signed the lease Marie King, a derivative of her real and prostitution name, and told the landlord she was divorced. 'She told me she wanted to open a beauty salon,' he said.

On 13 September 1993 she agreed to pay him £3,456 for the year in monthly instalments of £288 on the thirteenth of each month. She paid the insurance, the ESB and the phone bills but she didn't pay rates. She put the ESB in the name of Marie

Bridgeman and paid by direct debit every two months. She only signed one contract but the arrangement continued for over six years. She left for a few months in 1996 but came back and stayed in business for another three years. Over the years the rent increased to £1,400 a month but Marie didn't care. She paid it in cash in a brown envelope. She was finally thrown out of the building in Wexford Street in October 1999.

Tiffany's marked Marie's move into the big-time. She had the money and the experience and she used both to turn the big old building into a customised brothel. She put in basic furniture, beds or benches, the odd table and chair. She put in showers for the punters and a sofa in the sitting room for the women to wait for them. For security she installed a roll-up shutter in front of the door at the street and a closed-circuit TV system with the camera at the inside door and the monitor upstairs. 'This was so that the girls could see what was coming in just so they could see if young gougers were trying to get in to rob them,' she said. She later put in a video and recorded the customers going in and out.

The brothel was listed in the telephone directory first as 'Tiffany's Health Studio', then as the 'Dolce Vita Beauty Salon'. It was also advertised in *In Dublin* as 'Flamingo's'. It was open seven days a week from Mondays to Saturdays between 11 a.m. and 11 p.m. On Sundays it closed at 9 p.m. It only closed two days of the year — Christmas Day and St Stephen's Day. Six women worked there on two six-hour shifts which changed around 5 p.m. The women had keys. The early shift opened up and the late shift locked up.

Most of the women who worked for Marie heard about her operation through the grapevine. 'They would just come along looking for work,' she said, 'because they worked in other places.' She said she interviewed some in pubs and hotels, others over the phone. 'I'd know that they were professional girls by talking to them,' she said 'and they telling me that they had worked for other people before.' Loren, a 21-year-old English prostitute, got Marie's number from an Irish woman she worked with in Edinburgh. She phoned and called in to Wexford Street on a Sunday and started work on the Monday afternoon.

The women charged £60 for half an hour and gave £20 of that to Marie. The clients paid £60 no matter what sexual service they availed of. Some of the women could, therefore, avoid having full sex by offering the men the usual alternatives or something differ-ent like dressing up or spanking. They all made a lot of money.

'I work four or five days a week,' Michelle said. 'On average I see about four clients every day, on a good day about six or seven. That is £280 for me a day.' 'Today was very busy and I had eleven clients,' Celine said. 'I made £440 for myself. I also paid £20 ad money. So I have paid £220 to Marie today plus the £20 ad money.' The 'ad money' covered the £350 a fortnight it cost Marie to advertise in *In Dublin*. 'I used to hand it in to whoever would be there with "From Marie Bridgeman" on the envelope,' she said. When that finished, she tried to advertise in another magazine, *Patrick*, which was edited by the former *Irish Press* solicitor, and convicted forger and fraudster, Elio Malocco.

The women supplied the condoms while Marie supplied the condom bucket, a lurid indication as to how busy the brothel was. It was kept at the bottom of the stairs. The women threw the used condoms into it but it had to be emptied every night at 5 p.m. and 11 p.m. Marie supplied the towels and the cleaning products, shower gels, toilet paper and tissues. If these ran out, one of the women went out and bought some more, taking the cost out of the house money.

Marie usually rang around 10.30 p.m. to arrange to pick up the day's takings. If she couldn't get in she'd send Paul who, in later years, managed the brothel with her. One girl on each shift collected and minded the £20 house money and gave it to Marie or Paul when they called. The money was put into one of the brown envelopes, which Marie left in the closet. She also left her number in the book under the name Bernie and told the women to call her if there was a problem. 'She would usually tell us to deal with it ourselves,' Loren said. If for some reason neither she nor Paul could pick up her takings, one of the trusted women would bring it home for collection the next day.

Marie Bridgeman was making a fortune. She had six women each of whom saw around four men every day. For every one of those 24 men, she got £20. This, added to the £10 'ad money' every day from each of the women, gave her a daily income of £540, £3,780 a week and £196,560 a year in cash. In spite of this she earned the nickname 'Madam Mean' among some of her prostitutes. There was no heating in Wexford Street and the women only had an electric bar heater to sit around on cold winter nights. Marie complained about the electricity bills if they used it too much. They could, she felt, keep themselves warm by working.

Marie also banned outgoing phone calls from the landline phone and put in a payphone. When the men rang in, both the landline and mobile for the brothel were answered as Tiffany's. The payphone was answered as Flamingo's. Marie also fined the women £10 if they were late for their shifts and even though she provided a call-out service it was they who had to pay for the taxi fare out of their earnings.

When Paul started to run the brothels with her, the two of them carried out spot checks on the women to make sure they were handing over £20 for every customer. When they weren't there, the video kept an eye on business for them. 'If you do something wrong, the video is taken by Marie or Paul,' Tina said. They were able to count the men going in on the video tape and cross-check the number of customers with the house money they'd received. Paul even bugged one of the rooms and would sit in the car outside listening to the women's conversations.

Whatever about her relationship with her employees, Marie Bridgeman claimed she got on well with the Gardaí. She would report suspicious characters and co-operate with criminal investigations. She said officers in uniform came in to the brothels for a chat while on duty and sat down and had tea. She also claimed in newspaper interviews that members of the force were among her clientele that included politicians and high-profile figures. 'They did absolutely nothing wrong,' she said. 'They weren't taking advantage of us.' There was, however, never any evidence to substantiate these claims and it was more likely they were untrue. However, there was a certain amount of ambivalence to her operation and 'a blind eye' was turned to it for years. But that all changed in 1997 when one incident opened the Gardaí's eyes very quickly. They never again closed them on Marie Bridgeman.

On Tuesday 21 April 1997 two detectives from Harcourt Terrace, George Kyne and Seamus Butler, walked into Tiffany's. There had been a complaint to the Eastern Health Board that a child was working there as a prostitute and they were sent to investigate it. They spoke to the women there and became very suspicious of one of them. At first she gave them a false name, age and address but when they took her aside she admitted she was the child they were looking for. Tanya had celebrated her fifteenth birthday a fortnight before.

Tanya was from Lower Dominick Street in the north inner city. She had run away from a broken home and started drinking and taking drugs. She began working as a prostitute in the summer of 1996 on the streets around Fitzwilliam Square. Two weeks before

Christmas she rang one of Marie Bridgeman's numbers. Marie had by this time expanded her operation and was now running 'Lilly Langtry's' on Leeson Street and 'White Satin' on Queen Street. She hired Tanya when she was just fourteen years old.

This was a seriously disturbing development in the Dublin prostitution scene. One of the biggest operators was prepared to offer men a homeless, desperate and drug-addicted child for sex. Tanya first worked as a prostitute in Queen Street before Marie transferred her to Wexford Street. Still a child, young and vulnerable, Marie Bridgeman exploited Tanya for money. The word went around Dublin's vice circles that she had a young girl on her books. Men with paedophile interests turned up at her brothel especially to have sex with Tanya. Other brothel-keepers referred men on to her. If a client wanted to have sex with an underage teenager, Marie Bridgeman was the woman to see. Tanya had been working for her for five months by the time the Gardaí showed up in Tiffany's.

The two detectives immediately took the child into custody under the Child Care Act. They tried to get her to tell them what happened to her. They were anxious to help. They didn't want to charge her but they did want to go after Marie. She could be prosecuted as an accessory-before-the-fact to statutory rape. It was clear she was involved in child prostitution. But Tanya wouldn't co-operate. She refused to make a statement or give evidence against Marie. Without the child's help they could only pursue Marie Bridgeman for brothel-keeping.

Social workers at the Eastern Health Board were on strike during April and May 1997 and the night the Gardaí took Tanya out of the brothel they couldn't get her into care. There was no secure accommodation available. They had to bring her back to her father's home in Dominick Street. She didn't stay there long, however, and three weeks later she was back on the streets at Fitzwilliam Square. The Gardaí were watching her when she met a man and agreed to go back to the Burlington Hotel with him. Both of them were arrested and charged.

Tanya was brought before the Children's Court. Nobody wanted to see a 15-year-old charged and convicted of prostitution but the Health Board had no place for her. She needed help but she was a disturbed and difficult teenager. There had been trouble in some of the hostels where the Health Board had put her in the past. She was given bail but didn't show up for her next court appearance. She went to England and back into prostitution this time on the streets of Wolverhampton.

It was, however, a very different and unfamiliar vice scene there and Tanya soon found herself out of her depth. This was dangerous territory. She became so frightened after an incident there that she turned herself in to the police and asked to be taken home. She was looked after at the Brammersfield Children's Home before the UK Social Services paid for a flight and sent her back to Dublin. George Kyne and Shay Butler met her at the airport and took her back to the Children's Court. Judge James McDonnell sent her to Trinity House and she stayed there for two years until she was no longer the legal responsibility of the state. Damaged, scarred, exploited and abused, Tanya went back to prostitution.

The night Tanya was found in Tiffany's, Marie Bridgeman went down to Harcourt Terrace Garda Station to plead her case. She admitted that the 15-year-old had worked for her since Christmas but insisted that she thought she was over eighteen. 'The girl had worked right around town,' she said. 'She even worked along the canal long before she came near me.'

The next morning Kyne and Butler put the brothel under surveillance and saw enough to enable them to go to the District

Court and get a search warrant. That Wednesday evening, 22 April, they searched it and seized money, rosters, pornographic magazines, condoms, talcs and creams. The three women there admitted they were prostitutes working for Marie Bridgeman. A man found there said he came to buy sex.

Marie wasn't there for the raid but when she heard about it she went back to the Garda station for a second consecutive night. The Gardaí weren't able to prosecute her for the paedophile crime but they were determined to at least get her for prostitution. She was charged with managing a brothel and allowing the flat at Wexford Street to be used as a brothel. She pleaded guilty at the Dublin District Court on 6 March 1998. It was her first conviction. Judge John Neilan said there was no need for the court to hear 'all the gory details' and he fined her £500 after she promised she had moved away from prostitution.

It was a lie. She hadn't even closed the brothel and had no intention of doing so. She simply changed the name from Tiffany's to 'La Mirage' and continued on as before. The brothel became so busy that she had to employ a professional cleaning company to look after the towels. She signed a contract with Executive Towels and every Tuesday morning they collected fifteen bags of dirty towels and replaced them with fifteen bags of clean ones. 'I was under the impression that La Mirage was a health club,' a company representative said. Marie rented the towels and the bags from the company and paid £385.38 cash each month. They were specially labelled — 'La Mirage' was sewn on to them.

As was clear from her property dealings, Marie Bridgeman was making too much money to retire. She had sold the bungalow in Clonsilla in 1996 and bought a house in Bettyglen in Raheny in Dublin. It was the address she gave when she was charged and convicted. She registered the house in the name of Marie Keane.

'I bought it for around £60k and sold it for around £66k,' she said. She only stayed there a year.

On 2 July 1997 she took out a loan of £61,000 with the Irish Permanent. She bought a house on Glasanaon Road in Finglas and had the loan paid back in fourteen months. Then she moved again. On 11 September 1998 she took out another Irish Permanent loan for £90,000 and put another £28,000 in cash to it. This enabled her to buy her fifth house in five years on Oak Drive at Royal Oak in Santry. There was still £85,921 owed on the property in March 2000.

Marie could easily afford the mortgage repayments of £700 a month. She also had at least three bank and building society accounts. Two were in Wexford Street with the Irish Permanent and the Irish Nationwide while the other was with the Bank of Ireland on O'Connell Street. But she also kept money in a safe in her home. At one stage there was over £50,000 in cash in it. It was the money she made from Wexford Street and at least two other brothels, one in Camden Street and one in Myler Street in Cork. 'I took girls twice to the brothel in Cork,' she said.

Marie also had plans to set up a brothel in London. She opened an account in a bank in Kilburn where she could lodge the earnings. 'I was going to try and live in England,' she said. 'I tried to lease a sauna but I was done. I gave a man £21,700 sterling for the lease.' But that man 'Ronald' conned her into thinking he was going to sell her the lease on a place on the Willesden High Road in London. He took her money and that was the last she said she saw of it. The brothel never got off the ground. Her reaction was understandable. 'I was sick,' she said.

It could have been worse. 'The fella in England that swindled me out of £21,000 wanted another £10,000 more,' she said. 'I didn't have the money.' She also lost another £30,000 cash when the Gardaí raided Paul's house in Ratoath and confiscated it. She said she had given it to him because he told her he wanted to open a pool hall in Drogheda.

Even after losing over £50,000, she still had plenty of money left. She regularly went abroad on holidays with Kevin. They lived well and spent a lot of money. She was in New York, Portugal, Tunisia, Paris and Spain. 'I went to Spain about six times while I had Wexford Street,' she said. 'I spent a lot on taxis 'cause I can't drive. I looked after my friends. I bought clothes. I like clothes. I like drinking.'

Marie Bridgeman also knew what she didn't like and she didn't like paying tax. However, her earnings brought her to the attention of the taxman and she knew she had to give him something to keep him off her back. 'It was a "catch 22" situation,' she said. 'I knew the taxman wanted money and I was advised by a friend that if I wanted to stay in Wexford Street I would have to pay the taxman something. I didn't want to move on. Wexford Street was a good location. I wanted to stay there because business was good.'

Marie's 'friend' was in fact a financial adviser to other Dublin criminals and CAB had come across him before. She sent a letter to the Revenue Commissioners on 31 March 1998 but it was full of lies. On her tax returns she used the name Marie Keane and said she ran health studios. Not surprisingly, the figures she declared grossly underestimated the amount of money she was earning.

For the tax year ending 4 April 1992 she said she made £15,000. In fact she made at least three times that amount. Her 'friend', however, was very good at helping her to pay the least amount of tax. And even though she earned well over £100,000, the Revenue Commissioners sent her a tax bill for the year 1996/97 for £4,159. She only paid £1,404. 'I thought it was too big,' she said. 'I wasn't going to pay all that money (£4,159) to the taxman.'

The following year, based on the figures her 'friend' submitted, her tax bill was just £550. Even so she only paid £330 and she was bitter about having to pay even that. She felt she was being victimised, targeted, singled out and being picked on. 'I didn't want anybody to know what I was earning,' she said. 'I felt I wasn't liable to pay tax because it wasn't legal. Prostitution was illegal and I didn't know how long it would last. I knew I had to pay tax but I didn't think it was right. Everybody else wasn't paying so why should I.' But Marie wasn't paying enough and she knew it. The taxman was going to get her but he had to wait until Operation Gladiator was finished with her first.

On Wednesday 6 October 1999 Marie Bridgeman phoned her son Paul. She wanted to know what was keeping him. It was 11 o'clock at night and she was worried. She had sent him down to the brothel an hour ago to collect the money and he still hadn't returned. She rang the payphone. 'Flamingo's,' a woman replied at the other end. Marie asked to speak to Celine and she came on the line. 'Hello, Marie,' Celine said. 'I can't talk to you now, the police are here; that was Garda Noonan you just spoke to.' The brothel had been raided. Paul hadn't been arrested … yet! Celine handed the phone back to Martina Noonan. 'Is that you, Martina?' Marie inquired, 'tell the girls not to worry. I'll look after everything. I'm on my way.'

Marie was on her way alright — on her way down. The brothel had been under surveillance for a month. On Wednesday 8 September nineteen men were recorded going in for sex between 11 a.m. and 8 p.m. and that wasn't all that went in that day. The next day sixteen men called between midday and 7 p.m. Marie knew she was being watched and adapted her own counter-surveillance measures. One day she left 33 Wexford Street to buy fruit but hopped into a taxi and took the Gardaí for a spin around the city centre, out to Dorset Street and Christchurch and back to the brothel 40 minutes later.

The men they stopped and took statements from varied in age, background, cultures and in the stories they told. The brothel was popular with Chinese and Asian people who gambled in the club nearby. Some men admitted they were regulars but most claimed it was their first time. They all said they paid £60 for a variety of sexual services. 'I got a rub down and a bit of powder,' one said. Another said, 'This girl started making suggestive comments like you are a randy bastard and words in that vein. She took off different tops she was wearing and threw them in the air and let them fall on the floor.'

The women didn't always have to have sex with the clients. 'I'm Shirley,' one of them told the Gardaí. 'I do massage, oral sex; sometimes you have to dress people up and that. I don't do full sex, you're not expected to, that's why I like working here.' Shirley saw four men between 5 p.m. and 10 p.m. on the day of the raid and made £150. She got £40 for each but had to leave £10 'ad money'. She was 35 years of age and quite open and relaxed about it all. 'One I had to spank his bottom,' she said. 'Another I had to talk dirty to him, another one, a Scottish guy, and another one, both oral sex.'

At 10.20 p.m. on 6 October the Gardaí watched Paul Bridgeman go in to Wexford Street. 'Me mother rang me earlier on and she asked me would I mind going down to the brothel to collect the money for her as she was extremely busy,' he said. Marie was out celebrating her cousin's birthday. Paul had called earlier that evening but Celine, 'the trusted woman' who had the money, was with a client so he had to call back. The house money hadn't been collected for the last three days. Marie was afraid to go down because of the Gardaí and all the publicity there had been about the brothels. Celine handed Paul £910 in four envelopes.

Paul said it was his first time collecting. It was definitely his last. Next minute one of the girls came up the stairs and said, 'It's the guards.' Paul couldn't believe how calm she was. 'What!' he said incredulously. 'It's the guards,' she repeated nonchalantly. He took the envelopes with the money out of his pocket and threw them behind the wardrobe in the sitting room. 'I just panicked,' he said. The envelopes were found and his prints were all over them.

As seven Gardaí walked in, Paul sat hurriedly on a chair. The three women didn't care but he was worried. When Mark Kavanagh searched him, he found a three-square-inch piece of paper with lists of women's names, times and shifts on it. It was clearly a work roster but when Kavanagh showed it to him and asked him what it was, Paul snapped it from his hand. He then put it in his mouth and swallowed it.

In the meantime Mick Moran was chatting with one of the women who told him she had been with eleven men that day. 'Are you not sore?' he asked her. She turned her breasts to him and proudly declared, 'When you have a pair of these, not too many of them make it to down there.' She then proceeded to tell him all about her implants and the problems she had with them. One of them she said was a bit square. 'Here! Feel it, feel it,' she said. Needless to say the detective declined the offer.

Marie rang twice during the raid to assure everyone she was on her way. She was just having difficulty getting a taxi to the brothel. She arrived at 11 p.m. and agreed to go to the Garda Station. Paul was arrested half an hour later. He told the Gardaí they were welcome to search his BMW parked outside but he asked them to take it down to Kevin Street Station for him. He didn't want it clamped. When they showed him another roster they found in the car, he said he didn't know where it came from. But the three women all admitted they worked as prostitutes and implicated

Paul in the running of the brothel. 'I have been doing this since I was seventeen,' Celine said. 'It is Marie who gives out all the orders but it is Paul who organises the day-to-day running of the place and collects the money.'

Paul had a different story down at the station. 'I just want to say that I am not involved in the running of the place,' he said. 'I was just doing a favour for me Ma — she's me Ma.' He also admitted putting an advertisement in *In Dublin*. 'Once when me Ma was on holidays,' he said, 'I went to the *In Dublin* office and placed the ad for her. I just went in and handed over the envelope to the girl. There was £350 cash in the envelope.' But he insisted he didn't get any of the money from the business and he made and signed a statement to this effect without consulting a solicitor. At one point in the early hours Marie was allowed look in on him in the interview room. She asked him if he was OK and when he said he was she told him she'd wait for him and he could give her a lift home.

Marie supported his version of events by taking full responsibility for running the brothel. 'It is a brothel and I run it,' she said. 'The owner doesn't know what's going on up there. It's £20 for the book and the girls get £40 for whatever they do. I don't know. As far as I'm concerned it's a massage and a shower.' She also made and signed a statement and went home with her son at 3.30 a.m.

After six years Marie Bridgeman had to close down Wexford Street but she had already moved out to the suburbs on the south side of the city. She set up 'The Maples' brothel on Beechwood Avenue in Ranelagh in the summer of 1999 and ran it the same way as La Mirage except that the towels were brought to the laundry and the cost taken out of the house money. 'It was very discreet,' she said, 'you'd need a map to find it.' It wasn't as busy or as profitable as Wexford Street but she still made £300 a week from it. She ran the two brothels simultaneously for four months and employed the same women on the same terms in both. 'I always had three or four girls,' she said. 'I always treated my girls well — any of them would tell you that.'

She also insisted that it was safer and healthier for the women to work in her brothels. 'They protected themselves by the fact of their number,' she said. 'They were safe. If somebody who ended up being violent came back, we would refuse them. That was the way it worked. It was safe and hygienic.' She also had a good word to say about her customers. 'Most of them were good men. I only had a few bad experiences. I was attacked with a knife and at times it was dangerous.' The Maples ran for seven months before it was raided and shut down.

Paul Bridgeman didn't have a job. He had no other known source of income and yet he owned two houses, one in Finn Eber Fort in Finglas and the other in the Old Mill Estate in Ratoath. He bought the one in Co. Meath in October 1999 and was able to pay the ten per cent deposit, £25,000, up front in cash. He borrowed the rest and could afford not only to repay £1,115 a month for Ratoath but also another £450 a month on the house in Finglas.

When he applied for the mortgage on the house in Ratoath, he said he owned and operated two taxis and had an income of £64,000 in 1998. He doesn't own two taxi licences. He doesn't even have a PSV driver's licence. He paid an accountant in Dublin city centre to certify his income at £64,000. When CAB subsequently raided the accountant's office, they seized several files belonging to the Bridgemans and other brothel-keepers.

Marie and Paul were both arrested and charged on the same day with brothel-keeping. Marie was charged with managing Wexford Street and Ranelagh. Paul was also charged with managing Wexford Street and with assisting Marie in the management of

Ranelagh. However, he didn't wait around for the case to come to court. An incident in the New Year convinced him it was time to get out. On 6 January 2000 the Gardaí raided his house in Ratoath and found between £15,000 and £20,000 worth of cocaine. Paul Bridgeman was charged with possession of the drug with intent to supply and appeared at Kells District Court. He was remanded on bail and fled the country. He's still at large and believed to be living in Spain.

On 13 February 2001 Marie Bridgeman was convicted at the Dublin Circuit Criminal Court of keeping brothels for a second time. She admitted running La Mirage and The Maples. She was given an eighteen-month suspended sentence and fined £1,500. In her defence her lawyer said the Gardaí had no complaint about the brothel except that it was illegal! Afterwards Marie called for prostitution to be legalised.

'I was providing a service to the country,' she declared in the *Irish Mirror*. 'I think it should be legalised. It's needed. We know how to run them properly. This is a step back in time. It's about time somebody said it but there should be a red-light district in Dublin. I'm not saying we should go along the lines of Amsterdam and have women in the windows but we should have an area where people know they can go for this service. By that we could stop girls going out on the streets, slow the spread of disease and clean up the business.'

She also said brothels protected women from violent men. 'When they closed down the massage parlours, rape did increase I believe. These men, whatever their fantasies were, were left unsatisfied. And when that happens it can turn to rape and violence. Belinda Pereira and Sinéad Kelly were killed because they were out on their own. Now what you've got are girls working on mobile phones out of their apartments. They're leaving themselves open to be attacked, raped or killed. We would pay tax and women wouldn't be out on the streets or working on their own.' The truth was, however, that Marie wouldn't even pay the tax she currently owed and that's what got her into trouble with the law again.

Two weeks later she was arrested again, this time by the Criminal Assets Bureau. CAB knew that Marie was laundering her money and trying to get it out of the country before the Bureau could get to it. She claimed she was homeless and living with a friend in the Ballymun flats. In fact she had sold the house in Santry in a hurry for £73,000 and put her jewellery in a bank vault as part of her plan to liquefy and move her assets abroad. She was afraid of the CAB and took money out of her accounts to prevent them from seizing it. She had kept it for a time in a safe in the house.

Marie was also on the move. Five days after her conviction the house was empty and the patio door had been taken down and left in the hallway to make it easier to move the furniture out. However, she was put under surveillance and was seen going in and out of a house on Waterloo Road in Dublin 4. She was with a well-known, 40-year-old prostitute from Rathmines. The two of them were arrested and held at Donnybrook Garda Station. Marie was searched and found with documents relating to her financial affairs.

Marie wasn't happy being questioned by CAB. She was caught and she knew it and like a worm on a hook, no matter how much she wriggled, she couldn't get off. She felt she was hard done by. She felt sorry for herself. She felt she was being scapegoated, hounded and victimised. She put on the poor mouth during her interviews. She claimed she was broke and just wanted to be left alone to mind her mentally-ill son. 'I have no money at the moment,' she said. 'Any money I earned I spent on my home and family. I had very high overheads.'

She was vague on the details of her prostitution business. 'I can't remember how many girls I had working for me,' she said. 'I can't remember how much rent I was paying. I can't remember how much money I earned. I have no idea how much the girls got.' And she pleaded with the CAB for help because she was sick. 'All I know is I'm on medication and I have no money except from the house,' she said. 'All I can say is please get me my money.'

It was all nonsense of course. The CAB had discovered she was back in business this time in the prestigious suburb of Dublin 4. Marie was running a brothel on the ground floor of the house on Waterloo Road and had rented the apartments on the second and third floors. Using the name Marie O'Reilly she leased the house on 1 December 2000 and was paying £2,200 a month.

Detectives found £5,800 in cash hidden in the second floor apartment and a large amount of financial documentation. These showed she had bank accounts in Spain in the names of Marie Keane and Kevin Patrick Bridgeman, her maiden name and that of her eldest son. She also had property there and told CAB that night that she would leave the country if she could. 'I would leave in the morning if I got the money. I don't like the way this country has gone,' she said. 'All I have in the world is the money from the house and that's all.'

But Marie Bridgman didn't even have that. CAB obtained an attachment order for the money she got from the sale of her house in Santry and seized the cheque. Then the Bureau conducted a forensic examination of her earnings from prostitution and assessed her for tax on the money she made. It concluded that 'the earnings in the brothels for one year, total turnover, amounted to approximately £327,600; expenses came to £46,720 and net profit for a year would be £280,880.' And Marie had been running brothels for nearly a decade.

In fact Marie was liable for tax on the money she earned from prostitution and she knew it. She lied when she was shown all the lodgments to her bank accounts. She told CAB they were loans she had either taken from friends or loans she had given other friends in the past that they had paid back. She was also shown the false tax returns she filed for some years and asked why she didn't file returns for others. 'I wasn't bothered about filling in tax returns because prostitution was illegal,' she said. Then she tried to make a deal. 'I will pay a sum if we can agree an amount but I can't tell you,' she said. 'I haven't any money.'

Marie couldn't tell the CAB how much she owed so the Bureau told her. On 26 February 2001, the Bureau served tax assessments for five years on her; £126,600 for 1996, £137,900 for 1997, £138,000 for 1998, £153,000 for 1999 and £130,200 for 2000, a total bill of £685,700. Then Detective Sergeant Kevin Ring charged her with four counts of failing to make tax returns. She pleaded guilty to the two charges for the years 1995 and 2000 at the Dublin District Court, and on 25 October 2001 Judge James Scally gave her a six-month suspended sentence which was tacked on to the eighteen months already hanging over her from the Gladiator case. She died before she could settle the tax bill.

At 12.51 a.m. on 23 January 2003 Marie Bridgeman's schizophrenic son Kevin was arrested and taken to Ashbourne Garda Station. It was clear he was not a well man. He still had blood spattered on his face and didn't sleep during the twelve hours of questioning. He refused his right to suspend the detention period overnight to get some rest. At 12.31 p.m. on that Thursday afternoon he was charged with assault causing harm to his mother. It was a holding charge but Kevin was puzzled. 'Why does it just say harm,' he asked Detective Garda Michael English, 'She's dead, isn't she!'

It was also tragically clear in court in Navan that day that Kevin Bridgeman didn't seem to realise the seriousness of what had happened. The one person who loved and cared for him all his life was gone. Dazed and confused he spoke once out of turn during the hearing, when he wasn't being spoken to, uttering just one word, loudly 'No.' 'We have serious concerns over his mental capacity to understand the charge,' his solicitor Frances Barron said. He was remanded in custody for a psychiatric assessment and report. The judge directed he be put under special observation status and be given medical care. The case is expected to come to trial in 2004.

Not surprisingly Marie Bridgeman never agreed with the crackdown on prostitution. 'I really don't know why they did it,' she said. 'It's not like murder or anything like that. When you think of all the serious crime going on and the number of people missing, surely they have something better to do.'

She also argued that Operation Gladiator drove prostitution underground and made the women and the brothel owners far less willing to co-operate with or give information to Gardaí investigating more serious crime. 'All they've done is changed the industry. They haven't made it go away. We've been punished but there are dozens of other women involved now. Now all the girls are terrified. Nobody ever wants to be arrested. At least when we were in charge the Gardaí knew what was going on,' she said.

Following her second conviction for brothel-keeping Marie Bridgeman made the same announcement as she had made after the first. 'I'm finished with it now and I'm sad about that,' she said, 'They were some of the best years of my life. There was a great camaraderie. It was like a small village. We all knew each other and we all looked after the girls.'

And again, like the first time, she didn't finish. Instead she continued on for another two years. She was running two brothels before she died, one in Rathmines, the other in Drogheda. She was a madam to the end. The prostitutes knew her as Angie or Ruby. She may have had a name for being mean but the women said she was alright to work for. As she said herself, prostitution was the only thing she knew how to do.

4 The Lives and Crimes of Spoiled Brats

On Thursday 2 September 1999, Mary Hunt's husband took a phone call from a man interested in renting their apartment. It was the first of three nights that the apartment was advertised in the *Evening Herald*. He said his name was Reg Cullen and he left his mobile phone number. Mary rang him back and met him two days later at the apartment at the Winter Garden complex off Pearse Street in Dublin.

The meeting was arranged for 10.30 a.m. but both arrived early, Mary at 9.45 a.m., Reg fifteen minutes later. Six-foot tall with blue eyes and light brown, short hair, Reg had a bit of class about him. He was well-built, well-spoken and well-dressed in a white shirt with blue jeans. He wore a gold chain around his neck.

Mary showed him round the two bedrooms, the living room, the small kitchen and the bathroom, but she didn't have to try very hard to convince him to take the flat. Reg wanted to move in immediately. 'I was surprised as he showed little interest in the furnishings or fitting,' Mary said.

He handed her the first month's rent in cash, £700. He didn't have the money for the deposit on him but said he would have it for her in a week. Originally from West Dublin, he said he worked for a mobile phone company in England and was back in Ireland on contract for a month. He would be living in the apartment with his girlfriend who was eight months pregnant. No, he didn't want a receipt for the rent and, no, he didn't want to check the ESB meter. 'I trust you,' he told her.

At 2.30 p.m. the buzzer went and back came Reg with two other men and a woman. Mary let them in and left. On her way out she saw the heavily-pregnant woman whom Reg had mentioned, go into the apartment block. She presumed this was his girlfriend. Later she rang Reg to try and get the deposit from him. She gave him her bank account number in which to lodge the money and for a time wondered why it never showed up on her statement. He wouldn't meet her and Mary never did get her money. Two weeks later she found out why. She saw Reg's picture in the *Ireland On Sunday* newspaper in an article called 'The Lives and Crimes of Spoiled Brats'. She realised her tenant was Stephen Reginald Hutton. Her apartment had been turned into the 'Winter Garden' brothel.

It was Reg's pregnant partner Karen Leahy who was the brains behind the business. Born on 9 September 1969, she grew up on Collins Avenue in Whitehall, on the northside of Dublin. Her father retired from the prison service in the late 1970s and worked for a time as a security guard. Her sister Emma, who is five years younger, remembers Karen's childhood as troubled and difficult.

She said Karen suffered from eating disorders and tried to kill herself when she was just sixteen years old. 'It's been up and down since then,' she said.

Karen continued to suffer as an adult from a variety of illnesses including anorexia, bulimia, alcoholism and depression. She received medical treatment and counselling for her eating disorders and a variety of stress-related sicknesses. The mother of five children, she spent many unhappy years in different relationships until she met Reggie, the father of her two youngest children.

Karen was well known to the Gardaí. She was involved in prostitution for over a decade. Mary Jane worked for her before they had a falling out and she went to work for Thomas McDonnell. 'My job was answering the phones for Karen Leahy, to set up appointments for clients with the girls,' she said, 'covering the country areas of Cork, Limerick and Galway. I worked on a commission basis for the first few weeks and then on a percentage basis. My job also included collecting money from the girls when they returned from the country and handing it over to Karen.'

The Gardaí could not close her down in spite of numerous raids on the variety of addresses she worked out of, all over the country. On 16 March 1995, for example, one her brothels near Pembroke Lane in Dublin 4 was raided by a team led by Detective Inspector Tom Dixon, head of the Gardaí's Domestic Violence and Sexual Assault Unit. A file was submitted to the Director of Public Prosecutions but no prosecution followed. Four years later her business had an estimated annual turnover of £$\frac{1}{2}$m, tax-free. It was, therefore, not surprising that Karen Leahy became one of the prime targets of Operation Gladiator.

The Blandford Huttons were the new recruits to Karen's operation. Born into West Dublin wealth, their mother Joan Blandford leased and ran the Tuthills chain of shops. Samantha and her younger half-brother Stephen often used a different part of the double-barrelled surname. She was Samantha Blandford, or Blandford Hutton. He called himself Stephen, Reg or Reggie Hutton as and when it suited him. 'My mother remarried and sometimes I use the name Reg Blandford,' he said. 'I usually go by the name of Stephen Hutton.'

Thirty-year-old Stephen lived in England for ten years and worked as a jockey. He didn't ride too many winners and he came home with an addiction to cocaine. He continued to use drugs here and needed money to fund his habit, as well as his liking for fast cars, stylish clothes, fine wines, gourmet food and exclusive hotels.

A month before Christmas 1997, Dublin builder Michael Wallace called in the Gardaí after he noticed an extra £9,000 on his credit card bill. He still had his gold card but someone else was using the number. The thief spent £2,700 on tailored suits, booked five-star hotel suites in at least six hotels around Dublin and paid for flights to exotic locations like Venezuela. He even managed to send money from Wallace's credit card to the Caribbean and it was spent there.

Wallace only realised his card was being used when Bewley's Hotel rang him about it. Someone had booked the top floor and lived it up with a group of men and women on the best of food and champagne over one weekend. They had used Wallace's name and credit card number, and their extravagance led a hotel employee to casually ask another builder what Mick Wallace was like. That builder was a friend of Wallace's. When the description he gave of the man and his lifestyle didn't match the Bewley's customer, the hotel realised it had been conned. Wallace called in Visa and the Gardaí and they decided to put an alert on the card. It wasn't to be refused if used but the credit card company was to be contacted immediately.

On 2 December 1997, Visa rang Mick Wallace and told him his credit card number had just been used to book a suite in Jury's Hotel and Towers in Dublin. Ironically, the detective in charge of the case had just arrived at Bewley's to look at the hotel's security footage. He turned his car around immediately and headed straight for Ballsbridge. The Gardaí raided the room at Jury's and found Reggie, his sister Samantha and three other people there. They also found cocaine, speed, weighing scales and other paraphernalia associated with cutting cocaine for sale. Reggie took responsibility for the fraud and some of the drugs; both he and Samantha were arrested and charged.

Reggie was a wheeler-dealer, a chancer and a conman. He didn't have a regular job and was always looking for ways to make easy money. In June 1999 he had business dealings in a shop in Rathmines. Three months later he was negotiating a lease for a newsagents and handmade chocolate shop in Dublin city centre. The following month, on 20 October 1999, he was convicted of possession of drugs, stealing and five counts of fraud under the 1872 Debtors Ireland Act. He was sentenced seven months later and bound to the peace for two years.

Prostitution was to become his main source of employment although he claimed he got most of his money from selling so-called health products. 'I don't operate from any premises,' he said, 'it's all over the phone.' He had a tablet to stop smoking, a tablet to prevent balding and a tablet called Malpotane. Reggie advertised Malpotane in *In Dublin* and marketed it as a natural product producing the same results as Viagra. 'Malpotane,' the advertisement read, 'is a natural alternative to Viagra, which has done well in trial tests in the USA. Those seeking information should contact Kelly or Karl.'

Those who did ring the mobile phone number for Kelly or Karl ended up talking to Karen or Reggie. However, the number was also used for an escort agency so they first had to establish whether the caller was looking for their sexual or medical services. There was confusion at times but on the medical side the callers were told that Malpotane contained zinc and 'other ingredients' which helped combat impotency. If they wanted to try the product, they arranged to meet Reggie who handed them a clear plastic bag of mustard-coloured tablets. This was a three-month course. It cost £50. Dr Reggie's medical business was usually carried out in a car-park.

The tablets were subsequently analysed by an independent laboratory, the Chemical Analysis Laboratory (CAL). It found they contained nothing more than a mixture of fatty acids, Vitamin E and nicotinamide. Professor John Fitzpatrick, the senior urology consultant at the Mater Hospital in Dublin and the professor of surgery at UCD, said these ingredients are not a cure for impotency. 'I have never heard of Malpotane,' the professor said, 'and I have read up on all the medical literature covering this field. Those ingredients would not have any benefit at all in this case.'

Reggie's half-sister Samantha was a year and a half older than him but she also developed his taste for high living and illegal drugs. Born on 21 January 1968, she went to primary school in Dublin and a boarding school in England for her secondary education. 'I was born independent,' she said. She said she got her first modelling job at thirteen when she did a catalogue shoot for teenage clothes. She continued on to complete her A Levels and a commercial course but a woman with a penchant for being the centre of attention was never going to settle for secretarial work.

After she left school she continued modelling. She did a couple of photo shoots and even though she enjoyed the perceived glamour and expensive trappings that went with the job she never really made it in the business. Flamboyant and bubbly and strikingly good-looking, she was well known on the Dublin social scene. She went to parties dressed in leather hot pants and six-inch heels and turned up at one James Bond theme night wearing only a towel. She starred in a video for the heavy metal band, Dead Ringer, and partied in the VIP sections of the capital's clubs and hotels. She became very fond of cocaine and was nicknamed 'The Snow Queen'.

Samantha believed she was in demand both on a personal and professional level. 'Models go in and out of fashion,' she said, 'and for a while, my look was the fashion and I had the unique pleasure of turning down work.' But Samantha could have done with the money because she couldn't afford to pay for the lifestyle she was living. Drink, drugs, expensive clothes and exclusive nightclubs are not cheap and Samantha turned to crime to pay the way. She broke into one of her mother's shops, a newsagents in Clondalkin and stole £13,000 worth of goods and cash. She was caught and convicted of burglary and on 20 September 1989 she received a twelve-month suspended sentence. It was her first conviction.

Samantha went back to London and embarked on a new career. At 24 she flew to Los Angeles to launch her admittedly-short career as a professional female boxer. She says she spent a year touring Asia and the west coast of the United States working for Hollywood Hits and Knockouts. The production companies sent pretty women in spandex, lycra and full make-up into boxing rings to spar with each other. 'It was great fun while it lasted,' she said.

It lasted until Christmas 1993 when Samantha came home and bumped into an old boyfriend. She had known Gordon Parkinson since they were teenagers. 'My life changed forever,' she said, 'love is too important to let an opportunity for lifelong happiness to slip by.' She says she came back to Dublin and set up a company that sold gift baskets. She toned down her dress sense and lifestyle and appeared altogether more sensible, sober and mature. She and Gordon planned to get married.

But the fairytale was to have a tragic ending. The following year Parkinson committed suicide and Samantha said she tried to follow suit. 'I took 140 paracetamol pills and 60 sleeping pills,' she said, 'knocked it all back with a bottle of Southern Comfort and jumped into the canal in Clondalkin. I was only saved by a passer-by who fished me out with his cane and called an ambulance.' She was admitted to St Patrick's psychiatric hospital in Dublin. Samantha had her fair share of illnesses. 'She had arthritis from a young age and she was in and out of St John of Gods,' her mother said.

Following her treatment and release from hospital, she found a new boyfriend and went to Florida. It didn't work out for her there either and when she got a phone call telling her a relative had died she decided to come home. Before she left she bought a quarter ounce of cocaine and sent it to her address in Dublin, 'just so I would have something immediately I arrived,' she said. She arrived and so did the cocaine and when Samantha headed out on 2 December 1997 to meet Reggie at Jury's Hotel, she put the cocaine in her purse. 'While I sat talking to him the police walked into the room and after a search turned up incriminating drug paraphernalia. I was also searched and arrested on the spot.'

Samantha was caught with a small amount of cocaine in a plastic bag in her handbag. Three tinfoil 'wraps' of the drug with a purity of 0.4 per cent were also found under the sofa. A list with names, dates, weights and amounts was also found in the room. Samantha claimed the cocaine was for her own personal use but she was charged with possession with intent to supply. She offered to plead guilty to possession only but the prosecution wouldn't accept that and the case went to trial. The Gardaí said Samantha told them the three wraps of cocaine were hers. The verbal admission was recorded in a memo taken after her arrest.

'Admittedly, having a number of grams of cocaine was not the smartest thing I ever did,' she said later. 'The Gardaí, who believed that the existence of drug processing equipment in the room indicated I was selling drugs, gave me six months to hand in a major supplier of cocaine or they would hand me a Section 15. I was not prepared to co-operate.'

Section 15 is a charge of possession of drugs with intent to supply. It's a serious drugs charge and usually means jail on conviction. Samantha had no intention of going to jail and decided to fight the case all the way. It wasn't a particularly difficult decision. Samantha and Reggie weren't spending their own money on lawyers. They got free legal aid. The taxpayer looked after them. Free legal aid does not, however, cover barristers' fees. Nevertheless, Samantha hired an up-and-coming junior counsel Alan Toal to defend her.

One week into the hearing in September 1999 *Ireland On Sunday* published 'The Spoiled Brats' article which had enabled Mary Hunt to recognise Reggie. Samantha's defence lawyers claimed it had damaged her case. They sought and were granted an adjournment to seek a judicial review of the proceedings in the High Court. The trial was stopped. A second adjournment was granted but when no application for judicial review was made to the High Court the case proceeded as before.

On 10 January 2000 Samantha was convicted at the Dublin District Court of possession of cocaine with intent to supply. Alan Toal argued that Samantha could only be responsible for the drugs found in her handbag. He quoted case law but to no avail. Judge Murrough Connellan said he was satisfied there was enough evidence to convict on the more serious charge. The drugs, the plastic bag of cocaine in her handbag and the list with names all taken together showed, he said, that Samantha had the cocaine for supply.

The judge adjourned the case for two months for a probation report. When the day of reckoning came on 6 March, Alan Toal again made another eloquent plea, this time for leniency for his easily-led client. He blamed the media for subjecting her to 'unkind, adverse and scurrilous treatment'. 'She has always been vulnerable,' he said, 'and she will continue to be vulnerable. She became involved in drug abuse after graduating from college and went into a steady spiral down. She was a girl who has been in trouble for some period of time.'

He argued that the court was obliged to take a dim view of her treatment outside the court and asked to submit letters from her mother and others vouching for her character. Her mother stood by her throughout all her problems with drugs. Toal told the court that Joan Blandford wished her daughter had been born ugly. 'Her beauty,' he said, 'was the root of her downfall and spurred the steady spiral into a life she should never have known.' Samantha's mother was not very pleased when she heard him say this. But if beauty was a factor in Samantha's downfall, what was Reggie's excuse?

Either way, it was all academic. Judge Connellan wasn't having any of it. He said nobody's name had been blackened before the court. He also rejected the letters and said if anyone wished to make statements about Samantha's character they could step forward and do so. 'There is no doubt that certain people come before the court and one can deduce a certain lack of education that contributed to them slipping into the role they fulfil, but that is certainly not the case here,' he said. 'This lady benefited from a perfectly good upbringing and education. She is an intelligent lady, yet she involves herself in the drug scene or culture. There should be equality before the law and people who sell drugs should go to prison.'

Samantha was sentenced to six months in prison. The judge wouldn't allow her do community service instead. He refused to accept that she would benefit from a non-custodial sentence and further counselling. He struck out the less serious charge of possession and fixed surety in the event of an appeal. Samantha appealed the sentence immediately and never set foot inside Mountjoy Jail. 'I fought it for four years,' she said. 'I was convicted but on appeal the sentence was suspended. I went through a rehabilitation programme and am now clean of drugs.' On 26 July 2000 she was given a two-year suspended sentence in the Dublin Circuit Appeal Court.

However, in the middle of all that she was caught a second time with cocaine, this time abroad. Joan Blandford was a dedicated charity worker and Samantha worked with her during the drugs proceedings. She regularly travelled to Romania to help some of the children abandoned in orphanages there. In August 1998 disaster struck again. On her way home from one of those trips Samantha was caught at Bucharest airport trying to smuggle a gram of cocaine on to the plane. It was hidden in her bra.

'Being surrounded by twenty customs men in Romania is not an experience I would wish on my worst enemy. I had foolishly gone out on the last evening and bought something that vaguely resembled cocaine,' she said. 'I meant to flush it down the toilet in the airport but was halted at the gates.' She was arrested and charged but when she returned the next day to pay the fine, she was taken to jail. 'The next thing I knew I was holed up in a jail cell in Bucharest,' she said.

Samantha spent the next three weeks sharing that cell with three other women. Their toilet was a hole in the ground. They got ten minutes a day to exercise in a small area with four walls and a metal grid on top. Her mother spent thousands of pounds on legal fees to get her out. On the 23rd day she succeeded. 'I have no idea how the legal system in that country operates,' Joan said, 'but that was her punishment. That was the end of the legal proceedings.' Samantha was released and her mother took her home.

'After returning from Romania I was no longer the flavour of the month on the social circuit,' Samantha said 'and to my great regret I had to resign as director of the Romanian children's charity I was with.' She had to leave the board of the Tanner Romanian Mission Ireland. The Articles of Association for the charity state that any director must resign 'if convicted of an indictable offence unless the directors determine otherwise'. According to documents filed in the Companies Office both she and her mother resigned on 1 February 2000, three weeks after she was convicted for having cocaine for supply in Jury's hotel.

Samantha was no longer welcome on the Dublin social circuit because she was trouble. She was never known for her discretion but her exploits were now being written about in the court pages instead of the diary pages in the newspapers. A convicted drug dealer, she was no longer invited to elite parties or exclusive nightclubs. She was bad for business. She also lost a number of lucrative contracts including one with the Design Centre in Dublin's Powerscourt Townhouse Centre. The upmarket fashion retailer removed her face from their carrier bags. She moved back to the family home in St Patrick's Park, Clondalkin. She needed to do something and was not going to work in McDonald's.

Over lunch one Sunday Samantha announced that she was thinking of taking a job answering phones for an escort service. Karen Leahy was heavily pregnant and needed help with the prostitution business. Her mother strongly disapproved. 'Don't even think about it, put it out of your head, forget it,' she said to her. But a friend at the table didn't help when she said 'if she doesn't do it, I will.' Samantha decided it was the job for her. 'Due to all the local publicity about me I was unemployable,' she said, 'and when Karen offered me the position I jumped at it, more or less.'

Samantha got to know Karen through Reggie around Christmas 1998. He was her new boyfriend and Samantha sometimes stayed with them. Karen was running a lucrative prostitution racket and Reggie was working with her. Samantha listened in awe to their phone conversations with clients and employees. She was, as she said herself, 'fascinated by the whole thing'. In the summer of 2000 Karen asked her if she was interested in helping out. She wasn't able to continue interviewing girls and answering the phones to customers all the time. She was due to have Reggie's baby that October.

'I was pregnant and getting tired on the phone and I just couldn't keep it up 24 hours a day,' Karen said. Reggie suggested that she hire Samantha and the two women came to a verbal agreement. Samantha would take on some of the workload and would get paid ten per cent of the turnover. 'For this I took on the onerous job of answering the phone, taking their bookings, organising accommodation and advising them on what to wear,' Samantha said. She was as far as she was concerned back in the entertainment business only this time she was the agent. She pointed out, however, that ten per cent was less than an actor or a model agent's cut.

Samantha's approach to the business was that of a professional. She was polished, sophisticated, well-dressed and well-spoken. She had impeccable manners and a business-like approach towards the business of selling sex. She lent an air of respectability to it. She learned from Karen. She watched and listened to her on the phone and picked up what to say when a client rang. Later she also developed her own sideline at the top end of the market.

Karen was the boss and she ran a sophisticated operation. On 28 July 1999 she registered a business called Allied Corporate Entertainment Marketing and gave her family home on Collins Avenue as the business address. It's a lot cheaper and a lot less complicated to register a business than it is to set up a company. It only costs a third of the price and the registered owner does not have to comply with company law. Karen had previously been a director for six years of a company which sold clothes but it had been dissolved. Keili Manufacturing Ltd was registered but didn't file its annual returns so it was struck off the register in 1996.

Karen owned the name Allied Corporate Entertainment but the contact names for the business, Siona Ford and Michael Purcell, were both false. 'Siona Ford is me,' she said, 'and Michael Purcell is a man's name we use.' She rented a mailbox in the city centre and called it a suite. ACE marketing was situated at a prestigious and luxurious location — on South Frederick Street in Dublin 2. The mailbox was 'Suite 7'.

Once the business was established she rented apartments and houses from which to operate ACE brothels. She identified suitable properties from advertisements in the newspapers and sent Reggie along to con the landlords and get the keys. He was always polite and charming. He used a false name and handed over the first month's rent in cash. The promised deposit was rarely paid. They stayed as long as they could but the game was usually up within six weeks or two months. 'Karen couldn't rent the apartment,' Reggie explained, 'she would be too well known. I have leased previous apartments for Karen that we use as brothels.'

For years Karen ran brothels in apartments and houses all over the south side of Dublin. She also booked rooms in the Rathmines

Hotel and in the Burlington Hotel when the flat across the road was full. When the residents found out Karen was running brothels in one of the expensive properties she rented, they put pressure on her and her employees to get out. Once the Gardaí were called in, the business was no longer viable and it was time to move on. But Karen didn't go easily and she made sure her landlords remembered her. She left a trail of destruction and unpaid rents behind her. Nearly every house she left was damaged by systematic and deliberate acts of vandalism. She wrecked one house in Rathgar where she lived for eighteen months while repairs to another on Pembroke Road cost £40,000.

Karen didn't care what damage she left behind. She always had another upmarket address to move to. She had at least eleven more houses and flats in Dublin 1, 2, 4 and 6. She either lived in or set up brothels in Ballsbridge, Eastmoreland Lane, Wicklow Court, Charlemont Road, Upper Leeson Street, Alexandra Quay, Pearse Street, Haddington Road, Beggar's Bush Park, Temple Bar and Custom House Harbour. When she was living with Reggie in a bungalow near the entrance to the City West Hotel, two men tried but failed to throw them out. They called at 10.40 a.m. on 22 May 2001 and a row broke out because the rent hadn't been paid for some time. Reggie and Karen later complained they had been threatened.

For over two years Karen operated brothels and prostitutes under the name 'Penthouse Pets Exclusive Health Studio'. She advertised in *In Dublin*. However, when the Censorship Board took on the publisher, Mike Hogan, it toned down the content of photographs and the wording of some of the advertisements. First Penthouse Pets changed its name to 'Penthouse' and kept the same mobile phone number. Then it changed from Penthouse to 'Club Elite'. The first Club Elite advertisement appeared in *In Dublin* on

28 July 1999 with two new mobile phone numbers. When the magazine was banned, Club Elite's advertisement appeared in the *Dublin* magazine. The business was badly hit when *In Dublin* re-appeared but refused to carry any more advertisements. *Dublin* magazine ceased trading shortly afterwards.

Samantha took to her new job with gusto and began to con-centrate on The Executive Club. It was supposed to be for more discerning customers. Samantha told the *Evening Herald* all about it. 'The Executive Club,' she declared, 'Ireland's first one-on-one, ultra exclusive escort agency, run by me, Samantha Blandford under the nom de plume, Sheena Ford was like nothing else available in Dublin. The Executive Club made sex in the city erotic, instead of tawdry. Unlike the prostitutes who plied their trade at the massage parlours and the other escort agencies in Dublin, the other women who worked at the Executive Club were a class apart.'

'They were the type of women who could join a man for a drink or dinner in Dublin's most exclusive restaurants and not look out of place. Or they could take a bath with a client, watch an erotic video and spend time making sure the client was in the proper mood before getting down to business. Then there's usually time for a break and a second round, so to speak, before the client would shower and leave.'

'At any given time there would be up to ten women, all avail-able in different apartments or hotel rooms scattered around the nicer areas of the city. Dublin 4 was the preferred area for clients but sometimes further south along the coast or the airport was more convenient for the businessmen. The escort business has always been based on discretion and, as the agent in charge of the operation, I became the keeper of secrets.'

Of course all this was nonsense. It may have been what Samantha believed but the reality of the prostitution racket was somewhat different. Samantha may have seen herself as some sort of sexual pioneer but she was as unscrupulous as Karen and Reggie in her involvement in criminal activity. Under the veneer of erotic exclusivity, the three of them ran a seedy sex business. They defrauded customers, using false identities, and took large sums of money from people. Some should have known better. Others were just sad, lonely and vulnerable. One man made at least twenty cheques payable to ACE but when the Gardaí told him they managed to seize them before they were cashed, he just shrugged his shoulders. They told him they'd saved him thousands of pounds but he said he had plenty of money anyway.

The business operated by means of a maze of mobile phones. There were at least ten numbers, six Eircom (now Vodaphone), four Esat (now O_2). Most were pre-paid 'ready-to-go' or 'speak easy' phones which made the happy threesome who operated them more difficult to identify. Sometimes if a customer rang an '087' number he was transferred to an '086' number. Karen registered the main Penthouse Pets number in the name of Linda Doyle and paid the bill in cash, over £1,600 for one month.

One phone was registered in the false name and address of Michael Purcell, The Grove, Malahide. The bills were sent to ACE's post office box or suite. Karen also registered a phone in the name of Emma, her sister, and another for the Club Elite Escape Exclusive Health Studio in Samantha's name without her knowing. Reggie registered two mobiles in his own name and used his mother's address in Clondalkin while Samantha used her own phone but with a different SIM card for the Executive Club. Her mother's name was on the contract but she knew nothing about this criminal enterprise.

Karen set the business up to cater specifically for the wealthier client at the upper end of the market. The fact that it was run through what appeared to be a company created the illusion of legitimacy and respectability and made it more acceptable to professionals and businessmen. It was convenient to be able to pay for sex with cash, a credit card or with a cheque payable to ACE Marketing. 'Elite Escorts' accepted Mastercard and Visa. The name ACE was also carefully and cleverly chosen. An unsuspecting partner would never think that payments to Allied Corporate Entertainment on bank statements or Visa bills were in fact payments to prostitutes. It was the perfect front for the illegal activity.

Karen also had ACE business cards printed up in the false names of Michael Purcell and Siona Ford with landline, mobile phone and fax numbers on them. But to make her prostitution racket seem more exclusive she simply charged more, in some instances up to five times more than the average rate for straight sex. The men phoned Karen or Samantha and they'd send him to one of the brothels or set him up with one of the prostitutes.

At the brothel they were offered tea, coffee, wine or champagne along with their choice of lady. It was £100 for a half-hour, £150 for an hour and £300 for the executive service, which was Samantha's side of the operation. 'It would be for clients who didn't want to walk into an agency and risk being caught,' Reggie said. 'It would be more discreet.' Karen also operated a call-out service where the prostitute called to the man's home or office. The fee varied between £160 and £300. Most of these men paid by cheque and Karen put that through the business account and paid the women their cut in cash.

Samantha pretended the Executive Club was a dating agency. 'It (was) a private members' club, twenty at the most,' she said 'We organised one to one meetings between our members and girls belonging to the Executive Club. A brothel is just straightforward sex while the Executive Club was more personal and could be described as organised dates where the girls would go out on dates with the members and maybe have sex later on.' More rubbish! The dates with the women lasted an hour and a half. For more time the man paid more. The 'Executive Club' was nothing more than pricey prostitution.

For every £100 a man handed over, the prostitute got £55 while Karen got £45. For every £150, the split was £80/£70. Samantha got ten per cent of the total take. 'For example, if I had a client give £150, the girl would take £80, I would get £70 and then I would give Samantha ten per cent of the £150 which would be £15 in total,' Karen explained. 'If a client gave £300 then Samantha would get £30.'

At the beginning Samantha was earning about £300 a week but within two months she was up to £500. Customers paid for the time they spent with the woman, not for the service they received. This was completely the opposite to Tom McDonnell or other old-style brothels where the more explicit the sexual activity, the more expensive the visit. The longer the customer spent with Karen's woman the more it cost him and it didn't matter whether he talked to her, had sex with her or swung naked from the lampshades.

The women were marketed as no ordinary hookers and, to some extent, Karen and later Samantha were selective in whom they employed. There were no junkies, alcoholics or girls with pimps. There were no poor, ageing women, no frumpy mothers from disadvantaged areas trying to feed their kids and no women with strong Dublin accents.

'There were no young girls who didn't know what they were getting into,' Samantha insisted, 'and nobody was working to buy their child's communion clothes or support their drug habit.' They chose young ladies who could look well and upper-middle-class women from the wealthy suburbs. But that's not to say that good diction or a high standard of English was required. Foreign women were always welcome, particularly orientals. They conjured up notions of mystery and eroticism.

Karen and Samantha also claimed they employed bored middle-class housewives in search of excitement who were capable of giving intellectual stimulation as well as good sex to the clients. In truth, this again was all part of the marketing fantasy. In spite of all the flimflam and the trimmings, Karen Leahy's operation like all the others boiled down to the selling of sex. The difference was that the men tended to be better behaved and went out the door with far lighter wallets.

The women who worked for her were encouraged to believe that all this was fun. They were stars working in the entertainment industry. They all had 'stage names'. Karen called herself Sonia or Kelly, Samantha was Sheena. The women were known as Eve, Eden, Donna, Trudy, Shannon, Karla and Bianca. They worked shifts in the brothels on a roster basis. Some worked as many as 24 hours straight and took naps in the brothel but the norm was seven or eight hours.

Karen was flexible and the women usually worked when it suited them. The rosters were written in a red book and included the days, times, clients' names, girls' names, duration and commission due. 'They are records the girls keep of their clients,' Karen said, 'the times they were with them, the amounts of money due to me.' With one quick look she could see exactly how much she was owed from a day's business.

The women in the brothels took the money off the men and minded Karen's share until either she, Samantha or Reggie came to collect it. As well as renting the properties, Reggie was the chauffeur, the minder and the bagman. He liked to see himself as the muscle. Reggie and Karen drove around in his Isuzu Trooper and collected the takings but as her pregnancy advanced, Reggie collected more and more on his own. On Monday 20 September 1999, for example, Reggie called to the Winter Garden between 1.30 p.m. and 2 p.m. and collected £600 in cash. 'This is the money I take and give to Karen Leahy,' he said. He also drove the women to the brothels or the clients' homes particularly if one of them was running late or another had to step in to replace one unable to keep an appointment.

Karen's commission was left in the back of the red book in the brothel or kept in the handbag of one of the women at the brothel. She also kept notes of what she was owed on a piece of paper in her own handbag. This was a profitable business she was running. 'You could say they are the returns of the clients who got sexual services,' she said.

There were usually four or five women in an apartment or house at any one time. They provided their own condoms and washed the towels themselves. One or two of them operated out of their own apartments but the majority operated from the brothels. Most had enough problems without paying rent, fighting with or ripping off a landlord.

There were no phones in the brothels so the men couldn't phone in direct. All calls were channelled through Karen or Samantha, although there was one occasion when the heavily-pregnant Karen was so tired answering so many phone calls she diverted her mobile to two of her more trusted prostitutes. In general the women working for Penthouse Pets and Club Elite didn't know who was coming until the buzzer went downstairs and they let them in. 'I usually have a look out the window to see what they look like and that they are not knocking on someone else's door,' Trudy said.

When a man was let in to the brothel, he met all the girls and picked the one he wanted. He had already agreed a price on the phone and would have said what he wanted — regular, executive or domination. If an executive client was coming, Karen or Samantha would ring the brothel and tell the other girls to hide or get out while that client's prostitute pretended it was her apartment. The women didn't always do a good job and were often spotted by the executive customers crouching in the bathroom or the other bedroom. One man got really annoyed with this. He wouldn't pay any more than £150. Samantha had his mobile number and kept ringing him for the other £150 but he held his nerve and never paid her.

In fact most of the men who thought they were getting something special were conned. Some who paid £300 and thought they were getting the more exclusive Executive Club were sent to the Winter Garden brothel on Pearse Street to be with the same women who also worked for Club Elite and normally only cost £150. 'They were just getting us,' said 24-year-old Tina. 'The same girls worked for both agencies under different names. The clients were being hoodwinked into paying more.' Reggie admitted this was indeed the case. 'Sometimes they'd just clear out the apartment they're using at the time and say it was a girl's apartment.'

Twenty-four-year-old Frank felt particularly aggrieved. 'I didn't want to just walk in off the street,' he said. 'I wanted something more personal.' He rang Penthouse Pets and was referred to Samantha at the Executive Club. 'She said they would provide a girl that was suitable for me and that we could go for a drink. She said the price was £300. I understood that this was for either sex or a drink or just sitting in an apartment.' When Samantha told him to go to the Winter Garden, he pointed out to her that that was where the ordinary brothel was. Frank had phoned Club Elite before but Samantha thought quickly on her feet. She told him the company had a number of apartments in the complex.

In the end Frank's instincts were correct. He arrived at 8.15 p.m., half an hour early for his appointment with Bianca and was left waiting in the bedroom. 'I just watched TV and she was out in the sitting room on the phone,' he said. 'I left the bedroom and went back into the sitting room. I said I didn't want it that way. I meant I didn't just want quick sex. I wanted a social time.'

Frank had special needs. He brought his own ladies' lingerie but when he gave them to Bianca she wouldn't wear them. Frank was outraged. 'When she came out she was just wearing a pair of knickers and was topless,' he said. They stripped and he had oral and full sex. Bianca had a shower and got dressed in a separate room. He didn't bother. He was completely 'pissed off'. He went into her in the sitting room and complained. 'Is this it? Is it over?' he asked. Bianca told him his time was up. 'I was told by Sheena that the £300 was for an hour and a half but although I was in the apartment for over an hour I was only with the girl for about twenty minutes. I didn't get nor was I offered any massage.' He didn't get a refund either.

Business was booming. Karen was making a lot of money but in August 1999 she began to lose her grip on the operation. With the baby on the way, she was getting tired and losing focus and concentration. While Samantha appeared to be doing a good job she didn't have the same experience or nose for trouble as Karen. She wasn't as good at spotting a phoney. So when Liz Allen, a journalist from the *Sunday Independent*, applied for a job as a prostitute, Samantha hired her immediately. It was the beginning of the end of 'The Spoiled Brats' enterprise.

5 Cobra: The Connoisseurs' Club

Samantha Blandford Hutton loved her job. She was very good at it. She was meeting people. She was selling a service to them and she was being paid in cash. She was one of the Celtic Tiger's entrepreneurs. She worked her own hours and vetted prostitutes for Karen. The women were recruited through the advertisements in *In Dublin*.

'I rang and spoke to "Sheena" and told her I was interested in work,' Donna said. 'She just asked me details like age, description, height and had I worked before. I was told to call next morning to Haddington Road. I met two girls there and I just started work.' It was a simple as that. Samantha tried but didn't always get to meet the women before she approved them. It was quite easy to get a job at Club Elite or the Executive Club as the *Sunday Independent* discovered.

On Wednesday 18 August 1999, the newspaper's crime correspondent Liz Allen phoned the mobile number for Club Elite. A man answered. She told him her name was Claire and asked to speak to Kelly. She was, she said, looking for work. 'Have you worked before?' Kelly asked her. 'I worked in New York and have just returned home.'

Liz told Kelly she'd been earning $3,000 a week in the USA and was now interested in making serious money at home. However, she said she was worried about being arrested because she had read in the newspapers about *In Dublin* and the Garda crackdown on prostitution. Kelly warmed to her and told her her real name was Karen. She said she had nothing to worry about when it came to the police. She ran a very up-market agency. 'Most of my clientele are well-to-do businessmen who can afford £300 an hour,' she said. 'We're not like any of the other agencies. Any Joe Bloggs can afford £150.'

'There are no weirdos,' she assured her prospective employee. 'You just have to provide various types of sex and some of them don't even want sex.' She told Liz that one of her girls was going out for dinner with a client that night and was being paid £900. 'It's good money if you can play the game,' she said. The agency, i.e. Karen, got half of the pre-arranged price. If the client was happy and the girl had no other clients waiting, she could stay longer with him and negotiate a further fee. A portion of that would also go to the agency.

Karen arranged to meet Liz at lunchtime the following day in the lobby of the Burlington Hotel. Liz arrived at 1 p.m. and ordered a cup of coffee. Minutes later her phone rang and she realised she was talking to a woman sitting across from her on the left. She recognised Samantha. They had met before. Liz Allen was well known. Her picture was in the newspaper every week and she was regularly on television. But Samantha didn't know who she was. She came over and introduced herself as 'Sheena'.

Samantha told her about the agency and the type of work that Liz was expected to do. 'She said that I would be required to have regular intercourse, perform oral sex, dress up and also dance for some of the men,' Liz said. Samantha went into great detail describing the type of lingerie Liz would be required to wear at work, referring throughout to some of the clients and their requirements. She told her she would see two clients a night and get half the £300 each paid per hour. If she were to 'service' four clients for around 90 minutes each, she could walk away with £600.

Samantha didn't ask too many questions. She was too wrapped up in herself and the business and she just kept on talking. 'It's strictly a cash business, it's really fun,' she said, forgetting she was supposed to be talking to an experienced New York prostitute. 'You've got to know how to massage a man's ego as well as his body. You've got to dress very elegantly, nice short skirts and dresses, but not too cheaply and be good in bed. It's about manipulating men. It's so easy.'

Samantha also revealed details of a new project she was very excited about. 'Cobra, The Connoisseurs' Club' was a real money spinner and she decided there and then that Liz was perfect for it. Cobra was the codename for organised orgies. It was an ambitious project. There would be 400 or 500 members but only fifteen or twenty of them would be invited at a time to one of the club's nights where they could have sex with five or six prostitutes. The business cards had already been printed.

'It's a VIP evening,' Samantha told her. 'All the women are expected to dress elegantly and the men come in black tie. We take a house with lots of bedrooms and we expect you to get to know a good few of the men, spend some time in the Jacuzzi or sauna with one or two of them.' Samantha assured Liz she would not allow any of the men to monopolise her. She would make sure she 'met' as many men as possible that night. The men were paying £1,500 each and the women would have to put on a good show for them.

Samantha said the men were all thoroughly vetted and that the company had their addresses, employment and credit card details. She even had lunch with some of them herself to assess their suitability. She was absolutely categorical in her assurance that Liz would never be placed in a situation with someone the agency knew nothing about. 'Do I get paid extra for threesomes?' Liz asked her in an effort to project the image of a serious escort girl. Samantha's eyes lit up and she got very excited. 'When can you start?' she asked.

Then Karen popped in on the interview and introduced herself as the woman Liz had spoken to on the phone the day before. Karen was also full of reassurances particularly about the security of the women and the likelihood of her being arrested and charged. She had, she said, 'guarantees' that it was only massage parlours that Gardaí wanted to hit. Karen and Samantha liked Liz and wanted her. They asked her to start that evening at 5 p.m. Liz agreed and Samantha said she would meet her in the Holiday Inn next door to the Winter Garden brothel on Pearse Street. She said she would phone her to confirm exactly where she wanted her to go.

The *Sunday Independent* decided to continue with the investigation. At 3.30 p.m. another journalist, Campbell Spray, rang Elite from a friend's UK mobile phone. He said he was an English businessman 'looking for female company'. Samantha took his number and rang him back on it ten minutes later. She told him she had a number of women. He could meet one in her own apartment or at the company's premises. The fee was £300 for everything.

She asked him what sort of woman he liked and told him she could provide all types of girls — blondes, brunettes or black girls. Spray gave Liz Allen's description as his ideal girl and Samantha was delighted. She told him they had a new girl 'Karla' who just started with them and she sounded ideal. Karla, she said, was very sophisticated and had a very good dress sense. She was a very special lady and Samantha said 'she absolutely loved sex'. Spray also said she sounded ideal and agreed to an appointment at the Holiday Inn at 5.30 p.m. She gave him directions and told him she would call him again at 5.15 p.m. to ensure, as she put it, that everything was in place for his appointment.

Samantha then rang Liz confirming she had a client booked for her at 5 p.m. Liz had told her that her name was Claire but Samantha already had a Claire on her books and told her she was to use the name Karla. An hour later she phoned Liz again to ask her if she could go to the Holiday Inn to 'slip in' a client before the 5 p.m. appointment. She said she would keep the 5 p.m. client busy at the door while Liz finished up with the 4.30 p.m. client. Not surprisingly Liz didn't show up for her appointments. She got a few calls from Samantha and Karen asking where she was and what was keeping her but after a while these stopped. Campbell Spray, however, kept his appointment.

He was called at 5.15 p.m. and was told to go to the bar in Holiday Inn. He described what he would be wearing and was given a description of the girl who would meet him. He waited. Twenty minutes later he got another phone call to tell him Karla was running late. She would, he was assured, be along shortly. Three quarters of an hour later Samantha arrived and introduced herself as Sheena.

Samantha said that unfortunately Karla was delayed but assured him she was on her way. She sat down with him and tried to rope him into the Cobra Club. It was the hard sell for hard cash. He would, she told him, be picked up by a limousine and brought to a large house where there would be twenty girls. He would be one of ten or twelve men in dinner jackets but there would be gourmet food and as many women as he wanted. 'You could stay the night and be driven home the next morning all for between £1,000 and £1,500,' she said.

'You seem to be going in for this in a big way,' he said to her. 'Yes,' she replied, 'I see myself as the next Heidi Fleiss.' Heidi Fleiss was the US west coast madam-to-the-stars who provided prostitutes for famous actors, producers and directors in Hollywood. One of the names in her little black book was Charlie Sheen. Samantha told Campbell Spray that she'd been in the US a couple of times. Not only had she met Heidi Fleiss, she said, she'd also met Martin Sheen, the father of one of Heidi's biggest customers. Spray started to get bored and impatient. He asked her a few more times if Karla was on the way and Samantha continued to reassure him she was. She promised him he would not be disappointed. 'Karla is very good at sex. She knows the score and will do anything,' she said.

When 'Karla' finally arrived two hours late at 7 p.m., Samantha charged him £300 for an hour and a half with her but she told him 'nobody is counting the minutes'. Karla was in fact Eden, a professional make-up-artist-turned-prostitute who, unlike Liz Allen, was actually from the US. She had her own apartment on Merrion Street, just across the road from Government buildings. She loved her job, she was never afraid and she made a lot of money. Spray handed the cash to Samantha on the front steps of the hotel and once the newspaper's photographer had got a picture of him counting the notes into Samantha's hand, he made his excuses and left. The story was in the *Sunday Independent* the following Sunday.

Eden was an experienced call girl. She operated and worked in her own escort agency in Dublin for a time but said 'because of the censorship thing with the *In Dublin* magazine, business could not be advertised any more.' She was in no doubt what business she was in. She could define it. 'An escort agency is a cover name for a business providing sexual favours to males in return for payment,' she said. She went to work for Karen Leahy because she decided to link up with one of the capital's biggest agencies.

On 18 August 1999 she rang the number for *In Dublin* and spoke to Samantha. Her interview was held in the Camden Court Hotel in the city centre. 'We did not discuss services I would provide as it was clearly understood by both of us that it was sexual favours for men,' she said. 'I had been working my own agencies providing the same services.'

They agreed a 50-50 split on every £300 she made, but she often negotiated an extra payment on the side and spent more time with the client. She kept those earnings hidden from Karen and Samantha. It was her bad luck that her second client on her first day turned out to be a journalist. Karen and Reggie picked her up from her apartment and dropped her off at the Winter Garden brothel. Two of Karen's children were in the back of the jeep. Eden did the favour for Samantha that Liz Allen was supposed to do. She slipped in the 4.30 p.m. client before she met Campbell Spray in the Holiday Inn.

Karen ran two brothels in the Winter Garden complex. Eden was one of at least eight women working in them. Sonya was a 27-year-old from Donabate, the middle-class seaside resort in north Co. Dublin. Nineteen-year-old Bianca from Clondalkin also worked for another madam 'Tina' at the 'French Connection' brothel in Parnell Street. Mural was a Vietnamese girl with broken English who'd lived in Dublin for the past two years while Trudy was an Irish girl living in England. She flew home one week out of every four to work as a prostitute here. It was Trudy who trained Eve in and she was now the most popular woman in the brothel.

At 24, Eve was the dates and domination expert. She turned to prostitution after her parents threw her out of their Killiney home when she was seventeen. 'I was kicked out after my Leaving Certificate for staying out all night,' she said. First she worked in a variety of odd jobs and even managed a restaurant off Grafton Street for a year and a half. But she wasn't earning as much as she wanted and turned to prostitution.

When she first rang one of Karen's numbers looking for work, she was told it didn't always involve sex. 'It was mostly dates — where you go on dates with clients,' Shannon told her, 'that didn't always involve sex. The client pays for the company of the girl.' 'I asked her was it a parlour at £60 a go and she said no, it was not like that,' Eve said. 'She said they would ring back but they never did.'

Instead Eve went to work at Keith Thompson's brothel off Mary Street, in the north inner city. It was down a dark and dingy lane, beside a tattoo sign and up the stairs behind a hairdressers. She didn't like it. There were steel doors on the way in. She certainly wasn't impressed with one of Karen's competitors. 'It was filthy, filthy and the girls were filthy,' she said. 'I spoke to one of the girls there, I think her name was Elaine. She said Tony was coming to see me. In my opinion it was a brothel where men went for sex — the girls were sitting around in skimpy clothes. After seeing that place I was delighted with Elite.' Two days later Eve had a job with Karen.

Her first customer on her first night was a regular but a particularly strange individual. Trudy was the only other woman on duty and she told her what to do. He liked women in leather 'so I had my leather skirt on and my leather bra,' she said. Tom was quite literally an Elite customer. He got undressed, had a shower and lay on the bed. He got a sick, sexual pleasure from torturing his wife in a cruel, emotional fashion.

Eve posed for him with her clothes on. He then dialled his wife's number. When she answered, Eve had to ask for Tom. When his wife said he wasn't there, Eve was to tell her it was fine. Then she had to say she was waiting in a bar for him and he hadn't turned up. 'While I was saying this he was wanking himself,' Eve said. 'She asked me did I know him well and I said very well, as he had told me to say. He ejaculated himself and left. I didn't have to touch him.' For that Tom gave her £300. She left £180 on the mantelpiece for Trudy to give to Karen.

Eve didn't meet Karen until five days later when she called to the brothel to collect her money. She was very pleased with her and told her she had good reports about her. 'All the gentlemen said I was very pleasant,' she said. 'I don't know how she knew unless one of the gentlemen rang her back and told her.' After that Eve wasn't in the apartments much, only when she needed extra money. She concentrated on the Executive Club side of the business. She did the call-outs to homes and hotels as well as the specialist requirements.

'I go to the place and it's already easy to pick out the client,' she said. 'They would also know what I'd look like. Sometimes we'd go for dinner, drink, clubs, Leeson Street. Usually the hour and half is up when the meal and drinks are over but if the client says to me to go back to his hotel room and I feel like going I go. It's all included in the £300. If he was someone really ugly or really dirty I wouldn't have sex.' Eve had the numbers of Karen and Shannon (one of her more experienced prostitutes) in case something happened or she needed help.

Most men wanted some form of sex but she would often have to, as she put it, 'stand over them feeling myself and posing as they felt themselves'. But Eve was popular because she had a fondness for the kinky stuff. 'Domination is what I specialise in.' She handcuffed the men to the bed, took off her stockings, tied their feet and whipped them. She stood on their chests, slapped them, pulled their nipples, squeezed them and hit them with their own belt buckles. She was, however, sensitive to their needs. 'If they didn't want severe domination,' she said, 'I wouldn't use the buckle.'

She didn't have any whips. The men brought their own. She did, however, keep an egg-slice in one of the bedroom drawers. 'I prefer to do the domination than sex and I will always do it if I'm asked,' she said. It cost £150 for half an hour. Reggie was bemused by the fact that some men actually liked this. But he didn't care. They were making money catering for this niche market. 'Some fellahs want mild domination which is just being bossed around,' he said. 'I've actually gone into an apartment and there was a fella in an apron washing dishes. Most of the time it's sex they provide.' Samantha insisted the women were 'just like the men. They wanted fun, uninhibited sex and a break from the routines of their normal life.'

The high prices Karen charged meant most of the men were wealthy businessmen, tradesmen or educated professionals. They were, as Samantha put it, customers who could afford to pay for their women to be 'broadminded in the bedroom'. There were ambulance drivers, publicans, photographers, engineers, accountants, company directors and pension consultants. Most of them were from Dublin and the surrounding counties — Wicklow,

Kildare and Meath, although there were some from as far south as Waterford.

One Irish executive set up an appointment for two of his English colleagues who were in Ireland on business. They were staying at the five-star Berkeley Court Hotel. The 51-year-old director of a transport company drove the deputy managing director and the sales director of the British parent company down to the Winter Garden brothel in his black Mercedes. He waited nearby in Moroney's pub while one paid £150 for hand relief, the other £300 for oral sex. They were back for a drink in half an hour. 'When they were finished they joined me in the pub,' he said. 'While they did not tell me exactly what services they got, I assumed they had been looked after sexually as they seemed happy.'

Many of the Irish men had been to Karen's other brothels and knew the drill. Phone the number, state what you want, book a girl, agree a price and turn up in the general area before phoning again for the precise location. The prostitute and the client knew each other's pseudonym. 'Sheena told me they had a number of flats,' Frank said, 'and to go to the Holiday Inn on Pearse Street and ring her again and she would say what flat number it was.' He was Eddie and he was to ask for Tara. When he got there she buzzed him in. He walked into the foyer, through a second set of doors, into the courtyard and on up the stairs. It was an ideal apartment complex for Karen's brothels and there was plenty of parking nearby for the clients' top-of-the-range cars — BMW, Volvo, Lexus.

Regular clients noticed Karen had more than doubled her prices in a year. Bill paid £60 in 1998 for sex in the Appian Way. Now it cost £150 in the Winter Garden. Joe had been to brothels in Synge Street, Christchurch and Donnybrook and paid a lot less. It was also a lot busier and some days he and the other men had to wait in the sitting room until a bedroom was free. 'The woman let me into the apartment and brought me to a bedroom,' he said, 'but she took me out of it again because she said another girl had come back early and she was meeting a client in the apartment.'

Another regular John, however, thought the Winter Garden was one of the better places Penthouse Pets was based. 'The last time it was behind Beggar's Bush Park,' he said, 'but I didn't stay that time because I didn't like it.' Stephen was also happy with the service because he was able to ring ahead and book his favourite lady. He was particularly fond of the Vietnamese woman Mural since he first met her in the Rathmines Hotel. 'If she was not available, she (Siona) would tell me so and would make an arrangement to ring me on my mobile phone when she would be available,' he said. This was a perfectly satisfactory arrangement. On Saturday 18 August 1999 he turned up to meet her but she was having a meal break in the Holiday Inn. He relaxed and had a pint while he waited for her before going next door and paying £300 for an hour with her.

Samantha told Jack that for £300 he could have Mural for an hour and a half and if he wanted she'd dress like a schoolgirl. She also tried to entice him into parting with five times more to join the Connoisseurs' Club. 'She said I just missed a club night the night before,' he said. 'For £1,500 I could go to bed with as many girls as I liked. She said it was an exclusive club. The party started at 8 p.m. and went on all night. There were Cuban cigars and cognac available. She said the place was outside the city and there would be as many girls as I could handle available.'

When Mick phoned Samantha he was also given the hard sell about Cobra but he told her that £1,500 was way out of his league. He was one man who was actually under the impression that Samantha was running a legitimate dating agency. He told her he wanted a relationship and she explained that she had an escort agency where he could drop in and meet some girls and that he was under no obligation to stay. She gave him the price list and a description of each girl. He became suspicious when she told him 'each of them was eager to please and one of them was into French kissing,' but he went along anyway.

The 40-year-old was not impressed with Club Elite. He knew he'd made a mistake as soon as he walked in the door. He was brought into a bedroom while three other women sat out in the sitting room watching television. When he told Isobelle he had changed his mind and would call back, she misunderstood what he was saying and inadvertently insulted him. She told him if he liked there would be 'a more mature lady' on duty later. Mick was disgusted. 'I just left,' he said. 'It was obvious that those girls were just there to provide sex.'

Another customer Peter was concerned about all the attention the prostitution business was getting in the media. 'Around this time there was a lot of publicity about massage parlours in the papers,' he said. 'I got worried about being caught in one.' He said this to Karen but she told him about the Executive Club and got Samantha to ring him. She described what she said was a new service in detail. She pointed out how discreet it was and said there was no danger of him ever getting caught. She gave him the name Peter and told him to use it every time he called her number.

'I fell for her sell and booked a girl,' he admitted. He may have phoned the Executive Club number but Samantha packed him off to the Winter Garden and told him it would cost him £300 an hour. However, she forgot to tell the woman in the brothel because when he was finished he asked her how much and she said £150. He made out a cheque for £150 and left. 'Later that evening Sheena rang me and told me I owed her £150 as I had only paid half the fee due,' he said. 'She rang me on a number of occasions since looking for her £150. I have not paid it.'

But what Samantha lost on one man she made up on others. One she met in the Bleeding Horse wrote her a cheque for £350, £50 over the standard rate for an hour and a half with Bianca. Many of the men paid by cheque and made them out to cash or to ACE marketing. They were drawn on a variety of bank accounts all over the country; from the Trustee Savings Bank in Bray to the Bank of Ireland in Lisduggan, Waterford, from the Ulster Bank in Dun Laoghaire to the National Irish Bank in Malahide.

The cheque was the most popular method of payment for the men who used the call-out service. A man who said he was lonely signed two £300 cheques from the NIB in Malahide. He paid for two women to come to his home and as he put it keep him company. An AIB cheque was handed over by a man who paid for sex with a prostitute in his apartment on the Malahide marina. One of Karen's clients wrote a £160 cheque for a house call to Blackrock while another paid with a cheque in his and his wife's name which was drawn on their joint account. Another man wrote a cheque for £172 for a woman to come to him in Baggot Street while another handed a cheque to a prostitute who called and had sex with him at his office. It was drawn on the Ulster Bank branch in College Green. There was little consistency in the cost of a call-out. Karen, Samantha and the women charged as much as they thought they could get.

Samantha kept a record of the transactions in her so-called little, black book. It was an A4-sized, ruled diary. She kept it in her handbag. It contained the men's names and phone numbers — mobiles and landlines — and their addresses for call-outs. It listed their preferences, the girls' names, times and cash or cheque amounts. Some men were identified in the diary by their fetishes, for instance 'Stockings – Monkstown Gates on left, facing water'. Others were more straightforward such as 'Jerry £300 Tara', 'Paul — Café Java 3.30', and '2.45 Eve £160'. Frank's 8.30 p.m. appointment with Bianca was on page 76 with all his requirements — vibrator, lingerie, dressed/made up, his mobile number beside it. There was also a record of the first job Samantha had lined up for Liz Allen, 'Karla — Winter Garden 4.30'. 'The diary is a record of the enquiries I have handled since I started working with Karen Leahy,' she said. 'I kept this record so I could claim my commission. The ones ticked are those who kept the appointments.'

Not all the men kept their appointments and not all paid the agreed amount. Samantha kept a note of those like Peter whom she believed owed her money. On page 73 under Wednesday 15 August she had written 'Peter £300 Bianca' and a tick beside £150. She didn't give up easily. On the next page for Thursday 16th she had written 'Meet Peter' and his mobile number. Some of the names in her little black book may have been false but the contact numbers were real. Hundreds of men who were prepared to pay at least £300 for sex were in it. The numbers comprised the ideal target market for Cobra. Samantha could earn money and simultaneously compile a list of wealthy men whom she might just be able to persuade to pay a lot more money to go to expensive orgies camouflaged as corporate party nights.

Samantha said she only worked for Karen for around five weeks but the pages in her diary show it was closer to two months. During that time she conducted at least £40,000 worth of business. That figure represents the sum total when all the amounts of money in the book with ticks beside them are added up. In spite of the fact that it was she who wrote the amounts in the diary, Samantha still disputed the figure. 'Despite what the newspapers have said about the tens of thousands of pounds that passed through my fingers, the reality is that I saw little money,' she said. 'It wasn't about money really anyway. It was more borne out of a fascination and desire to see if I could create something unusual and successful.'

It is highly unlikely the men knew their details were kept on file and no doubt it would be of great concern to them even today. The information could have been extremely useful to blackmailers. The Gardaí seized the diary. Reggie also kept a record of the different places he rented and the false names he used. Karen, too, kept a diary but while the Gardaí discovered diary pages listing names and cash amounts, the actual book was never found.

The operation to close down Karen's business started almost by accident. The caretaker at the Winter Garden complex first noticed something wrong on 11 September 1999. He found a set of keys for the apartment in the open letter box. This was the way the women let themselves in. 'This was a breach of the complex rules,' Walter McCormick said, 'and I (tried) to meet someone from the apartment to tell them not to leave the keys out.' He finally spoke to a black-haired girl but his suspicions were aroused.

Over the next few days men whom he didn't know and who didn't live in the complex started coming up to him and asking for directions to the apartment. He noticed other men finding their own way to it. 'These men were calling constantly from approximately 11 a.m. until 8 p.m. when I finished work and left,' he said.

Then he discovered there were at least four women in the apartment, one blonde and three brunettes. A few days later an oriental girl arrived. They stayed there all day, only leaving for short periods to pop out to the shops or the chipper. It was then he realised the apartment was being used as a brothel. He told his boss, the property manager, about it and he called in the Gardaí. They knew about it already.

A team from Operation Gladiator had the apartment under surveillance. There were detectives watching it from inside the courtyard and outside on Pearse Street. The surveillance teams were in radio contact over the four-day operation. Half of the 24 men stopped and questioned admitted paying a total of over £2,550 for sex. Six others told the Gardaí they didn't have sex for a variety of reasons. One man called for Bianca but she was busy. He decided to go for a walk around the block until she was free but was instead stopped by Gardaí. Another was the company director who brought the two English businessmen down. Two other men who called left because they didn't like the set-up or any of the women. The other two were caught during the raid. One was in the apartment, the other arrived during the search.

Two weeks after the caretaker's suspicions were aroused, the women in the apartment knew something was wrong. They caught glimpses of men watching them and got worried. They were afraid these men were stalkers or creeps. They didn't expect them to be the police. On Wednesday 22 September they panicked and rang Karen. She was having lunch with Reggie and Samantha in the ILAC centre. 'Karen got a call from one of the girls saying someone was messing with the buzzer,' Reggie said. He drove them down and parked the jeep in the underground car park. Karen breezed in and used the opportunity to collect her commission from the book. They were there fifteen minutes when the Gardaí knocked on the door. Mural answered it and six detectives walked in.

It was the middle of the day but all the curtains in the apartment were drawn. Megan and Bianca were in the sitting room. Karen, Samantha and Reggie headed for the kitchen but Detective Inspector John McMahon, the officer in charge, went after them. Eve was in one of the bedrooms with a man. Detective Garda John Cribbin described what he saw. 'I observed a naked man lying on a bed face down and a woman, who was dressed in a very short PVC mini-skirt and a black bra, sitting on his naked buttocks.' Sergeant Mary Delmar explained to Eve she was not under arrest and free to go at any time. Eve handed her the egg flip and £80 which she had hidden in her bra. The man got dressed quickly, made a statement and left.

It was clear the apartment functioned solely as a brothel. There was no one living there. The Gardaí found no personal clothes, bed sheets, female toiletries or substantial amounts of food during the search. In the bathroom there were bottles of shower gel, shower wash, skin toner, shampoo, razors and aftershave, so the men could shower and shave after sex. In the bedrooms there were condoms, used and unused, baby lotions, tissues and toilet rolls. There was also a skirt, pants, bra and knickers. They were all made of PVC, with compliments slips from the Skintight Company. There was also another rubber skirt and a black wig. In the women's bags the Gardaí found handcuffs, condoms, KY Jelly, vibrators and assorted ladies' clothes.

Karen Leahy remained calm and in control. She told Detective Inspector McMahon the brothel was her responsibility. 'There were four girls but only two on duty,' she said, 'The Chinese girl had called in to see Sam.' Karen had the Club Elite mobile phone on her and admitted it was hers. When she was cautioned she replied 'that's OK.' Karen, Samantha and Reggie were arrested and taken to Store Street station. On the way in the car Garda Mick Moran asked Karen what her own mobile number was. When she told him, he knew it was also the number for Penthouse Pets.

Karen's and Samantha's phones rang all evening with men looking for sex. The phones were left singing on a table in the station. During the five-minute journey Karen missed seven calls. When they emptied their pockets and handbags, it was clear they were loaded. Karen had two cheques, each for £300, £830 cash, the brothel mobile, a £1,655 paid mobile bill, commission records, a foreign currency advice slip, ACE marketing business cards and the keys to the apartment. She claimed that only £270 of the cash was commission and the rest was her own. Reggie handed over £3,560 cash, a £900 bank draft, an ICS building society book in the name of Emma Leahy (Karen's sister), his own mobile and eighteen cheques worth £4,772. One of the £300 cheques was payment for Malpotane. Samantha also surrendered her mobile, a second SIM card, her diary and three ACE business cards.

Karen and Reggie spoke freely during the subsequent Garda interviews. She was heavily pregnant and the Gardaí took no chances with her. During the course of the evening they made sure a doctor examined her. 'Do you take responsibility for running the brothel,' Detective Inspector John McMahon asked her. 'Yes, I do,' she replied, 'but I want to say that I am a single mother of three children expecting a fourth and I have no other way of providing for them. While I know that what I do is wrong, I feel that I have done no harm to anybody and I am only trying to provide for my family.'

Reggie made a number of calls from the station and ensured the children were looked after when Karen couldn't contact her father. He admitted collecting the money but claimed he wasn't directly involved in the business. 'Although I played an active part in the running of the brothel,' he said, 'I made no personal gain whatsoever. All the money went to Karen Leahy. I'd collect £500 a day, sometimes it would be more depending on how busy the girls were.'

He had simple explanations for the cash and the building society book. The £3,650 was what was left of £4,000 he got from his mother. Karen's sister Emma, he said, had left her ICS book in his car. He also had a simple explanation as to what he was doing in the brothel. 'The only reason I was there,' he said, 'was to bring Samantha and Karen there and then drive them away from it.' At the end of the interviews he signed the notes and initialled the pages. There was no animosity between him and the Gardaí. It was raining when they released him so he asked them for a lift back to his jeep. They were going back to continue the search anyway so they dropped him at the basement car park in the Winter Garden.

Samantha, however, was a different kettle of fish. The Gardaí weren't even sure what age she was and there are still four different dates of birth on file for her. She told them she was prepared to talk about her role in the business on condition that nothing was written down. She said she had been strongly advised by her solicitor not to make a statement. A pattern developed during the course of the interviews where she started off telling lies before the truth, or at least part of it, was gradually coaxed out of her.

First she said, 'I do not have any part in the running of a brothel.' Then she agreed, 'I have on occasion answered the phone for a friend of mine who runs an agency.' Then she told them 'the agency organised female company for male clients but I didn't know if that included full sexual intercourse.' And finally she admitted, 'I am aware the agency does provide sex as requested by the client.'

She also admitted she knew it was a brothel but emphasised, 'I got no money for doing this for Karen.' She insisted throughout that she would stop talking as soon as the Gardaí started writing so a detective who sat in for about an hour of this had to excuse himself, leave the room and write down all he could remember outside.

In the second interview Samantha admitted she was paid for setting up men with prostitutes and gave her side of the *Sunday*

Independent sting. She said the allegation that she hired Liz Allen was not true. 'I explained that any clients she would meet were signed-up members of an exclusive club and that most of them are people that we would know very well,' she said. 'I also told her she would have calls from travelling businessmen who would require female company.'

She complained that Campbell Spray had tricked her. 'He brought me outside the hotel and he paid me £300 in cash which is something I don't normally do.' She only realised she'd been stung when she opened the newspaper the following Sunday. Samantha claimed there was nothing illegal going on. The girl was going one-to-one with Campbell Spray, she said, and this was not against the law. She was right about the law but not about her own role in it. To commit a prostitution offence there must be more than one woman involved. However, Samantha was organising prostitution and that was against the law.

All three were released without charge that night and a file on the case was sent to the Director of Public Prosecutions. Karen's two mobile phones were given back to her. The following week the Gardaí checked them and found they were operating again. Karen had the SIM cards re-issued but she retained the original numbers and re-opened the brothels in new locations.

Samantha and Reggie also went back to work for her and ten days after the raid it was business as usual for all three. Samantha's distinctive voice and telephone manner was easily recognisable on the phone. The Gardaí received a complaint about an advertisement in the *Golden Pages* for a dating agency 'Blondelle Blues'. Reggie's mobile phone number appeared in the advertisement. He was also running a sweet shop in Dublin City centre and although they never proved it detectives suspected he was putting the punters' credit cards through the shop's machine. One of the women who worked behind the counter was a prostitute who worked for Marie Bridgeman and was well known to the Gardaí because she was the one who told them about her breast implants.

On 16 February 2000 Karen, Reggie and Samantha were arrested and charged with organising prostitution and managing brothels. They said nothing and were brought before Kilmainham District Court. They were released on £3,000 bail each. For the next year and a half they gained a certain notoriety around the District and Circuit Courts because they turned up for the subsequent appearances dressed in hooded, full-length capes.

Reggie was the first to be convicted. On 15 May 2001 Stephen Reginald Hutton was fined £6,500 and given an eighteen-month suspended sentence at the Dublin Circuit Criminal Court for helping to manage the Winter Garden brothel. Detective Inspector John McMahon said Reggie was now working with Karen in a legitimate business, a shop in Abbey Street in the city centre.

Four months later on 30 October Karen and Samantha were also fined £6,500 and given an eighteen-month suspended sentence. Ironically while Karen, the brains behind the operation, was only convicted of brothel-keeping, Samantha was done for managing a brothel and organising prostitution by controlling the activities of prostitutes. She made legal history. She's the first person in Ireland to be convicted of organising prostitution. She said later she thought this was 'hilarious'.

Samantha's lawyer said she was suffering from severe depression. She was a cocaine addict he said but now she was drug-free. Judge Elizabeth Dunne took a lenient approach. She said by admitting their guilt both women had saved a great deal of court time and embarrassment for the men who used their brothel. 'Both were involved in a sordid, despicable and distasteful way of making money and they exploited those who were working for them,' she said. 'Having heard the circumstances of both, I see nothing that justifies their involvement in such activities but I feel that I can deal with it in a non-custodial way.'

But Samantha wasn't happy with those comments and later declared: 'To the judge who made the heinous accusation against me (i.e. of exploitation) I ask, if given the option of a Lada or Mercedes, would she not choose the car more representative of her position, income and lifestyle. The men who chose to use the Executive Club made that choice every time they picked up the phone and called me.' Karen and Reggie had three months to pay the fines. Samantha was allowed five months. The Gardaí estimated the business generated an annual turnover of half a million pounds.

Six weeks later Samantha blamed the legal system for the fact that none of the men who used the prostitutes had to appear before the court. 'I could have pleaded not guilty,' she complained. 'This would have provoked a media circus of proportions this country has never seen. If nothing else it certainly would have been fun. Imagine if all the customers the police had interviewed would have been required to appear as witnesses and be cross-examined by my lawyer in detail. In one fell swoop, I would not have been the sole victim of a media witch-hunt. I would be one of the 300 or so of the cream of Irish society who were caught out.'

This simply wasn't true. None of the clients the Gardaí took statements from were, as Samantha called them, 'the cream of Irish society'. There were no politicians, public figures or media personalities. Samantha also said she was writing a book as part of her rehabilitation. She promised, rather tantalisingly, that it would be a good read. It has yet to be published. At least one publisher turned her down.

'I feel no guilt whatsoever arranging meetings between willing adults,' she defiantly declared. 'My only mistake was to set up the Executive Club in one of the most morally-backward and sanctimonious countries in the world and my only shame is that an excellent business opportunity is gone forever.' But this morally-backward and sanctimonious country had not, however, heard the last of Karen Leahy and Samantha Blandford Hutton. There were more victims to be exploited in a cruel, cynical and criminal fashion.

6 A Woman of Substance

I t was a routine call-out. Two uniformed Gardaí arrived at the recently completed City West Hotel and Conference Centre in West Dublin. A woman was shouting and roaring abuse at the staff. She was very drunk. The hotel management had asked her a couple of times to leave but she refused — loudly. When they arrived the two Gardaí were greeted by a very aggressive and indignant Samantha Blandford Hutton.

'She was going berserk outside,' Garda Keith Mallon said. They warned her that if she didn't calm down she would be arrested. With that she became more aggressive and continued screaming and roaring and trying to get back in to the hotel. She was arrested but wouldn't go quietly. She fought and kicked and screamed and scratched. She bit Keith Mallon so hard on the arm that she left the tracks of her teeth in his elbow. She also performed a striptease when Gardaí brought her to the station.

Samantha said afterwards that the incident was an attempt by her to commit suicide. 'At the time I was recovering from drugs and was at my most vulnerable point,' she said. 'I was almost pushed over the edge by this incident. This is what pushed me to the point where I almost attempted to take my life a second time and was arrested for resisting a garda's efforts to stop myself from approaching the edge of the roof of a building.'

It was also her defence when the case came up in Kilmainham District Court a year later. Her solicitor, Michael Finucane, said she was suffering an acute psychiatric condition at the time. She was, he argued, going through a difficult time and was making a serious attempt to take her own life. He submitted a report from Dr John Connolly, the Head of the Irish Association of Suicidology.

The judge said she could not look at the doctor's report with the same 'rose-coloured glasses' as Mr Finucane. Judge Gillian Hussey said any stress caused to Samantha by media publicity mentioned in the doctor's report was self-induced. However, she took pity on her. On 14 February 2002 Samantha was given a three-month suspended sentence and fined £900. It was her twelfth criminal conviction. Her record now included assault, burglary, drug dealing and organising prostitution and yet she never spent a day in jail for any of her crimes.

In a series of unprecedented full and front-page interviews, the *Evening Herald* published a series of articles over four days entitled 'A Woman of Substance'. The newspaper reporter, Brian O'Connell, spoke to Samantha about her life, crimes, opinions and feelings. Amongst other things Samantha talked about her life before and after her conviction for prostitution. 'I started working again and opened a number of businesses,' she said. 'One of them being a cleaning company, the other an elite escort agency. The former has proved to be enormously successful and the latter proved to be my latest undoing.'

In fact the opposite was the case. Samantha was lucky she wasn't sent to jail because of the latter but it was the former that proved to be her undoing. By rights the articles should have been called 'A Woman of Substance Abuse'. The cleaning company may have been 'enormously successful' for Samantha but it was just another money-making scam founded upon the exploitation of poor, vulnerable and isolated people. In this case those exploited were again mainly women. But this time they were foreigners trying to earn some money here — South Americans, in a strange country a long way from home.

In January 2001 word reached a rural village in Western Brazil that there was work in Ireland, a country over 7,000 miles away. Neusa da Silva Resende was a widow who lived in Sidrolandia, a village on the borders of Paraguay and Bolivia, with her 24-year-old son and 15-year-old daughter. She got a call from her brother who lived 150 kilometres away in the state capital Campo Grande. He had met a Brazilian woman in Sao Paulo who had told him there was work available for her as a cleaner in Ireland, and her flight and accommodation would be paid for.

Sidrolandia is in an agricultural region of the vast state of Mato Grosso do Sul. The state is famous among wildlife enthusiasts for the Pantanal, an open swampland larger than France. But work is hard to come by there and Neusa was offered a cleaning job in Ireland on money she could only dream of earning at home. She was told she'd be flown to Dublin and would be paid €1,523.69 (£1,200) a month after tax. She would also be provided with a place to live. If she didn't like it, she could always come home. She believed there was only one catch, that she'd only have to re-pay the cost of her move if she didn't work up to the end of the year. Neusa needed the money to support her elderly parents and pay for her daughter's education. She decided to give it a go.

The widow left her home and family in Brazil and arrived in Dublin on 30 May 2001. Like many Irish people who went to America she hoped to live comfortably but work hard. She planned to save money and send as much home as she could. She came alone. She knew no one here. She hadn't a word of English. She knew nothing about Ireland. The representative had arranged everything including her work permit. She was put up in a house in Kingswood Heights in Tallaght and quickly knuckled down to doing what she was here to do, working as a cleaner for Samantha Blandford Hutton's company.

At Hand Cleaning Services was a limited company with an address at Samantha's home in St Patrick's Park, Clondalkin. Samantha was a founder director and was later joined on the board of directors by Reggie. The company was set up on 3 April 2001 but two years later it still hadn't filed any accounts.

At Hand had a number of lucrative contracts and its cleaners worked all over Dublin and the surrounding counties. They cleaned the offices of Hibernia Computer Services in Ballsbridge, Golden Vale in Tallaght, uPVC Windows in Clondalkin, JVC Recycling on the Cookstown Industrial Estate and the clubhouse at St Margaret's Golf Club. But, as Neusa soon found out, the company had some rather unorthodox work practices. Its employees were expected to be, to say the least, extremely versatile, flexible and understanding.

Neusa waited three weeks for her first pay cheque and discovered she was not going to be paid what she was promised in Brazil. She was left short by over €577 (£454.76) a month. She was only paid €949 (£747.60) and never told why. Then Samantha started to deduct €29.20 (£23) every week without her permission. It was to pay the company back what it cost to bring her to Ireland. This left her with €200 a month less than she would have got if she claimed the dole and rent allowance. She told Samantha she hadn't enough to live on, but Samantha ignored her. She continued to ignore her for three months. It was only when Neusa refused to work for her if the deductions continued that she stopped taking the money from her pay packet.

Then Neusa discovered that for Samantha's company the employment legislation was an optional extra. Gone was the promise of an eight-hour day and five days a week with overtime paid at reasonable rates. Her wages were paid in cash. She was handed a brown envelope with her name on it. She said she never got a payslip or any information relating to tax, PRSI or other deductions required by law, nor did she receive holiday pay or annual leave entitlement. There was no overtime. When she queried this, she was told there was no such thing as overtime in Ireland.

Neusa had to work twelve hours a day. She was also told to be available for immediate rostering starting at any time between 7 a.m. and 7 p.m. When her eldest daughter came to Ireland to see her, Neusa was refused holidays. Francini Louise, who was by now sixteen years old, ended up working with her mother while she was in Ireland. This was also illegal but it was the only way they could be together. 'I didn't get one day off to go out with my daughter,' she said. 'She kept saying, "This is a first world country. This is absurd." She was here for six weeks in July and August and every day of her holidays she worked.' Not surprisingly Francini was never properly paid for the work and she returned to Brazil on 26 August 2002 out of pocket.

The work got harder, the hours got longer and the wages got smaller and smaller. Neusa often worked from 8 a.m. to 2 a.m. the following morning without a break. It was slave labour. She never worked less than forty hours a week. In July 2001 she worked 105 hours a week for which she was paid a basic €196 (£155), around €1.80 an hour. She wasn't paid for the 65 hours overtime. From August to September that year she worked between 75 and 80 hours a week, again for basic pay and no overtime.

Neusa often went five to six weeks without being paid and then, when she did receive a cheque, she was told not to cash it. Once when she did try to convert the cheque to cash, Samantha gave out stink to her. She phoned her and ordered her back to work immediately. She told her she was to stay away from the bank. She was not to attempt to cash the cheque until Samantha told her there was enough money in the account to meet it.

Samantha kept her employees working for her through a combination of charm and bullying, promises and threats. When she wasn't driving them to the limit, she was re-assuring them that the company was growing and getting stronger financially. She told them her main concern was that the job was done properly and she didn't care how many people it took to ensure that. The workload would, she said, be shared amongst a larger group of cleaners as soon as they could be recruited and therefore conditions would improve for those who stayed.

The problem for Neusa was that even if she wanted to she couldn't leave and find another cleaning job. Her work permit was job specific. It was issued through her employer and that meant Samantha had a hold on her. She couldn't work for anyone else. She had no savings and no other form of income open to her. She could not claim social welfare and, because her accommodation was tied in to her job, she would have nowhere to live if she left.

After eight months of this, Neusa decided she'd had enough and in February 2002 she went home. Samantha missed her immediately. She phoned her in Brazil and asked her to come back. Neusa said she promised her that things would be different and so much better. She was to come back and bring her sisters. There was plenty of work and 'better pay for everyone'. Neusa says she turned on the charm, "'You've been a wonderful worker. I've never had a moment's problem with you. I can't afford to lose you. The firm needs you", and so on, she said. I said we had far too much work and could not keep it up, and she said, "Well, if you have anybody else in your family bring them over too.'"

More in hope than in faith, Neusa returned to Dublin the following month. Her sister, Nilce Mara da Silva, came with her leaving her husband and 4-year-old son behind in a shack with only walls and a roof. She hoped to earn enough money in Ireland to pay to put the doors and windows on their home. She started working for At Hand Cleaning Services on 7 March 2002, the day she landed in Dublin. She wasn't legally entitled to work because she only had a tourist visa but she said Samantha told her she would get her a work permit and deducted money from her salary to pay for the paperwork.

Three months later the permit still hadn't arrived and Nilce Mara decided to go home. The sisters met Samantha but she persuaded them to stay by offering them more money. When they said they had too much work to do, she asked them to bring more people over from Brazil. She promised to organise work permits for all of them.

The following month their sister, Nilma Benedita, and her husband, Elis Pereira da Silva, arrived. They also came to try and earn some money here to improve the quality of their lives at home. They left their two infant boys aged one and two behind. 'You have to appreciate how bad things are where we come from,' Nilce Mara said. 'There are no jobs and no hope of a job.'

In a wealthy city in a wealthy country, it was a classic tale of impoverished immigrants arriving full of hopes and dreams and struggling to make a better life for themselves. But the family's hopes were dashed very quickly here. By the time Elis and Nilma arrived on 25 July, Neusa and Nilce Mara hadn't been paid for a month. They couldn't afford the bus fare for both of them to go to the airport to meet their sister and brother-in-law. Neusa went to meet them on her own.

After a three-day journey Elis and Nilma arrived in Dublin. Along with Neusa, the three of them made their way back to Tallaght on the bus. They had to change in the city centre and carry their luggage from one bus stop at one end of town to the other bus stop at the far end. They paid their own air-fares to Dublin. It cost them over €1,000 each. They took out a loan to get here because they had been promised a refund. They never got the money back from Samantha.

All four Brazilians lived together in the house in Tallaght. They worked together as a team and endured the same long hours under the same atrocious conditions with no breaks or rest periods. Samantha promised them all new and better rates of pay — €350 a week for Neusa, €320 for Nilce Mara and between €250 and €300 for the new recruits. These never materialised. All four were left short or without their wages and still no overtime was paid.

Neusa and Nilce Mara worked 84 hours a week as standard. Nilma and Elis only had to work 40-hour weeks in July and August 2002 but then they weren't paid for them. By September 2002, Nilca Mara was owed more than €10,000 (£8,290). This represented two weeks wages plus compensation for not being paid at the proper rate from the start. Her sister and brother-in-law were owed at least €1,500 (£1,200) each. 'We were five weeks not being paid and we had not anything to eat in the house,' Neusa said.

The family worked in strange and mysterious places, arriving in a strange and mysterious way. They were picked up in the morning and driven to work in a van with blacked-out windows. Black plastic bags were glued to the sides and the back of what Samantha so eloquently referred to as 'the company van'. The workers could not see nor were they told where they were going. The next-door-neighbour Rose Cooney watched in amazement as the cleaners piled into the back of the van early in the morning only to return late in the evening or in the early hours of the following morning.

'I get up at 6.45 a.m. because I do cleaning myself and I have to be down in Ballymahon by 7.30 a.m. so I used to hear the van, beep, beep, picking them up,' she said. 'I saw them getting into the van and I also saw the black sacks going over the windows. They would have to cover the van themselves. I brought it to my husband's attention. I thought it was appalling. I said, there is something wrong but I never knew because they did not understand English.'

When there was no van, Reggie turned up in a sports car to drive them to work. 'There was no room in the back,' Neusa said, 'we were all squashed in with the vacuum cleaners, and the cleaning liquids would spill all over us.' Neusa remembers cleaning 'every type of building.' The van brought them to dimly-lit houses where they dusted and picked used condoms off the floor while scantily-clad women and men walked around them. They were taken at least fifteen times to a building site in Kilcock, Co. Kildare. It wasn't a job for female cleaners but they swept up and had to scrape blobs of cement and mortar off the floors and windows. They weren't given tools and did it with their hands.

Samantha's mother subsequently denied this claim. 'I worked in the building site,' Joan Blandford said. 'I never saw a bag of cement to be moved. The houses were all new but the builders were gone. They had to be cleaned, the glass and the floors.'

However, the Brazilians said they even cleaned Samantha's home and spent the August bank holiday weekend cleaning the van. The van driver drove it down to them. Reggie followed and drove him off in the sports car.

Desiree O'Rourke, a retired solicitor, was also shocked at the way the company treated the Brazilians. She had some work done on her house in July 2002 and called in 'At Hand' to clean up after the builders. Neusa, Nilce Mara and Elis were dropped off at her home in the morning. She thought they were only going to work four or five hours there and was quite prepared to have them come back and finish the job over a couple of days.

That's what she expected to happen but that's not the way things were done in 'At Hand'. The man who dropped the Brazilians off told Desiree the job would have to be finished within the day. 'The Brazilians worked from 10 a.m. until nearly 9.30 p.m. that night and I was actually quite concerned about them,' Desiree said. 'They had no provision for food. I gave them lunch and I gave them their dinner and they were amazed at this. It struck me at the time. I was very concerned about them when I saw the things they had to do.'

The Brazilians were told that these extremely harsh and exhausting conditions were the way things were in Ireland. They knew no better. They came from a country with no social welfare and little protection for workers. They believed this until Francini Louise, who could speak some English, realised this was not the case. Samantha was on holidays at the time and conditions had seriously deteriorated. Some days Elis and Nilma were collected for work while other days they were left behind. On 16 August 2002 they finally brought the matter to a head.

Elis and Nilma approached Samantha and asked her why they weren't being paid what they were owed. They presented her with a list of all the hours they had worked. They insisted they be paid properly and in full. But Samantha denied hiring them and refused to give them any money. When Neusa heard this she broke down and cried.

Samantha relented and said she would pay her sister and brother-in-law but only if they worked on the Kilcock building site. They were told to clean out rows of newly-built homes. There was so much stuff that by the end of the first day they hadn't even cleared the first house. When darkness fell the company driver still hadn't collected them. They were promised €50 a house but weren't given a cent. After one particularly difficult week Elis decided they had had enough.

Elis's decision to quit came at a bad time for Samantha. She had a big job on the next day and needed all four cleaners. She resorted to her usual tactic, a combination of charm and bullying. 'They said to us that Elis and Nilma would have to leave the house,' Neusa said, 'and I said we are all staying together.' Samantha sent the driver to Tallaght with €200 for Elis and Nilma. When he phoned her on the mobile and told her none of the Brazilians would work until they were paid what they were owed, he was instructed to take the €200 back. 'I gave him back the money because I was afraid,' Neusa said. 'He was very intimidating.'

The next day all four, along with Neusa's daughter Francini, took the bus into town. Francini spoke English and discovered the existence of the Equality Authority. The phone calls from Samantha began while they were at the bus stop and continued as they made their way along Clonmel Street to the Authority's offices. 'She phoned us about fifteen times to tell us to get off the bus and go to work,' Neusa said. They were met by a member of the legal section and were told there were no solicitors on duty. They left with an appointment to see one three weeks later.

On that day, Friday 6 September 2002, they approached Samantha to see if they could resolve their problems without having to take legal action. They told her they were going to a solicitor but said they would work if they were paid up to date. But Samantha turned nasty. She was not prepared to put up with what she saw as troublemakers, that is those who interrupted or interfered with her immoral and illegal operation. She told them she'd sack anyone who consulted a solicitor and ordered Nilma and Elis to get out of the house in Tallaght immediately.

That was the last straw. They had had enough. They decided there and then to stick together. It was time to stand up to Samantha. They refused to leave the house and from then on they got no more work or money. They had already written to and called in to the Labour Inspectorate of the Department of Enterprise, Trade and Employment. They kept their appointment with the Equality Authority and met the solicitor, Sheila Larkin.

Sheila Larkin listened to their story but explained that it would take her some time to deal with the problem. She wrote to Samantha pointing out to her that she had broken the labour laws and asking that she pay the money she owed immediately. She sent the letter by courier to make sure she got it. Samantha phoned her the following week and told her that Neusa was the only one who worked for her. She said she didn't hire the other three in spite of the evidence to the contrary. 'I said to her I had seen a cheque made out to her (Nilce),' Sheila Larkin said, 'and she said no. She denied it.'

The week after their meeting with the solicitor, Samantha sent the van around three mornings in a row (9, 10 and 11 September) to bring the da Silvas to work. When they didn't go, she wrote them a letter. She said if she didn't hear from them by the following Monday 16 September, she would take it that they didn't want to work for the company any more. The language she used would lead one to believe she was the most upstanding and understanding of employers. 'I will treat your refusal as a resignation,' she wrote, 'and will make arrangements to pay you what you are due, including the balance of your holiday pay and issue a P45 termination certificate.' She didn't say who would decide what they were due.

The next day, 12 September, Samantha wrote them another letter. The language was again polite and sweet but the message conveyed was anything but. She told them they had to get out of the house. She said the lease on Kingswood Heights had expired but she had found a property more suitable and convenient for the company. She told them they were to leave the house clean and tidy 'as we found it', and have the keys ready to hand back to the landlord. 'The new house is in Clondalkin and is available to any member of staff wishing to rent it under the same agreement,' she said. 'The company van and driver may be used over the weekend of the 28th and 29th to move your belongings to our new address.'

The use of the phrase 'available to any member of staff' was clever considering the first letter the day before made it clear Neusa was no longer a member of staff. Samantha used the same phrase in a letter to Sheila Larkin at the Equality Authority. It was full of irrelevant detail in relation to the expiry of the lease in Tallaght and the decision to rent elsewhere. She made no reference to the way she had mistreated the family and had no response to their claims against her. The fact was that Neusa and her family were being sacked and evicted and now they faced the additional risk of deportation. They couldn't get other jobs, none of them had work permits. Neusa's permit had expired on 2 August. She had applied for it to be renewed in July but she was still waiting.

Meanwhile, the man who owned the house in Kingswood Heights knew absolutely nothing about all this and was shocked when he found out what was going on. The first he heard about it was when a Garda Inspector from Tallaght told him that the Brazilians had got a High Court injunction preventing him from evicting them. He rented the house to Samantha but she put the da Silva family in it and charged them rent. He told her he wanted the house back by 6 October. He had no dealings or agreement with the da Silva family and had to hire a solicitor to protect his interest.

Samantha was also trying to protect herself from the trouble that was on the way. She wrote more letters. She got an employee of the Brazilian Embassy in Dublin to translate one of them into Portuguese before sending it to Neusa. She forwarded copies in English and Portuguese to Sheila Larkin at the Equality Authority. But the Department of Trade and Enterprise had already promised to send an inspector to At Hand Cleaning Services. They were investigating the family's complaint under the Contract Cleaning Employment Regulation Order. Such an investigation could lead to Samantha being prosecuted under the Industrial Relations Acts.

The Brazilians, however, hadn't time to wait. Samantha's letters had frightened them. They were extremely upset but when they went back to Sheila Larkin the news was not good. 'Basically I could not represent them,' she said. 'They had no money and they were not entitled to legal aid.' She put them in touch with a Portuguese-speaking priest who spent eighteen years on the missions in Brazil. When Fr Pat McNamara, a Holy Ghost Spiritan, went to see them they were cold and hungry. The heating in the house had been cut off and they were living on milk and biscuits. They had already gone to their next-door neighbour and begged for help. In spite of the language differences Rose Cooney could see they were in dire straits. 'The three women came crying and knocking on my door,' she said, 'They were saying "no food, no job, no nothing".'

The first thing Rose Cooney and Fr McNamara did was to buy them food. 'We went, the two of us, up to the local supermarket and I did a decent buy for them because they had nothing in the house,' he said. 'They were really appreciative.' Then Fr McNamara took them to another solicitor. He walked in the door and presented the Brazilians to him. 'I have four people here who are to be sacked, evicted and deported in the next two days,' he announced.

Donal Taaffe specialises in cases where foreign workers are exploited. The da Silva family was lucky to have been introduced to a sympathetic and generous solicitor who was shocked and saddened by what he heard. He engaged a barrister, Oisín Quinn, and both of them took on the case for free. The family did not, therefore, have to wait for the lumbering mechanisms of the State to trundle into action to protect them. They were able to take Samantha to court themselves.

Samantha came out fighting and denied everything. She said they were illegal immigrants. She correctly pointed out in her affidavit that none of the family had work permits and, therefore, none of them were legally entitled to remain in the State. In rather pompous language more commonly used by an obnoxious immigration officer, she said Neusa could be sent home. 'She is now in breach of the conditions attaching to her permission to land,' Samantha said. 'Her current status is thus a person liable to deportation pursuant to Section 3(2)(h) of the Immigration Act 1999.'

This in spite of the fact that she had helped Neusa complete the permit renewal forms in her own home in St Patrick's Park. She had also told her not to worry when it didn't arrive. She said delays of three or four months were to be expected within the Department of Enterprise, Trade and Employment. But when Neusa went to the offices of Garda National Immigration Bureau in August she was told her permit was ready. The only outstanding document was a form to be submitted by Samantha.

Samantha also denied that Nilce Mara, Nilma and her husband Elis Pereira had ever worked for her. She said she had no role in bringing them into the country. 'To do so would be an offence under Section 2 of the Illegal Immigrants (Trafficking) Act 2000,' she said. She pointed out that Neusa had admitted she was responsible for bringing her sisters and brother-in-law to Ireland. Samantha had, therefore, implied Neusa was trafficking in illegal immigrants.

There was, however, substantial evidence to the contrary. Samantha once paid Nilce Mara by cheque and the Brazilian woman kept a copy of it. She had signed it herself and the envelope it came in had 'Mara, 4' written on it in her handwriting. In addition one of the company's customers, Dr Tony Holohan, said Neusa, Nilce Mara and Nilma cleaned his house one morning in August. 'They arrived in a taxi and were accompanied by Ms Samantha Hutton who apologised for the fact they were late in arriving,' he said.

Nilce Mara, Nilma and her husband Elis came to Ireland on three-month holiday visas but they said Samantha told them they could work legally for 90 days. When those visas expired, they all filled in application forms for work permits and gave Samantha copies of their passports. Nilca Mara also completed her application form in Samantha's home. She told them their applications were being processed and continued to roster and collect them for work. She later claimed any dealings she had with Nilce Mara were only 'to allow her the companionship of her sister'.

The da Silva family believed they were entitled to work because Samantha was processing their applications. If they thought otherwise, they would hardly have written to the Government department responsible for issuing those visas and complained about their pay and conditions. But once they challenged Samantha, they lost any hope of getting work permits through her company so that they could remain here legally. In fact she later admitted she had no intention of applying for permits for them. She swore that three of them never worked for her and that Neusa was 'constantly disruptive and recalcitrant'. She did, however, concede one thing in her affidavit — 'It is true that all the plaintiffs are Brazilian nationals.'

On 26 September Donal Taaffe secured a High Court injunction to stop Samantha sacking and evicting them. He had already served papers on At Hand Cleaning Services Ltd at its address in St Patrick's Park but these came back unopened. The injunction and subsequent orders ran until the case came to trial. Samantha responded with a counter-claim. She denied everything and said Neusa had damaged her business with individuals and companies she worked for such as Brian O'Connell, Laurenta McManus and Galtee. She said the claim was vexatious and she was now seeking her legal costs and damages. But Samantha wouldn't put her money where her mouth was, and when the day of reckoning in the High Court finally arrived on 29 October 2002 she wasn't even represented. A solicitor who had been representing the company asked to be discharged because he couldn't get any instructions from the company as to what he was supposed to do.

In true theatrical fashion and in the manner she believed she was accustomed and entitled to, Samantha did manage a walk-on part during the proceedings. The company director appeared in court for a short time at the start of the hearing to let everyone know how traumatic all this was for her. She told Judge Peter Kelly she was 'at her wits' end' and was going to 'end up in a mental hospital if it keeps going as it is'. She spoke of her difficulty meeting the legal costs and claimed she couldn't afford counsel.

The company, she said, had been damaged by the case which had already received substantial publicity. At Hand had lost three contracts. She claimed it had few assets — four industrial hoovers worth between €900 and €1,000. At least that was what they were worth when they were new. She said it was unfortunate that the case had come to the High Court and asked if it could be transferred to the Labour Court. The case, however, went ahead. The judge told her that a limited company could only be represented in court, not by its director but through the agency of a solicitor. In effect, he added, At Hand was not represented although he told her she could remain in court to hear the proceedings if she wished. She left a short time later, well before the case finished.

Rose Cooney was disgusted by Samantha's behaviour in court and she told the judge how she felt. 'It is absolutely appalling that she can come in there and tell lies to the court, the director or whatever they call themselves and worked them to the bone,' she said. 'Worked them to the bone, that is what she done with them. I am ashamed to be Irish, that is all I can say, and so is my husband. I have five children of my own and I have taken on these people and trying to speak their English and whatever, bring them into my house. Their heating has been cut off at the moment so they have no heat now because they are being run out of where they are.'

Rose Cooney felt passionately about the way the da Silva family had been mistreated. She couldn't stop herself and apologised to the judge, but her honesty and integrity was compelling. Mr Justice Peter Kelly, who found her to be a true Good Samaritan, allowed her to continue. 'You are perfectly entitled to give your evidence,' he said. 'I'm not benefiting anything from these people,' she told him. 'I am after been helping these people for the last seven to eight weeks. In actual fact I have been feeding them along with Fr McNamara as well.'

It was clear from his judgment that Mr Justice Kelly felt the same. He saw the injustice of it all. 'The working conditions,' he said, 'were reminiscent of those which obtained in the time of Charles Dickens.' The company, he said, knew it had hired people who were not entitled to work here and, therefore, moving them around in the company van 'was done covertly and with a good deal of subterfuge attached to it.'

He found Samantha had exploited the family in a cruel fashion. They were, he said, the victims of a trick. They were vulnerable to such a hoax because they came from a very poor part of Brazil and had little English. In spite of her denials, she employed them, broke an agreement with them and 'behaved in a quite despicable fashion' towards them. Her treatment of them, he said, was 'shameful'.

He awarded Neusa €32,510.87, Nilce Mara €10,525 and Elis Pereira €1,143. Nilce and Elis were also awarded €1,000 each for their air-fare. He also awarded Neusa €5,000 and Nilce Mara and Elis €2,000 for emotional upset, distress and disappointment — a total of over €52,000 in damages. He deducted €4,500 from that because At Hand paid €2,500 to the Brazilians after the first hearing and another €2,000 on the morning of the second one. 'I want a receipt for that', Reggie told Donal Taaffe.

Nilma wasn't in court to hear the judgment. She had already gone home to look after her two infants. Reggie's cash allowed Nilce Mara to follow her. The costs were put at €15,000 plus 21 per cent VAT, which the judge said was a substantial reduction on what the actual costs should be. They were also awarded against Samantha. The bill was over €70,000.

But not everyone was impressed with the victory. 'Ah, what did they win?' Rose Cooney asked after court. 'They were working for seven months for nothing. Dickens, going back to Dickens' time, she treated them like slaves. If those Brazilian women had stolen a loaf of bread, they'd be in jail. Where's the justice is what I want to know?'

But Joan Blandford believes her daughter is the victim of the injustice. 'They were not ill-treated. They had lunch with us in my home every Sunday,' she said. 'Neusa had Christmas dinner with us. She spent New Year with us.' She denies almost all the Brazilians' claims and said Samantha didn't defend the case because she couldn't afford to. 'It had already cost €12,000,' she said. 'It would have cost another €20,000 and Sam hasn't a bean.' But that means that neither the Brazilians nor the lawyers will get paid a cent of the €70,000.

Naturally Joan Blandford, who has supported her daughter through thick and thin, continued to defend her in the face of severe criticism. 'Sam's not as bad or as black as she's been painted,' she said. 'That company was 100 per cent legitimate. She was working her butt off and she fell flat on her face. She's had a hard life. She was never given a chance. They never leave her alone. No matter what she does they never leave her alone.'

It may also be possible to see this saga as a genuine attempt by a disorganised woman to run a legitimate business which she couldn't cope with after one director left. But throughout all her enterprises Samantha doesn't seem to have realised the damage she has caused to herself and others. She has consistently rationalised her behaviour. She perceived herself as the hard worker who provided a service to people whether in the cleaning or sex business. There may be no malice in her and over the years she has suffered with illness and addiction, but she didn't seem to realise that while some of her actions were chaotic, others criminal, they have had drastic consequences. The fact is she's lucky she has never been sent to jail.

It was all very different eight months before when Samantha told the *Evening Herald* that At Hand had proved enormously successful. If this was true, it was hardly surprising considering the low wages, the long hours and the Dickensian conditions endured by its exploited employees. Even before Mr Justice Peter Kelly delivered his damning judgment, Samantha claimed the company was hopelessly insolvent. The judge said he hoped the family would get their money but the reality was they never would.

The apparent bankruptcy of a successful business in the space of a few months is ideal material for an investigation by the Director of Corporate Enforcement. That's precisely what the Brazilians' solicitor, Donal Taaffe, asked him to do. However, the Director wrote to him on 1 November 2002 and told him that a Mr Peter Durnin was considering the matter and would be in touch. 'I should say,' the letter continued, 'that it may be some time before he reverts to you.'

The da Silva family came to Ireland from a remote and agricultural part of Brazil. They were used to working hard and that is how they were able to keep going through such a physically and mentally draining experience. They came here to work hard and earn money honestly to improve the quality of their own and their family's lives. They would never have been able to earn the kind of money they were promised here in Brazil.

As it turned out they weren't able to earn it here either. They were victims of another one of Samantha Blandford Hutton's exploitative enterprises. They went home with less money than they came with. They took with them painful memories of a time which cost them financially and scarred them emotionally. They will never be as trusting again. Two of them, however, did come back to Ireland and by March 2003 Neusa and Elis Pereira were happily working for the ISS cleaning company in Intel in Leixlip.

'There was a lot of anguish and a lot of hurt and a lot of bitterness about what they had been promised. They let off a lot of steam,' Fr McNamara said. 'But they recognise they were seriously misled and they realise that it is not like this in employment in general in Ireland.' Despite their experience the da Silva family are extremely generous and have no bad feelings about the country where they were treated so badly. Elis Pereira was admirably dignified in his summary of the situation. 'We were not lucky,' he said, 'we met the wrong person, that is all.'

Charlotte Godkin also met the wrong person when she went to work for Karen Leahy. But while Samantha used a combination of charm and bullying when it came to exploiting employees, Karen leaned towards violence and false imprisonment. The difference in approach, however, meant that while Samantha ended up in the civil courts and managed to stay out of prison, Karen was brought before the criminal courts and ended up in the women's prison at Mountjoy Jail.

7 *Karen the Kidnapper*

Charlotte Godkin was 25 years old when she started working as a nanny for Karen Leahy. She grew up on a farm near Brittas Bay in Co. Wicklow. She looked after children from the time she left school. For the previous six years she worked in Dublin, Wicklow and in Florida. In the summer of 1998 she worked for a family in Clonskeagh in Dublin. 'In all my years working as a child-minder I never had any problems with the families I worked for and none of them ever complained about my work,' she said. But all that was about to change in October 1998.

Charlotte rang Karen after she saw an advertisement in the *Evening Herald* and went to see her at a house in Sunbury Gardens, Dublin 6. It was all very civilised. Karen's father, Dan, brought her in and gave her a cup of tea. He showed her around the house and pointed out the child-minder's room. The previous occupant had gone home. She was a French girl who had looked after the three children during the summer. Dan then left Charlotte to wait in the sitting room as he was in and out minding the three children, two boys aged eight and four and a girl aged two.

At 3.30 p.m. Karen came home to interview Charlotte. She was an hour late. The advertisement had been in the newspaper for some time and Karen had rejected a number of previous applicants. But she liked Charlotte. 'I was impressed with her as she had waited the hour and minded the kids,' she said. They talked for another hour as Karen explained the job to her and the way she'd worked with the two previous child-minders. She lived an unpredictable life not governed by any particular routine and she told Charlotte she would have to live in. She also told her she'd split up with the children's father.

Karen was now passing herself off as a legitimate businesswoman. She was running a discount type of shop in Rathmines, which sold things like toys, cutlery, crockery and cheap trinkets. She was also registered as a partner in a business called Glencairn Health Products which claimed to sell and distribute food supplements. Karen had a warehouse on Keeper Road in Drimnagh. She stored wholesale goods for the shop there and some of the so-called medical products like Malpotane which she and Reggie sold over the phone. When the Gardaí searched it, they also found furniture which had been reported missing from some of the previous houses she'd rented. Between this and her prostitution business, she hadn't time to mind her own kids.

Charlotte took the job without finding out how much she was to be paid. As a reference, she gave Karen the telephone number of a family she'd worked for in Brittas Bay. She moved in the following week but never signed a contract. The job entailed cooking for the three children and cleaning the house.

'I wanted her to run the home and look after the kids,' Karen said. 'I wanted someone that I could trust and that would be capable of looking after the kids.' Charlotte moved to Dublin because she had ambitions to get a better job. She planned to do a computer course the following year. She also wanted to take up martial arts again. She had done some judo classes in America.

Karen lent Charlotte her own keys and told her to get a set cut for herself. A few days later Charlotte asked her how much she would get. Karen told her £150 a week as well as food and board, and promised her every second weekend off. She had to give notice if she wanted other time off. 'She could have any time off she wanted provided she told me in plenty of time,' Karen said. 'My sister or my Dad could look after the kids if she wanted time off.' 'I asked her if she would draw up a contract stating my duties, my pay and my hours,' Charlotte said, 'but she said no.'

Charlotte's room was at the top of the house, on the third floor. The children's bedrooms were there too. Karen slept on the second floor with her boyfriend, Ernie Kenny. They had been together for about a year and he moved into Sunbury Gardens in April 1998. Originally from Castleknock in Dublin, Ernie was notorious in his own right for being 'a bit of a thug'. He had seven convictions for road traffic and public order offences such as being drunk and disorderly, and using threatening and abusive language. However, a celebrity chef and his wife experienced a particularly violent, frightening and sinister side of Ernie's character when they were driving home from their Dublin restaurant on 27 September 1997.

Derry Clarke is an award-winning chef. He has represented Ireland in cookery competitions and has appeared on RTÉ television. He and his wife, Sally Ann, own and run one of Dublin's most exclusive restaurants, L'Ecrivain on Lower Baggot Street. The night they met Ernie Kenny, Sally Ann Clarke had locked up the restaurant and was driving home. She stopped her Mazda sports car at traffic lights at Fitzwilliam Place when Ernie pulled up behind her in a Toyota Camry. He jumped out, banged on her car window and told her he was a Special Branch detective. He showed her a fake badge and ordered her to pull over.

Sally Ann Clarke was terrified. Ernie was apoplectic with rage. He accused her of changing lanes rapidly which caused him to brake hard and hit her. He claimed he had already flashed his lights at her twice before she stopped at the traffic lights. But Sally Ann didn't believe him and didn't want anything to do with him. She rolled down her window an inch and told him to go away. She didn't believe he was a policeman and suspected this was an attempted abduction or robbery. Ernie told her she had contravened a section of the Road Traffic Act but when she asked him which section, he couldn't tell her. She drove off and Ernie chased her for five miles. He caught up with her again at traffic lights in Kimmage in south Dublin.

By this time Derry Clarke was also on his way home. It was a pure coincidence that he arrived at the junction of the KCR garage to find a man standing at the driver's door of his wife's car screaming in the window at her. The chef nudged the back of Ernie's car forward. Then he got out of his car and asked Ernie what he was doing. At first Ernie ignored him. Then he showed him the fake badge and walloped him across the face with his mobile phone. He broke Derry Clarke's nose in two places, gave him two black eyes and drove off, leaving him on the street with blood pumping from his face.

Ernie Kenny was clearly not a man to be trifled with which made the set-up at Sunbury Gardens all the more puzzling. Even though Ernie was now her new boyfriend, Karen's old boyfriend John Nolan called in from time to time. He was also known to the

Gardaí as a conman. He was involved in a scam run by the convicted fraudster, Clive Bolger, in which they got car loans for cars that didn't exist. Bolger used false registration plates and VAT numbers to take over £60,000 from the banks. The scam came to light when the registration numbers chosen by Bolger were higher than the number of cars sold in Dublin that year.

The Garda Bureau of Fraud Investigation was called in and 44-year-old Nolan was one of four people convicted for the scam. He pleaded guilty in the Dublin District Court on 21 March 1997 to obtaining money by false pretences. He and two others, Patrick Gallagher and Patrick Shovlin, the owners of Blake's Restaurant in Santry, were given the Probation Act. Bolger was given a three-year suspended sentence at the Dublin Circuit Criminal Court on 12 January 1999 provided he paid back £12,000 to AIB Leasing and Finance.

At the time the scam was being run, John Nolan was in a relationship with Karen Leahy. He was the father of their 4-year-old boy and 2-year-old girl and he originally rented the house in Sunbury Gardens with her. 'On one occasion when he called he was very drunk,' Charlotte said, 'and I let him in even though Karen had told me not to.' Nolan admitted their time together was often stormy. 'During our stay in Sunbury Gardens,' he said, 'we had a volatile relationship which resulted in a number of rows. The glass in the front door was broken in one row we had.'

At first Charlotte was happy with the work and she got on well with the family. The two eldest children stayed most of the week with their grandfather Dan. He picked them up on Sunday and dropped them back on Friday. Charlotte only had to mind the 2-year-old during the week and all three at the weekend.

Karen never told Charlotte what she worked at but she heard the gossip and rumours. 'I was only a few weeks working for Karen when I was talking to another woman,' she said. 'This woman told me that Karen had been a prostitute and was now running her own brothels and escort agency. I did not let on to Karen what I was told.' The house at Sunbury Gardens was never used as a brothel.

The first sign of trouble appeared within weeks. On Saturday 7 November, Karen flew out to Spain for a two-week holiday and left £150 for the shopping. She also left £40 in a card for the three children but no wages for Charlotte. She hadn't stocked up on groceries or supplies either. The money was gone within three days.

First of all Charlotte ran out of nappies and rang Karen's friend, Liza Brophy, for help. She couldn't get her the first time she rang. The second time Liza came and gave her some household and birthday money for the youngest child. Liza also paid her wages but when she couldn't get over to the house, Charlotte rang Dan, Karen's father, and asked him for £15. 'She said she would give it back to me,' Dan complained, 'but she never did.'

Karen disputed this version of events. She claimed that she bought £200 worth of groceries and made out a fourteen-day calendar before she went so Charlotte could decide what days she wanted off. The night before she left she put two £20 notes in a card for her son's birthday. 'I sealed it and left it on the desk in front of the stairs so he would see it.' Karen said.

Three days later she rang Liza from abroad to see how things were. Liza told her she had a call from Charlotte and had to go to Sunbury Gardens to give her £20. 'At the end of the holidays I discovered that Charlotte had been on to my Dad, my sister Liz and a guy called Jason. She got £15 from my Dad, £20 from Emma and £110 from Liz,' Karen said. But Emma said she never gave Charlotte any money. 'There was no food in the house when I got back,' Karen said, 'and when I asked her about this money she made some excuse about the child needing special food. I should have addressed the problem at this stage.' Three weeks later the real trouble started.

At around 7 p.m. on Wednesday 16 December 1998 the atmosphere in the house dramatically changed. It became volatile and criminal. Charlotte was downstairs with the 2-year-old in the TV room. Karen had just come home. Suddenly Charlotte heard shouting in the hallway. Karen burst in to the room and said there was £1,200 missing. Liza Brophy was with her. Karen accused Charlotte of taking it. There was, she said, no one else who could have stolen it. Charlotte was the only one downstairs. The cash had been in an envelope. It was the children's Christmas money and now it was gone.

Karen retraced her steps. The money had been in her handbag and she had left that in the hall earlier in the day. She'd been speaking to Ursula, the interior designer, upstairs and when she came back down she took the bag shopping. 'I went around to three or four wholesalers buying goods for my shop,' she said. 'I was behind on lots of my regular domestic payments. I had a list of payments that I had to make. I had spent £380 in Harold Elmes, £253 in Fitzpatrick's beside the M50 and £100 in the Delph Centre in Ballymount Industrial Estate. I counted the money while sitting in my car. I put £1,200 into a white envelope which was my budget for Christmas and the next few weeks. I put the envelope in my handbag.'

Karen said she saw the white envelope in her bag at 4.30 p.m. when she delivered the goods to the shop. Then she went for a drink with Liza Brophy and got home just after 5 p.m. She left her bag beside the bench in the hallway and went upstairs to see the decorator. Her friend, Niall Fay, was also up there trying without much success to put a bunk-bed together. 'Niall was supposed to be fixing a bed,' Ursula said, 'but he didn't appear to be doing much.'

When Karen came down again she said Charlotte was standing in the hall and Karen told her she would not be home early.

Karen went to a toy shop in Tallaght and that's where she said she discovered the money was missing. The envelope was gone when she opened her handbag to pay at the checkout. She left her shopping behind her and headed for home. She rang Ursula back at the house but was told that there wasn't a white envelope on the desk in the hall.

Niall had gone home at 5.30 p.m. so the only other people in the house were Charlotte and the kids. Karen was sure Charlotte had stolen her money even though Charlotte, according to Karen, swore she hadn't. 'I felt completely betrayed,' Karen said.

Liza Brophy, who had come back with Karen, was also convinced Charlotte was a thief. She had been in the house earlier at around 5.30 p.m. and came in to say hello to the baby. Her phone rang and she went out to the car to talk. Liza wasn't happy either. 'Charlotte,' she said, 'I told you earlier that Karen was upstairs and to tell her I was waiting for her in the car.' Charlotte didn't remember this. 'Karen and Liza were screaming at me and accusing me of taking the kids' Christmas money,' she said. But then the two women turned nasty and violent.

First Karen pulled Charlotte's hair. Then she started punching and pounding her on her head with her fists. Liza told her she'd put her through the window. They didn't believe her when she said she hadn't been in the hall earlier and hadn't taken the money. 'We are stripping this house from top to bottom until I find my money,' Karen said.

'Karen threatened to tell Charlotte's parents everything and that she would go to the Eastern Health Board, every agency, and print notices in the paper and make sure she would never be employed as a child-minder again,' Liza said. Karen punched and pushed her out into the hall. She picked up a hammer there and told her what a good job she could do on Charlotte's legs with it.

The interrogation went on for hours. There were intermittent bursts of shouting, screaming and violence. Ernie came home while it was still going on but he decided to keep out of it. At 11.00 p.m. the children were still up, watching and listening as their mother continued to argue with and attack the babysitter. When Karen hadn't extracted an admission of guilt from Charlotte by midnight, she ordered her to her own bedroom. She told her she was going to lock her in.

'I went to her room. She came up with me. She had the key in her hand,' Charlotte said. 'She closed the door and locked me in. I lay down on her bed and stayed there for the night.' The bedroom was on the second floor. The decorators had taken the phone out and left it on the landing because they were working in the room. Charlotte couldn't climb out or call out. 'I could not have escaped,' she said. 'The room was too high for me to get out.' Karen went back downstairs and drove off to get a takeaway.

At 8.30 a.m. the next morning Karen arrived back with the key and unlocked the door. Charlotte was not to be released, but transferred to another cell. 'You are going into my bathroom and staying there until you tell me where you put the money,' Karen told her. She was taken down to the bathroom on the first floor and locked in.

Karen came in three or four times during the day to accuse her of stealing the money and 'stashing it away somewhere'. Twice or three times Karen again tried to punch an admission out of her, hitting her on the head with her fists. Charlotte kept telling her she hadn't taken the money but Karen refused to believe her. 'She locked me in each time after she left,' she said. 'I tried the door on three or four occasions and it was locked.'

Charlotte spent all day Thursday locked in the bathroom. That evening she was taken downstairs to the dining room. Karen had taken Charlotte's handbag from her room and she searched it in front of her. 'She threw the contents on the floor and made me pick them up,' Charlotte said. While she was collecting her belongings the phone rang and Karen answered it. 'I heard Karen say Charlotte's not here and bang down the phone,' Charlotte said.

At 11.30 p.m. Karen ordered her to search her room and belongings to see if she could find the money. 'If you find it, bring it down,' Karen told her. But Charlotte used the opportunity to pack her bags to be ready to get out. While she was there, Karen and her 2-year-old daughter came back upstairs. The infant fell asleep on Charlotte's bed.

Ernie said he also went up to the bedroom to try to get the money from Charlotte. 'She denied having any knowledge of the money,' he said. 'I believed her that she did not take it.' The search yielded nothing and Charlotte was escorted back down to her cell one storey below. She was locked into Karen's second-floor bedroom for a second night.

Karen went downstairs and went berserk in the kitchen. She flew into a rage and smashed cups, saucers, glasses and plates and threw them all over the floor. She broke bottles of sauces and cartons of milk and scattered jars of jam on the tiles. There was food splashed and spattered all over the walls and floor. 'I don't care, I want my money, I want my money,' was all she said. After smashing up the kitchen she stormed out of the house and didn't come back till after 2 a.m. Ernie put the kids to bed. The next morning he and his friend, Niall Fay, couldn't believe the state of the place.

Fay was a waiter and student who knew Karen because his friend went out with her sister. He said he worked for Karen doing odd jobs around the house and garden. He was there two or three times a week. He couldn't believe the state of the kitchen. 'There was a mess everywhere in the kitchen, all over the walls and the floor,' he said. Niall and Ernie spent two hours cleaning up. Karen stayed in bed. Ernie fed the children in the front room. 'I did not want them in the kitchen as there was glass everywhere,' he said.

Karen woke Charlotte and marched her down to the bathroom again. The decorator was coming so she had to get her out of the bedroom. She spent most of that Friday there. A few times during the day Karen went in and hit her. She took some of her clothes, a black and white rugby shirt, a blue sweatshirt and a blue t-shirt from her room. She brought them into the bathroom and cut them up with a scissors in front of her. 'You better think strongly about where you stashed the money,' she said as she dangled the rags in front of her face. She threw the shreds at her and they landed in the toilet and on the floor. Then she punched her a few more times on the head before storming out and locking the door behind her.

Liza also came upstairs in the afternoon and attacked her in the bathroom. Charlotte said she heard Liza's voice and that of another man she didn't know. Suddenly the door opened and Liza walked in and slapped her around. 'Liza accused me of taking the money plus £300 from Ernie and I said I did not take it,' Charlotte said. 'She hit me on the head with her hands and left the room.' Both Liza and Karen had now also accused Charlotte of taking money from Ernie but Ernie never said she did.

At one stage Charlotte heard Karen say to Ursula, the interior designer, that she had definitely taken the money. Ursula knocked on the door and asked her if she was OK. 'I said no,' Charlotte said, 'it was unfair that I was locked in and needed a phone call to prove my innocence.' But Ursula seemed to think she took the money and suggested to her to give it back and it would all be over. When Charlotte again protested that she didn't take it, Ursula replied, 'You did because there was nobody else here.' Ursula then tried to open the door but couldn't. Karen arrived and shouted in at Charlotte that she did take the money and she could rot in hell. But Charlotte told Karen she would get someone to pay her back. 'I only said this to her,' she said, 'so that I could get out of the house.'

Charlotte hadn't been given anything to eat or drink all day. She was getting worried and by evening time she knew she had to escape. First she tried to pull the bathroom door open but the handle came off in her hand. She threw it on the shelf. The bathroom window was at the front of the house so she started shouting and banging on it. She broke one of the panes of glass and shouted for help. 'I could see two men walk past,' she said. 'One stopped and looked at me and walked on again. I shouted at him to ring the guards.'

One of the neighbours was leaving his house at about 6.30 p.m. on Friday evening. 'As I was at my gate I heard a female voice say, "help, help",' he said. 'It was not a scream but you could clearly hear the word help.' He ignored the call. He said he thought it was a domestic dispute and decided not to get involved. He arrived home at around 11 p.m. but heard nothing.

Two other neighbours' children who played with Karen's son also heard that Charlotte was locked in the bathroom. The two 9-year-old boys told their parents that Karen's son had told them the babysitter had stolen £300. Neither parent believed their son's story. One ignored it while the other told her son he shouldn't be going around saying that. The boy, however, insisted it was the truth but told his mother it was a secret and that he wasn't supposed to tell anyone. Neither set of parents allowed the Gardaí to speak to their children about the incident.

Charlotte was by now very frightened. Ernie Kenny came upstairs and told her to calm down. 'I heard Charlotte screaming from the bathroom it was not her who took the money,' he said. 'I asked her to come out and tell me where the money was. Charlotte said … Karen was a mad woman and would kill her.'

'I told him that I knew that Karen was going to kill me,' Charlotte said, 'and he said she wouldn't because he would be by my side and he would not let her go near me.' Charlotte started shouting and screaming out the window for help. Ernie started to get worried, not about Charlotte but about Karen and himself. He was afraid Charlotte's family would miss her and call the Gardaí. There had already been one phone call for her but Karen had told the caller she was busy.

Just after 7 p.m. on Friday 18 December Karen and Ernie opened the bathroom door and stood there looking at Charlotte. Ernie turned to Karen and told her to let Charlotte go or they'd all end up in Rathmines Garda Station. Karen, however, was unmoved. 'I want all her clothes dumped in a skip until the money is returned,' she said. Charlotte told Karen she'd write a cheque to pay back the money. She was petrified and just wanted to get out of the house.

Karen thought for a moment. Then she walked into the bathroom and announced she was letting Charlotte go. But as she was making her way down the stairs, Karen started shouting after her accusing her again of stealing the money. Ernie was directly behind Charlotte carrying her bags. He quietly told her to keep going. Karen refused to give Charlotte back all her things. She kept a black suitcase and a black and yellow sports bag. 'Fair is fair,' Karen said to her, 'you stole my Christmas money and I deserve to keep your clothes.'

At 7.15 p.m. Charlotte Godkin walked out the front door of the house in Sunbury Gardens and headed to Rathmines village.

She had been held against her will since Wednesday night. She took a taxi to the Four Provinces pub in Ranelagh. She had once worked in the disco there. She knew the barman and asked him to mind her bags for a while. 'She was very upset,' he said. 'She told me that she had been locked in a room for two days or so. I advised her to go to the police.'

Charlotte didn't have a drink in the pub. She went to the Garda's Dublin headquarters at Harcourt Square. Ironically the building which houses much of the force's specialist units — the Fraud Bureau, the Special Detective Unit, the Domestic Violence and Sexual Assault Unit — is one of the few Garda buildings in the capital that doesn't function as a Garda station. She met Detective Christy McInerney from the National Bureau of Criminal Investigation and he took her to Rathmines Garda Station.

'From Wednesday night until I left the house I was in fear of my life of Karen and Liza,' Charlotte told Detective Sergeant George McGeary. 'When I was leaving this evening Karen said she could have me killed in the house and thrown me in the canal and no one would ask any questions. I believe she is capable of doing this.' Charlotte complained of mild headaches and pains in her neck and was examined by the Garda doctor. He found minor tenderness and swelling and gave her pain killers. 'In my opinion,' Dr Y. M. Fakih said, 'the injuries would be consistent with the history given by Ms Godkin.'

George McGeary believed her story and was anxious to search the house as quickly as possible. His superior officer, Detective Inspector Tony Brislane, went to Judge Catherine Murphy's house that evening for a search warrant. She heard the story and she was satisfied the Gardaí needed to move fast on this one. They organised a search party and four Gardaí went to the house. Karen and

Ernie had gone out. One of Karen's prostitutes, Mary Jane, was minding the children. She had no option but to let them in.

They found a number of items that substantiated Charlotte's story. They found a 4lb lump hammer with a wooden handle lying in the hall. When they went upstairs they saw the broken window in the bathroom. The handle was missing from the door. Garda John Forde went in but couldn't find the handle and key. He closed the door to see if it was possible to open it from the inside and found it wasn't. He had to get Garda Matthew Conway to let him out.

There was brown-stain glass on the landing and Charlotte's shredded clothes were strewn around the floor. They also found her suitcase and sports bag in the hall. They photographed the scene and took away the evidence in sealed brown bags. Mary Jane wouldn't tell them her name and said she couldn't contact Karen. They left but decided to come back later.

At 1.45 a.m. the following morning two detectives, George McGeary and Donal Regan, went back to the house. This time Karen let them in. She knew George and called him by his name. Two of the children were asleep on a sofa in the sitting room. The other was in bed upstairs. Ernie Kenny was also asleep on the sofa with half a glass of beer still in his hand. Mary Jane was sitting in the armchair. Karen invited the Gardaí into the kitchen for a chat. It still looked like a bomb had hit it. There was broken delph and glass on the floor. There was congealed food on the walls and a broken picture in the hall.

McGeary told Karen about Charlotte's allegations but in response she told him she knew Charlotte had taken the £1,200 from her handbag. She also said Charlotte had stolen other smaller amounts of money as well as her clothes and her mail. McGeary told her she should have reported that to the Gardaí. At

2.05 a.m. he arrested her on suspicion of falsely imprisoning Charlotte Godkin.

Karen whinged about the unfairness of it all. She moaned that all the Gardaí had to do was ring her and she would have gone to the station of her own accord. Ten minutes later Ernie was also arrested. He also complained that he had done nothing wrong. Both were taken to Rathmines. They were held under Section 4 of the Criminal Justice Act and could be questioned for up to twelve hours. The time could have been suspended if either of them wanted to sleep. It was 2.50 a.m. Both kept the clock ticking. They wanted to answer any questions there and then. They were both released by 7 a.m.

Karen's version of events was — not surprisingly — very different to Charlotte's. She said she thought Charlotte was brilliant at first because she was 'brilliant with the kids'. Then she became concerned because she didn't appear to have any friends or a steady boyfriend. There were no phone calls for her and Karen claimed she got no answer from a number Charlotte gave her in Brittas Bay.

Then came the allegations of criminality. 'From time to time I'd notice that silly amounts of money were going missing out of my bag,' she said. 'They were small amounts. She would ask me for money to go to the shops and never give me the change. I recall going to bed one night when I had three £50 notes and one £20 note in my handbag. I left the bag on the desk in the hall. The next morning I missed one £50 note from my bag.'

Karen admitted she never approached Charlotte about the missing money even though she believed she had also stolen £200 from Ernie. Instead, she said, she started taking her handbag to bed. She said, however, she did confront Charlotte when she caught her stealing the mail. She said she found letters she had never seen before while searching her room for the £1,200. 'I went downstairs and asked her about it,' Karen said. 'She said that she was sorry and that she was just curious.'

Then in marked contrast to her earlier claims about Charlotte having few friends and no boyfriend, Karen accused her of bringing 'numerous strange men' into the house while she was away. 'The day I came back from holidays,' she said, 'she had two strange men sleeping in the house.' Liza Brophy backed her up on this one.

'Charlotte had a different man in the house every day,' an apparently shocked Liza said. 'Well, she had about six different guys in the space of the two weeks Karen was away.' Karen said she told Charlotte not to bring any more strange men back to the house and that that would have annoyed her. Now Karen had given her a motive to tell lies about her.

From strange men to strange behaviour, Karen then claimed Charlotte acted suspiciously. She came and went at different times. She wore Karen's clothes. She neglected her work and Karen said she noticed she bought cheap German wine. 'Everything began to deteriorate,' she said. 'The house was in a mess. She was drinking and she wasn't doing her work. She was subbing her wages from me a week in advance.'

And yet while all this was going on, charitable Karen insisted she cared about Charlotte. She was, she said, worried about her and tried to reach out to her. 'We had dinner together. I told her that I was upset about her sleeping around. I told her she could talk to me about it. I told her that her problems had upset me.'

The finger of suspicion for the theft of the £1,200 was, however, firmly pointed at Charlotte. She had, Karen said, left the house for a few minutes on the day of the theft, probably to hide the money she had stolen. Karen told both her friend Niall and Ursula she'd had a dream that the money was hidden in the grounds of a hospital or convent. Niall suggested they search the park in Sunbury Gardens so the two of them went around the area searching for a white envelope with £1,200 in it. They didn't find it.

Karen also said that Charlotte had shouted at her numerous times and made it look like it was in fact Charlotte who had locked herself in. She said Ernie told her on the Friday evening at around 5.30 p.m. that Charlotte was in the bathroom and wouldn't come out. Overall she portrayed Charlotte, maliciously and falsely, as a boozer, a liar and a vindictive and spiteful weirdo. She was, according to Karen, a thief with no friends or boyfriend, who slept around and brought strange men into her home at all hours of the day and night. Karen was shown the hammer and admitted it was hers. She signed the Garda statement and was told she was free to go.

While Karen never asked for a solicitor, Ernie told the Gardaí that he didn't need one. He said Karen told him that Charlotte had taken £1,200 from her bag. He said there had been numerous screaming matches between the two women with Karen demanding the money back and Charlotte denying she ever took it. He also said Charlotte had locked herself in the bathroom and wouldn't come out. 'I heard her slam the door closed. Once you close the door in that bathroom you cannot open it from the inside as there is no door handle on the inside' he said.

Ernie portrayed himself as the honest broker. He said he re-assured Charlotte that he wouldn't let anything happen to her and then told Karen to settle the row. 'I told her to sort this thing out, get Charlotte out and get her out of the house,' he said. He also claimed that Charlotte had admitted stealing small amounts of money and said he found letters belonging to him and Karen in Charlotte's room. He also had a different ending for the incident. 'They started shouting again so I shouted, "that's it! Enough! Out you go!" She walked out the door with her handbag, two little bags and a sort of sports bag and down the road. That was the last time I saw her,' he said.

There were others who didn't have a good word to say about Charlotte either. Karen's previous partner, John Nolan, was not impressed with the woman hired to mind his children. 'My opinion is that she would have been unsuitable for baby-minding and untrustworthy,' he said. Karen's sister, Emma, said she felt Charlotte was so nice when she first met her that she grew wary of her. 'She seemed very obsessive about cleaning and food,' she said. 'The two weeks that Karen was away she drank a good drop of wine most nights and went out a good few times about 1 a.m. One morning I came downstairs Charlotte was drinking with two fellows. This was at 7 a.m. On one occasion before Charlotte went out she asked me could she bring a fellow home with her. When I asked her who it was, she said she did not know yet.'

Karen's friend, Niall Fay, said she was a peculiar woman who got on well with the 2-year-old but not with the other two children. He was annoyed with her because he believed one day she left Karen's 9-year-old son locked out of the house. His girlfriend, Megan O'Doherty, agreed.

'She was very submissive at times and in general I found her slightly different to the average human being,' she said. 'She crept around the house and would not go out until around twelve o'clock at night.' They also said Charlotte tried to borrow money from them and accused her of bringing strange men back to the house. 'When Karen was away on holiday, Charlotte drank a lot,' Megan said. 'I saw the vodka go quickly and she drank a lot of wine.'

Ursula Flannery, the interior designer, also said she thought Charlotte was a bit strange. 'The baby seemed to spend a lot of time wandering around on her own,' she said, 'and I had to put on her shoe at one stage and I had also to answer the phone on a number of occasions.' She also said she asked her to get bulbs for her at 11 a.m. on the Thursday morning because the light in the room she was decorating was poor, but Charlotte didn't return from the shops until 4.30 p.m. Her assistant said Charlotte asked her and the other assistant if they were Ursula's child-minders. They had their painters' clothes on at the time.

The decorators said that Charlotte asked them if Karen had gone out, and then left the house on the Thursday for ten minutes. They also knew there had been trouble in the house and that money had gone missing because they talked about it at a café in Rathmines on Friday morning. They went for breakfast at 9.30 a.m. because they couldn't get into the house to start work. They also knew Charlotte had been locked in an upstairs bedroom overnight. 'At the time the whole thing seemed confused and complicated,' one of them said.

But Karen's friend, employee and co-attacker, Liza Brophy, was particularly scathing about Charlotte Godkin. She said she had numerous rows with her over money while Karen was on holidays. On one occasion she said Charlotte had threatened to leave the baby without nappies. 'I told her not to pull that trick on me,' Liza said. She also claimed that the baby had suffered a cut near her right eye while Karen was away and was clingy and didn't want to go to Charlotte. She said Charlotte told her the baby had fallen in the sitting room. And to top it all off she accused her of being particularly promiscuous while Karen was away. 'Charlotte had a different man in the house every day,' she said.

Liza also had a mysterious tale to tell the Gardaí. One day she said a strange man called to the house looking for Charlotte. She wasn't there but the man was specifically looking for £30 Charlotte owed him. Liza said that Karen paid the debt. 'I gave Karen the change of a £50 note,' she said, 'and she paid the man.' Karen

'Condy the Country Pimp':
Young and old, the many faces
of Thomas McDonnell

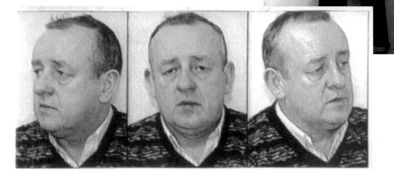

	EARLY		LATE
MON	CLARE – MONICA – NIKKI	MON	TONI – ~~[crossed out]~~ MIA NADIA – ZOE.
TUE	~~[crossed out]~~ TONI – ZOE.	TUE	NIKKI – EdEL – CLARE – ZOE.
WED	NADIA – EdEL – NIKKI	WED	ZOE – TONI – MONICA – EdEL
THURS	CLARE – EdEL – MONICA	THURS	MONICA – LEANNE – TONI.
FRI	CHRISTMAS	FRI	Day
SAT	STEPHENS	SAT	Day
SUN	EdEL ~~[crossed out]~~	SUN	NIKKI – MONICA.

The prostitutes' roster for
Christmas week 2001.
Women with children worked
as prostitutes in the early
hours of Christmas morning.

IMPERIAL TRADING COMPANY LTD.

PHONE: 6612 696

24a GRATTAN STREET

OFF LOWER MOUNT STREET,
DUBLIN 2.

The brothel's business
card with the 'nun on
a motorbike' logo.

The New Imperial
brothel, subsequently
sold by the Criminal
Assets Bureau.

'Madam Mean', Marie Bridgeman.

Kevin Bridgeman (left) on the day he was charged with assault causing harm to his mother Marie.

Marie Bridgeman's roster for Tiffany's brothel on 5 October 1999. 'R' and 'N' indicate 'regular' and 'new' customers. $^{1}/_{2}$ indicates a half-hour session, which meant £20 for Marie and £40 for the prostitute.

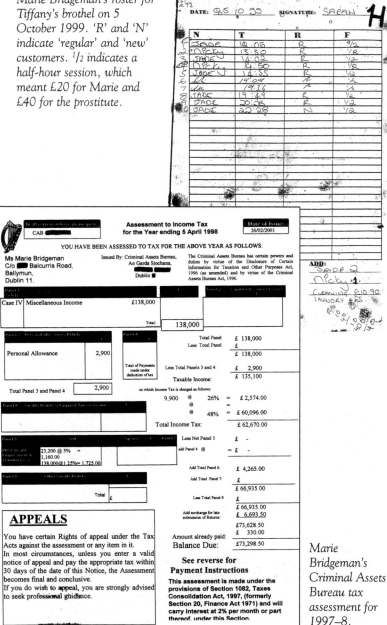

Marie Bridgeman's Criminal Assets Bureau tax assessment for 1997–8.

'A Woman of Substance', Samantha Blandford Hutton.

'Private Dancer', Samantha Blandford Hutton performing for the camera in July 1992.

Stephen Reginald Hutton leaving court after he
was charged with managing the Winter Garden
brothel.

Karen Leahy after her conviction for falsely imprisoning Charlotte Godkin.

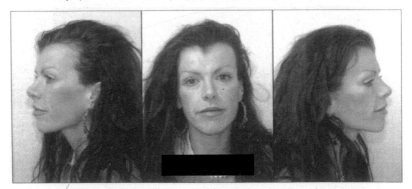

A page from Samantha's 'little black book', with records of her clients' names, addresses, telephone numbers and special requirements.

(From left) *Neusa da Silva Resende, Elis Pereira* and *Nilce Mara da Silva, following their victory in the High Court over Samantha Blandford Hutton.*

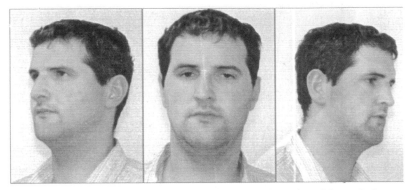

Ernie Kenny following his conviction for violent assault on the celebrity chef Derry Clarke and his wife Sally-Ann as they returned home from their restaurant L'Ecrivain.

Keith Thompson opening up the brothel Club 59 for business.

Liza Brophy in dark glasses, leaving court after her conviction for falsely imprisoning Charlotte Godkin.

Charlotte Godkin, the child-minder that Karen Leahy locked in a bathroom.

Brothel-keeper, businessman and sex-shop operator, Brian O'Byrne.

The In Dublin magazine advertisement for Brian O'Byrne's brothel, the New Acorn.

Caught in the act! A brothel raid, 16 April 1998.

Club Six, the bunker-like brothel with boarded-up windows…

…and the way it was portrayed in an advertisement.

'The Man Who Didn't Know', Mike Hogan outside the Four Courts.

'Hooker with a Heart', Justine Reilly relaxes in one of the brothels.

DUBLIN PROSTITUTES

Dublin Prostitutes

Dublin prostitutes is the website for adults seeking to make contact with prostitutes in Dublin, Ireland. Find Dublin street prostitutes easily with our definitive guide to red light districts in Dublin. If you prefer a more high-class service, you may browse our detailed and extensive Dublin escort services listings. Dublin Prostitutes lists both Dublin escort agencies (brothels) and Dublin independent escorts, and unlike our competitors, we list ALL the escorts in Dublin.

InDublin - Dublin's Famous Escort Contact Magazine

Visit InDublin Escorts Magazine

Browse hundreds of Dublin escort ads for Dublin escort agencies and Dublin independent escorts. Get involved with Irish adult classifieds and discussion boards. Read Dublin escort reviews, find Dublin escort jobs, your guide to Dublin adult entertainment including lap dancing clubs and street prostitution, the latest Dublin adult news and much more - Only in InDublin - Dublin's famous escort contact magazine now online!

Visit InDublin Escorts Magazine

Related Irish Adult Links

Free Irish porn sites featuring real Irish women, real Irish men and Real Irish couples and many more. Irish interest adult websites... Irish Escorts Ireland brings you a selection of the best adult links you'll find for Ireland below:

The home page for dublinprostitutes.com. Since In Dublin stopped taking brothel advertisements, the internet has become the new way to find a prostitute in Ireland.

The Academy brothel in
Rathmines, the first
brothel seized and sold by
the Criminal Assets
Bureau.

'Corridors of love!' –
inside the Academy.

The Academy's Jacuzzi
room.

'The Policeman',
Peter McCormick…

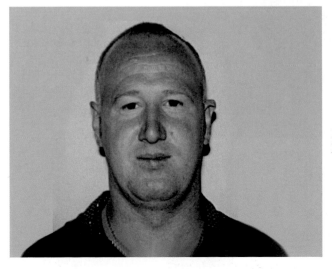

…and 'The
Beast', Martin
Morgan.

Detective Chief Superintendent Martin Donnellan, Head of Operation Gladiator.

The Real Policemen: Detective Chief Superintendent Felix McKenna, Head of the Criminal Assets Bureau.

Pat Byrne, the Garda Commissioner who ordered the first concerted investigation into prostitution and brothel-keeping.

Detective Chief Superintendent Sean Camon, Head of the National Bureau of Criminal Investigation.

didn't even tell the Gardaí this one.

Liza also supported Karen's claims that money had been stolen from her and Ernie even though Ernie didn't mention this to the Gardaí. Liza said Karen was all heart in spite of her advice to the contrary. 'I told her to get rid of her,' Liza said, 'but she would not sack her as it was too close to Christmas.'

As regards the assault and false imprisonment, Liza's version of events was that there was just a lot of shouting. She never saw anyone hit Charlotte Godkin and she certainly did not hit her either when the row started or in the bathroom. She was quite emphatic. 'I did not threaten Charlotte at any time,' she said. 'I did not assault Charlotte at any time. I did not see her or go into the bathroom to her any time. I never touched Charlotte.'

Unlike Karen and Ernie, Liza voluntarily went to the station on 22 December and made a statement. She didn't have to be arrested and as she left she walked past Charlotte. She was sitting waiting on a bench in the public office with her head slightly bowed. They didn't look at or speak to each other.

But one of Karen's former employees, a prostitute, later told a different story than that of her family, friends and other employees. The babysitter the night of the raid, Mary Jane, might have been expected to support her one-time boss but didn't. 'I was working in one of Karen's apartments in Sussex Road in Donnybrook,' she said. 'Karen Leahy rang me on Friday 18 December and said that she would collect me as she wanted to talk to me.' Mary Jane said Liza Brophy had told her two days earlier that Charlotte had stolen £1,200 from Karen.

On the way to the house Mary Jane asked Karen about Charlotte. 'I still have the bitch locked up,' was Karen's reply. They got there around 6 p.m. and Mary Jane went to make a cup of coffee. It was a house of horrors particularly for the children.

'The kitchen was in an absolute mess,' she said. 'There was food on the walls and the ceiling.'

Karen's 9-year-old son came in. 'We're not going to have a Christmas,' he said. 'I told him everything was OK and he would have a Christmas,' she said. 'Mum was angry and she was breaking everything,' he said. 'I told him everything would be OK.' 'Charlotte is in trouble. She took Mum's money. Charlotte is locked in the bathroom,' he said.

Mary Jane went back to the living room but she could hear Karen shouting at Charlotte and Charlotte pleading with Karen. 'I could hear people going up and down the stairs,' she said, 'I then heard the crash of the big picture in the hallway being smashed.' 'There goes my mum again,' the 9-year-old commented stoically.

Mary Jane went to Karen. 'You cannot keep a human being locked up in a bathroom,' she said, 'you will have to let her go.' Karen and Ernie came back to her a little while later and Karen told her she had let Charlotte go. They wanted to go out for a while so Mary Jane agreed to mind the children.

The next day she went for something to eat with Karen and Ernie after they had been released from custody. 'At the meal,' she said, 'Karen told me that the police would be interviewing me and Ernie would tell me what to say.' Two days later she claimed Ernie had that chat with her, a coaching session in Sunbury Gardens. She said he told her to say she didn't know Charlotte and knew nothing about her being locked in the bathroom. She said she was told to say she was working in the warehouse for Karen dealing with medical supplies. 'Ernie told me not to say anything about Karen's prostitution and escort agency or about her medical company called Glencairn which sells Viagra,' she said.

Initially, Mary Jane refused to talk to the Gardaí. They spent two months trying to find her without success. Karen didn't help them either. She told them that she didn't know her surname. However, on 19 February 1999 Karen threw her out of her flat on Pembroke Road. Karen had rented it and she now wanted to turn it into a brothel and move women in.

'I refused to let them in, and Liza and Karen threatened me,' she said. 'They both called up to me with a big guy called Reggie. This guy threatened to throw me down the stairs.' Mary Jane fled to a house in Goatstown but made herself available to the Gardaí and made a statement to Detective Sergeant George McGeary. She also agreed to give evidence in court.

The Director of Public Prosecutions now had a job to untangle this web of claims and counter-claims, and try to figure out some sort of truth. He had to decide if Karen, Liza and Ernie had a case to answer and whether this was a criminal or civil case. There were so many confusing and contradictory statements that it was difficult to establish what really happened at the house in Sunbury Gardens the week before Christmas 1998.

Charlotte insisted she was locked in on Wednesday and Thursday because she said Karen accused her of stealing the money on Wednesday. Mary Jane supported her on this but every other witness said Karen only missed the money on Thursday. The decorators and Karen's friends also told the Gardaí that they saw or spoke to Charlotte in the house on Thursday and Friday when she was supposed to have been locked in the bathroom.

The DPP also had to consider the possibility that Charlotte had stolen the money. There was witness evidence that she left the house with the baby for ten minutes on Thursday afternoon. Ten witnesses had made statements criticising her or accusing her of stealing the money. Charlotte said she never admitted at any time to taking any money from Karen. She also denied asking Liza Brophy or Niall Fay for money. She said she didn't have a drink problem, she didn't have a steady boyfriend and she didn't sleep around.

The DPP put aside the claims that Charlotte may have stolen the money because she was never charged with theft. Ernie Kenny wasn't prosecuted either but Karen and Liza were charged with assault and false imprisonment. However, by that time Karen had other problems. The owners of the house wanted her out of Sunbury Gardens. Karen was very fond of it and referred to it as 'home' and 'my house'. She wasn't prepared to go quietly and she forced them to go to court to evict her.

It wasn't easy for landlords to get people out of their properties even if they suspected they were involved in criminal activity. For example, in one case a company called Deep Drill Developments told the Circuit Civil Court that they thought their property was being used as a brothel. 36–37 Lower Ormond Quay, which stretched into 33–34 Great Strand Street, was only yards from the Four Courts in Dublin. It included a 'tiger room' and a dungeon but appeared to be a cross-dressing club, not a brothel. A Dublin publican, Brian Winters, and his wife, Helaine, who lived in Foxrock, denied it was being used as a brothel. They also gave Judge Michael White an undertaking it would not be used as one.

The house at Sunbury Gardens was a luxurious three-storey, five-bedroom Victorian house. Karen's old boyfriend, John Nolan, rented it for £1,500 a month but hadn't paid rent in five months. He owed over £7,000. When he and Karen broke up he left, but Karen, who had no lawful tenancy, stayed on as a trespasser. The house was so good that she decided to live in it with her children. The two diplomats who owned it lived abroad but wanted it back. They were shocked at the way it was being mistreated. The case came before the Dublin Circuit Civil Court on 19 March 1999.

Anne Webster, an Irish consular official based in Paris and her husband, Gerard Clarke, told the court their home was being ruined. Scraps of food were stuck to the walls and ceilings. Overspills from the baths and wash-hand basins had destroyed period lath and plaster ceilings and cornices. The first-floor bathroom was flooded. The sunken marble bath was smashed and water had seeped down through the ceilings on the ground floor. Glass from broken pictures was scattered around. Cutlery and broken delph were strewn on the floors. Garda John Forde, one of the search party who raided the house in December, gave evidence for the couple as to just how bad a condition the house was in.

'It is vandalism of the worst possible nature,' Judge Liam Devally said, 'It cries out to heaven for someone to do something about it immediately.' The judge said that every further moment Karen Leahy was left in possession of the house meant a very valuable property stood in grave danger of being destroyed to an extent that it would make it financially prohibitive to restore adequately.

The judge granted the owners immediate possession and awarded them £7,500 against Nolan in rent arrears and £5,800 against Karen. Needless to say, neither Anne Webster nor Gerard Clarke ever saw any of that money. They were left with the bill for the damage to the house and they had to pay their own legal costs. They were left severely traumatised by the whole episode while Karen and company simply sailed away to their next criminal adventure.

Two months later Ernie Kenny was up before the Dublin Circuit Criminal Court for the road rage attack. He pleaded guilty to assaulting Derry Clarke and careless driving. His defence counsel, Andrew Flynn, said that Ernie had told the Gardaí that he feared for his own safety but admitted he had used an unnecessary amount of force. He asked the judge to take into account that there was no disfiguring of Derry Clarke's face even though the chef couldn't go to work the day after the attack. He had to cancel an appearance on RTÉ that morning and was unable to appear on several shows afterwards. He lost money and publicity. His wife, Sally Ann, was much more deeply affected. She had been in fear of her life and became apprehensive every time she had to travel home.

Andrew Flynn also asked Judge Kieran O'Connor to consider Kenny as a man who had learned his lesson but the judge felt the 28-year-old father of three would benefit from further instruction. He said he had to protect women on their way home from work from 'blackguards' like Ernie Kenny. On Wednesday 12 May 1999 he sent him to jail for a year for the attack. He also disqualified him from driving for four years and directed that he pay £1,000 compensation to the Clarkes. But by this time Karen had moved on from Ernie. She was now with Reggie and both she and Liza Brophy decided to fight the kidnapping case. It was another three years before it came to court.

The trial began on 2 July 2002 and both women pleaded not guilty. They adapted a curious strategy. They denied the charges but didn't take the witness stand to defend themselves and give their side of the story. They never said that they didn't imprison Charlotte Godkin. They never addressed the real issue of imprisonment either in statements to the Gardaí or in court.

Detective Sergeant George McGeary gave their side of the story by reading out their statements in court. Perhaps they didn't give evidence because they would either have been forced to admit their guilt or commit another offence, perjury. But they forced Charlotte to go all the way with them and prove her case against them. She had to convince twelve of her peers that they had locked her in the loo.

Karen and Liza's strategy failed. On the second day of the trial Karen changed her plea on one of the three charges and admitted cutting up Charlotte's clothes. However, the next day the jury unanimously found her guilty of the assault. They didn't believe any of the outrageous allegations she made against Charlotte Godkin. They also convicted her, but by a majority verdict, of falsely imprisoning Charlotte.

Liza Brophy was also found guilty of false imprisonment. Six days later she was jailed for three months. Judge Yvonne Murphy said the appropriate sentence was nine months but she took into account the fact that Brophy suffered from diabetes, had a young dependent son, and had offered Charlotte €5,000 compensation. Karen's sentence hearing was put back until the autumn.

Charlotte Godkin was deeply affected by the incident. It damaged her physically and mentally. She couldn't go back to work until the women were convicted and then she only gradually returned to child-minding. Emma Leahy loaned her sister Karen €10,000 she could ill-afford. Reggie handed it over in a white envelope on the afternoon Karen was sentenced. Charlotte is still taking a civil action against her captors.

Karen Leahy's senior counsel, Ciaran O'Loughlin, tried hard to keep her out of jail. He referred to her troubled and traumatic life. He said she earned €300 a week and was now in a stable relationship with Reggie who earned €500 a week. He pointed out how difficult a custodial sentence would be on her and her five young children. He even apologised on her behalf for the trauma her irrational action caused Charlotte Godkin. 'The build-up of stress for years,' he pleaded, 'led to her flying off the handle.'

He suggested the judge impose a longer sentence than would be appropriate but suspend all of it. 'The gravity of the offence would be recognised by the length of the suspension which will hang over her for years,' he said, 'but she will not be separated from her family. There are a lot of things to be said in Ms Leahy's favour.'

He also succeeded in having details of her conviction for brothel-keeping excluded by arguing the offence was not committed before this one and therefore could not be deemed a previous conviction. This was important because it meant she was sentenced as a first-time offender and the court could treat her more leniently.

Karen and Reggie dressed up for the day. She wore a brown trouser-suit, white blouse and high heels. He was in a dress suit — long coat with tails — pin-stripe trousers and a silver tie. But this time Karen was going to jail. The judge took a dim view of the fact that she had fought the case by attacking Charlotte's personal integrity and had tried to portray her as a liar and a thief.

'Ms Leahy's medical report suggests she was psychologically traumatised but this is inconsistent with her approach to the trial,' Judge Yvonne Murphy said. 'Ms Leahy was entitled to have the matter fully investigated but through the proper channels. She has a personality-type that reacts with aggression to others. Young people must be protected by law from this crime.' On 15 October 2002 Karen Leahy was sent to prison for the first time in her life. She was sentenced to eighteen months for the kidnapping and six months concurrent for the assault.

It was a sad irony that at over 80 years of age, retired Assistant Chief Officer Dan Leahy had to walk back through the gates of Mountjoy Jail, the place where he spent most his working life, in circumstances he least expected. He found himself in the same position as so many other fathers he had admitted and supervised at visiting time over the years. The shoe was now on the other foot. It took courage for Dan to go and see his daughter in the women's prison. At least he didn't have to do it for long.

The judge suspended nine months of Karen's sentence because of her health problems and she swore to be bound to the peace for a year. She was well treated in the Dóchas Centre, the women's prison at Mountjoy Jail, where women live in rooms with televisions, not in cells. She was allowed out to be with her family at Christmas. She was given temporary release on two more occasions after that, each time for two weeks to allow her to get treatment for her anorexia. The second period of temporary release became permanent. She didn't have to go back to prison. By February 2003 Karen Leahy was free. She had served less than a third of her sentence.

8 The Businessman

Brian O'Byrne is a legitimate businessman. He started off with a credit union loan of around £5,000 in 1998. Now he has two shops with a turnover of hundreds of thousands of euro a year. He employs ten people, most of them on a part-time basis — young people, students, foreign nationals. They work harder, he says, and give him less grief. He pays his tax and PRSI contributions. He pays rent on the retail space and all his products are licensed and legally sold here. His customers are consenting adults and strictly over 21 years of age. He's still in the sex business but now he is upfront, on the street and above board.

The 41-year-old runs two sex shops in Dublin city centre. They're both called Shauna's — one is on Capel Street on the northside, the other is on Aungier Street on the southside. They sell a wide and bewildering variety of sex condiments — videos,

DVDs, vibrators, toys, dolls, pussys, pumps, magazines, oils, sprays, strap-ons and creams. The prices start at around €10. The videos cost €30, the DVDs €50. The shops have video booths where customers can pay 40 cent a minute to watch pornography. At that rate it costs €48 to watch a two-hour video. It's cheaper to buy one.

There are around fifteen sex shops in Ireland and that makes Brian O'Byrne one of the biggest operators in the country. He is no longer afraid of the knock on the door from the Fire Department, the Health Inspectors, the Revenue Commissioners or the Gardaí. He says he doesn't entertain any of the requests he receives for strange and illicit material, and he has no time for paedophiles, necrophiles or those seeking bestiality. He has left his criminal past behind him.

Born on 31 January 1962 Brian O'Byrne grew up in Inchicore in Dublin. He lived a normal life until he was about 30. Only then did things start to go wrong for him. His marriage split up. He was unemployed and he started getting into trouble with the law. His ex-wife took a barring order out against him but on 7 April 1992 he broke it. He was arrested at Thorncastle Street in Ringsend and charged with two offences — breach of the barring order and dangerous driving at the same place on the same day.

Three months later he was arrested again, this time at Emmet Road in Inchicore. He was charged with breach of the peace and possession of two knives with intent to intimidate or injure. Ten days after that he was in trouble again. This time he was charged with causing £60 worth of damage to the driver's door of a car. In the eyes of the law he was now deemed to be violent and known to carry weapons.

O'Byrne was convicted of all charges on 20, 21 and 22 January 1993. He got six months suspended for breaching the barring order and was disqualified for a year for the dangerous driving. He appealed the convictions and that enabled him to stay on the road for another year and a half but ultimately it was a decision which cost him two weeks in prison. The Circuit Court judge not only confirmed the barring order sentence but also sent him to jail from 10 May to 23 May 1994. He suspended the remaining five and a half months of the sentence. There was some comfort for O'Byrne in that he successfully appealed the driving disqualification. It was reduced from twelve to three months.

After he came out of prison he drew the dole and lived at Rathdown Square off the North Circular Road. The following year, 1995, he was again arrested nearby on Blessington Street and subsequently convicted of common assault. It was his fifth conviction. He had no job and enrolled in a number of FÁS and back-to-work schemes but these didn't lead to any steady employment. He decided there was money to be made in vice and by 1998 he was making so much money he came off the dole. He has been in the sex business for nearly a decade but he didn't always operate on the right side of the law.

O'Byrne knew Marie Bridgeman and saw how easily she was making money running brothels. He went into business with a former girlfriend from south Dublin. They set up brothels on the northside of the city on Richmond Street, North Lotts and Parnell Street. O'Byrne borrowed the money to get himself started from people he knew he had to pay back. The 'New Acorn' was on North Lotts, a dark, narrow road between Middle Abbey Street and the River Liffey. He leased the building under the name of Patrick Butler.

The New Acorn was dark and dingy and even though O'Byrne spent £3,000 on renovations, it didn't look much better after it was done up. He customised it. He had showers and a closed-circuit television system put in. He furnished it with sofas and beds. There was no heating and the women had to huddle around electric bar heaters to keep warm as they waited for clients. Some complained they waited all day to get nothing.

O'Byrne's other brothel at Parnell Street wasn't much better. 'Club 6' may have been advertised as a health studio but it looked more like a bomb shelter. Unknown to its owners, it was literally a red-light area with fluorescent lamps illuminating rooms that looked liked cells. Each consisted of a bed and a table with the usual array of baby oils, powders, condoms and creams. It offered strict mistresses for bold boys and a two-girl special. It was also a little more flexible on the prices with different charges for different sexual services — hand £40, oral £50, full sex £60.

The punters rang the intercom and walked in through two doors while all the time they were monitored on camera. O'Byrne supplied the towels. It cost him around £15 a week to have them cleaned. He didn't have a contract with any particular laundry, 'I go everywhere and anywhere,' he said. The women supplied their own condoms, powders and oils. O'Byrne said he was able to buy anything he needed wholesale because at one time he owned a sandwich bar, the Deli Bakery in Bolton Street. When he moved out of the business, he continued to use the account number for Musgraves Cash & Carry.

He and his business partner hired the women. If they phoned in and he was happy with what he heard, he told them to come in and start work. Crystal was an English girl who came to Dublin to make money. 'I didn't do an interview,' she said, ' I rang and started straight away.' O'Byrne had the same financial arrangement with the women as Marie Bridgeman and most of the other brothel owners around the city, £60 for sex — £20 for him, £40 for her. Courtney was the mother of two children aged five and three. At 27 she still lived in a council house with her parents, children and brother. 'I am working to support my kids,' she said.

There were at least four women working in each brothel. The New Acorn was by no means one of the busiest in Dublin. Each woman saw only about seven or eight men a week. However, even with this low average of one a day they were still earning £300 cash a week each and with four girls each handing over another £160, the New Acorn was still making £640 a week for its owners. The prostitution business was profitable even when business was slow. Courtney worked for O'Byrne in all three brothels before changing her name to Megan and moving on to work for Karen Leahy.

It wasn't long, however, before O'Byrne came to the attention of the neighbours, the business community and ultimately the Gardaí. Like Marie Bridgeman and Thomas McDonnell, he had been operating before Gladiator was set up and it was the local detective unit in Store Street that first moved to close him down. The investigation method remained the same. For three months, between January and March 1998, The New Acorn was under surveillance. The clients were stopped coming out and statements taken from them. O'Byrne and his partner were also stopped and the brand new car they were in was searched. He knew the Gardaí were on to him but it didn't deter him.

On 6 March 1998 the New Acorn was raided. The two women and one man there were questioned and, when O'Byrne arrived, he was arrested and taken to Store Street. He knew why he had been taken in and didn't want a solicitor. He admitted he was in charge of the brothel. He said he'd taken out a short lease on the place and had only been operating there for the previous four weeks. 'Why didn't you take our warning and quit the business?' he was asked. 'I borrowed money to open the one in the North Lotts,' he replied. He didn't borrow it from a bank. This was a debt he knew he couldn't welch on. Even though part of his operation was busted, he made sure he paid his moneylenders back with interest.

O'Byrne exonerated his partner and took full responsibility for running both brothels. 'I'll take the rap myself,' he said, 'I'll make a statement. Nobody else was involved. I only got involved in this because I owed money.' It wasn't the truth. He also promised that he would quit the business. 'I will close down both of these premises and I will not be involved in anything like this again,' he said. This wasn't the truth either. It was a promise he had no intention of keeping and four days later Club 6 was also raided. Two weeks after that O'Byrne was arrested and charged with four counts of brothel-keeping.

On 8 September 1998, the day the case came up for trial, O'Byrne was gung-ho and ready to fight. His instructions were communicated to the State which was in turn prepared to prosecute. However, it was pointed out to him that he should take a look down the back of the court. One of the witnesses against him was a solicitor with a practice on the northside of Dublin. He had been caught naked with one of the prostitutes in the New Acorn. He had made a statement admitting paying for sex and his evidence would have been convincing and damning. It would also have cost him his job. The Law Society takes a dim view of its members consorting with prostitutes. O'Byrne changed his mind and pleaded guilty to two of the charges. He was remanded for sentencing to the following week.

On 15 September 1998 Detective Garda John Stratford gave evidence about how O'Byrne ran the brothels and how much money he was making. The judge, Desmond Windle, took a particular interest in the figures and estimated O'Byrne made between £18,000 and £20,000 in four months. He asked O'Byrne, rhetorically, if he had paid any tax. He dealt only with the first charge, ordered him to pay £5,000 to the court poor-box and bound him to the peace for two years. The second charge was put back for nearly a fortnight until a report could be drawn up to see if he was suitable for community service.

It was at this second hearing that O'Byrne's real feelings towards the prostitution business became known. There were, he said, at least a half a dozen men and women organising sex-for-sale outlets who had been convicted in the courts in the past ten years. This, he felt, was unfair because, while the gay community was able to operate saunas and bathhouses, the straight community was being prosecuted.

'We're being discriminated against at the moment because since homosexuality was legalised none of the gay saunas have been closed down,' he said. 'What the authorities seem to be saying is that it's OK to have places catering for homosexuals, and I've nothing against those guys, but it's not politically correct for consenting heterosexuals to do the same.'

He warned that the brothel owners of Dublin might get together to lobby the government to change a law which he felt discriminated against them. He announced he was considering discussing the setting up of a representative group with other people in the capital's sex industry. 'The gays got their act together and lobbied to have the law changed,' he pointed out, 'and maybe it's time we did the same. Guys like me want to pay tax and be above board.'

Brian O'Byrne was talking politics — some said it was just nonsense. 'It's a bit like the pirate radio stations which were being closed down for years and eventually they came along and legalised the whole thing,' he said. He made these views known in a report for the probation and welfare service which prepared the community service report on him for his court appearance.

It was perhaps because of these views that the probation service had 'some reservations' about his suitability for community work.

His lawyer said he was willing and able to do it so it gave him the benefit of the doubt and so did the judge. Judge Thomas Fitzpatrick sentenced him to 240 hours instead of six months in jail. He walked out of the Richmond Court on 27 October 1998 vowing to open a sex shop in the city. In the meantime, he went straight back to business. He never did get around to establishing that lobby group. It may have looked like he was arguing a point of principle. In reality, it was all about the money.

The Gardaí may have closed down New Acorn and Club 6 but by that time O'Byrne had moved on. He was running another brothel at Synge Street. He rented the house eight months earlier in January 1998 for £950 a month. He told the landlord that he had just sold a string of cafes on the northside of Dublin and was now 'exploring a number of business opportunities'. He didn't tell her that business was prostitution and the opportunities he was exploring were illegal. She gave him the lease the night he moved in and asked him to sign it and send it to her solicitor. She never found out if he did.

The brothel on Synge Street was a split-level, three-bedroom house. Two bedrooms were in the basement, one was on the first floor. The bathroom, kitchen, and sitting room were all on the ground floor. O'Byrne put a monitor in the sitting room and a camera over the hall door. The women could watch the punters come up the steps outside and knock on the blue front door. They could also check them out through the peep-hole before opening the main door.

The two downstairs bedrooms were for sex. O'Byrne moved in and lived in the bedroom upstairs. This room doubled as his office. The women never went up there. 'The table upstairs is set for show,' Angie said. He didn't insist on a dress code for them and most arrived to work in jeans and runners. It didn't matter to him what clothes they wore as long as he was paid when they took them off. There was also some evidence, if not of a referral service, that men could get information about O'Byrne's brothels in his sex shop. At least two men said they found out about Synge Street in Shauna's.

The brothel went under a variety of names — 'Monkey Business', 'She Devils', 'Club Central' and 'Centrefold Girls'. 'The girls picked the names,' O'Byrne said. The women were also marketed and advertised individually as personal trainers or masseuses. One of them was in fact a qualified beauty therapist with a CIBTAC diploma in beauty, therapy and massage.

Aimee worked on and off for O'Byrne for nearly two years but never got a chance to practise those skills as a beauty therapist. She answered an advertisement in *In Dublin* and was told to come in and start as a prostitute the next day. She only worked for half the year between September and February. 'I have elderly parents who can't work,' she said, 'I'm the only one who can bring in money. I work to make our lives a bit easier at Christmas.'

Aimee worked afternoon shifts from around 1 p.m. until 8 p.m. two or three days a week. The punters rang up and she or one of the other women gave them the 'sales pitch' and told them where to come. 'It's £60 fully inclusive, that's massage and extras,' she said. 'My name is Aimee, the agency is called Shauna's.'

O'Byrne collected his £20 per client 'book money' from the press by the fridge. He paid the rent, the phone bill and supplied the towels. The women supplied the oils and the condoms, although as prostitutes they got them free from the Health Board. They were also responsible for keeping the house clean. 'Brian's mobile number is on my mobile which I use to find out if I'm working or if I can't come in or if I have a problem with a client,' Aimee said.

The brothel was first advertised in *In Dublin*. O'Byrne tried to get VAT invoices from the magazine to claim the tax back from the Revenue Commissioners. It was ironic that a brothel owner who was asked by a judge if he had paid tax on his earnings from prostitution tried to claim back some of the expense he incurred advertising those brothels. He never got any VAT invoices from *In Dublin*. When it moved out of the adult advertisements market, he put his adverts into the international pornographic magazine *Penthouse* and the Irish gentleman's magazine, *Patrick*.

'I gave the details to a bloke in England,' was how he suc-cinctly explained advertising in *Penthouse*. On page 78 of the autumn 1999 edition of *Patrick*, issue 4, volume 1, there appeared a number for Amy/Holly and a separate one for Laura under 'Adult Contact'. 'Shauna's Adult Shop' was also advertised on the next page and customers said they heard about the brothel there. Tom got the address for Synge Street after he asked the assistant in Shauna's if he knew a good massage parlour. 'The fellow knew what I meant was a place where sex would be offered,' he said. Tom called in and paid £60 for oral sex.

The brothel attracted men from every county and country. Mohammed got away with paying £55 for sex when he told the woman that was all he had. She didn't have time to argue. It was a busy day and all the women were occupied. O'Byrne had to come down and let him in, and Mohammed had to wait for a while on the couch in the hall before the woman arrived and led him downstairs. Frank wasn't so lucky and had to pay full price. He was told it was £60 and had to go to the bank to get it before he was let in. George was up in Dublin for the day when he decided to drop in for a talcum powder massage and hand relief. 'I did a bit of shopping and then I rang one of the ads,' he said.

O'Byrne wanted to put more phones in the house to keep up

with the demand. He told the landlord he had a PC and would probably need to get a second line to get on the Internet. 'I told him that he would have to get my permission before he started to bore any holes in the wall,' she said. He never bothered getting back to her. He registered six phone numbers to the address without her even knowing. The landlord also complained that O'Byrne was often late with the rent. He was supposed to set up a standing order and pay it every month but instead lodged money directly to her account. He and his partner regularly forgot to lodge it, she said, and she often had to remind them. 'They were not regular payers and I had to chase them up,' she said.

Phone lines are an extremely valuable commodity in the sex industry. They are the lifeblood of the business because they are the means through which the customers contact the brothels and the women. O'Byrne's phone numbers were particularly valuable. They had been in operation for a long time and as such were established brothel numbers. People who rang them once held on to them and rang them again when they wanted sex. The numbers, therefore, represented a loyal and lucrative customer base, a focused, distilled, specialist market. They were currency and hard cash in this part of the criminal underworld and they ensured brothels kept their old customers while continuing to attract new ones.

When caught, most brothel owners just closed down the operation that was busted and started again. Those advertising with *In Dublin* changed their numbers. But O'Byrne kept his numbers live. He continued to pay the bills and moved them on with him from brothel to brothel. Therefore, punters who might only call a brothel once in six months could still use one of O'Byrne's even if it had changed addresses. A client who turned up at North Lotts only to find his old favourite brothel closed down could still phone the old number and find out its new name and location. The numbers also meant O'Byrne could continue to recruit staff as well as hold on to his customers. Prostitutes rang the brothels looking for work.

A number set up for a brothel on Parnell Street on 16 August 1997 was transferred to the Richmond Street brothel, then on to a third brothel, Club 6. When Club 6 was closed down, its number moved again to the New Acorn brothel. On 6 March 1998, the day it was raided, the number was moved to a fifth brothel at Synge Street. It was disconnected on 26 November 1999. One of the other numbers for the New Acorn brothel was set up on 19 December 1997. This was also moved to 'Centrefold Girls' at Synge Street on the day of the New Acorn raid and continued to operate there for another year.

O'Byrne's numbers were landline numbers which gave the client a greater sense of security and safety. They were a source of comfort to his older, 'yuppie' and middle-class customers who were afraid of being robbed, ripped off, or beaten up. They knew, in case anything happened, the person who paid the landline bill could be traced. The brothel-keeper who operated with a ready-to-go or speakeasy phone could not.

In what was by nature an uncertain and transitory business the landlines represented stability, consistency and reliability. This was reflected in their market value and many brothel owners were prepared to pay well for them. 'I kept them because they were "established" phone numbers,' O'Byrne said. 'At the time (1998) I could have sold them to other people in the industry who would have paid up to £1,000 each.'

O'Byrne not only transferred old numbers and advertised them under the name of the new brothel, he also re-directed old numbers to new ones. Therefore, a customer who rang one of the New Acorn numbers, after it was closed down, was diverted to the Centrefold Girls number at Synge Street. At least two other numbers were diverted to Centrefold Girls and She Devils. The client may have originally paid for sex on the northside but from now on he was going to have to travel to the southside to buy it. These numbers were also advertised in old copies of *In Dublin* and were particularly valuable after the Censorship Board banned the magazine and it stopped carrying the brothel advertisements.

The banning of *In Dublin* marked the beginning of 'the heat' coming down on the capital's brothel owners. It led to the closure of a number of brothels in Dublin that couldn't survive without the oxygen of advertising. Those like Brian O'Byrne who stayed open benefited from the demise of some of their competitors. There were more clients available to the smaller number of brothels still open and there were more experienced prostitutes looking for work. He was now getting more money from the punters and less hassle from his staff.

Holly was one such case. She was an English woman who came to Ireland to be with her boyfriend. She lived here for sixteen years. When after five years their relationship broke up, she became a prostitute and has been 'on the game' ever since. She worked the streets around Leeson Street and Fitzwilliam Square before moving into the brothels in 1997. She worked in Arches brothel in Thomas Street in the south city. Diane was the 'madam'. She was a blonde-haired, middle-aged woman who 'spoke very well'. But Diane got worried when the *In Dublin* controversy began. She closed down Arches, and Holly was out of a job.

'I couldn't get work because of the publicity in relation to *In Dublin*,' Holly said, 'A lot of telephone numbers I rang were dead numbers.' She was unemployed for two months before she rang one of O'Byrne's landline numbers. She found it in an old copy of

In Dublin. In two days Holly was back in business but she soon found out that while she had been out of work some things had changed.

Holly rang O'Byrne looking for work on Monday 26 October 1999. He told her he wasn't looking for staff but said he would rent her a room and whatever she did in it was her business. 'He kept saying I don't care what you do in the room but all I want is £100 a day,' she said. 'He kept saying to me, "I don't want to know what you are doing, just once I get my £100 every day."' She started work two days later. O'Byrne was in the same business but he had adopted a new system to try to avoid getting caught again.

This time O'Byrne tried to run the business like a seedy New York red-light hotel where the rooms are rented by the hour for astronomical prices. Instead of taking £20 book money for every client, he sub-let the rooms in the house in Synge Street for £100 a day. He was now the landlord, not the brothel-keeper. He tried to pretend he was no longer in the prostitution business. He told any of the women who rang looking for work that he wasn't hiring. But instead, for a fee, he offered them facilities — a room in a house with showers, heat, light, telephones, towels and security. They could work as prostitutes but he didn't want to know about it.

O'Byrne only let the rooms in the house to women and every woman there was a prostitute. The women, therefore, decided how much to charge and what sexual services to offer. Some brought handcuffs, belts and ropes for the clients who wanted bondage. The price was still £60 for half an hour but they charged £80 if they could get away with it. 'The fact that I am paying a standard £100 for the use of the room I can vary my time and my prices,' Holly said. As part of the precautions he was now taking, O'Byrne kept a low profile. He didn't meet the women and distanced himself from the activities of the brothel as much as was possible. He made his money by collecting the rents from the rooms every evening after the women had gone home.

The prostitutes worked out the shifts amongst themselves. Usually two women were enough to cover the day, one working 11 a.m.–8 p.m., the other from 1 p.m.–10 p.m. O'Byrne left the towels for them in the press, on the stairs or on the sofa. Then he left them alone. The punters rang in and the women told them where to come, who to ask for and how much it would cost. The women kept a record of the business among themselves on a piece of cardboard on the worktop in the kitchen. 'I am down for 2, 3.15 and 4.30,' Aimee said pointing to the roster, 'and the R stands for regular client.'

Holly was never introduced to O'Byrne. When she started work, his business partner showed her to her room and gave her her mobile number to call if she had any problems. But she was sure he was the man who lived upstairs. 'I presume it's him as he opens the front door himself and goes straight upstairs,' she said. 'Brian always holds his head down when at the front door. He never comes downstairs. We are only allowed upstairs to open the front door.'

When the business took off, he stopped doing that too and hired a man to look after the place. There was a 'young skinny guy with mousy hair' who let the women in in the morning and cleaned up a bit. The used condoms were thrown in the bag under the sink but Holly said she sometimes took hers home and burned them in the fire.

O'Byrne knew the prostitution business was unpredictable and was, therefore, understanding and flexible when it came to collecting the rent. 'Sometimes I might only leave £80 for Brian,' Holly said, 'and I'd make it up the next day and leave £120 for him.' The system was extremely profitable for O'Byrne. He was guaranteed £200 a day and with both women sometimes working seven days, some weeks he made £1,400 cash.

O'Byrne had little or no dealings with the running of the brothels, to protect himself from prosecution. To the uninitiated he was the landlord or another tenant renting the upstairs part of the house. But he was mistaken if he believed he could claim he didn't know what was going on and wasn't part of it. Ignorance is no defence of innocence and O'Byrne was neither when it came to prostitution. In reality the system was a clumsy attempt to circumvent the law. It ended in failure and when the Gardaí burst in again he didn't even try to use it as an excuse.

On 15 October 1999 Mary Delmar bought a copy of *Penthouse*, the pornographic magazine. It wasn't her usual leisure reading. This was for professional, not personal, reasons, strictly business, no pleasure. The detective sergeant turned to page 112 and found adverts for Centrefold Girls, Monkey Business and She Devils. The adverts confirmed her suspicion that Brian O'Byrne was still in business.

On 8 November the Gardaí began a surveillance operation which lasted four days. Statements were taken from nine of the twelve men who were seen going in and out over a three-hour period. At 4.12 p.m. on 11 November 1999 they recorded Brian O'Byrne bringing in a large bag of towels. Three quarters of an hour later the Gardaí went in after him.

Aimee opened the door and let the seven of them in. Detective Sergeant Mark Kavanagh went downstairs and into a bedroom where he found a man 'lying naked on a bed with a female kneeling beside him; she appeared to be masturbating him.' 'I was going to have sex with the woman,' the man told Kavanagh, 'but you arrived while I was having a massage.' This time a Garda had actually witnessed sexual activity in a place advertised as an escort agency or health studio. That evidence would prove crucial in prosecuting O'Byrne.

The search turned up the usual incriminating evidence that the house was a brothel — used tissues, condoms, rosters, oils, canes and creams. But there was also six telephone bills all addressed to the house in Synge Street and all either in O'Byrne's name or in both his and his business partner's name. The bills linked him to phones that linked him to the brothels. They enabled the Gardaí to build a solid case against him because they formed a trail of evidence that led to him as a brothel-keeper.

The numbers on the bills rang into two phones in the house. The one downstairs behind a curtain in the sitting room was connected to a caller I.D. unit. It had no dial pad so the women couldn't make calls. They could only receive them. The second phone was upstairs in O'Byrne's bedroom. There was an answering machine beside it and when Detective Garda Mick Moran pressed it, it played the following message in a seductive woman's voice; 'Hello, Shauna here. We are located on the northside at (landline number), southside at (landline number) and now in the city centre at (landline number). Shauna is also available on 086–(mobile number).'

The Gardaí also found copies or draft copies of the Dublin sex guide, *The Ultimate in Instant Contacts*. This was what O'Byrne described as an adult contact listings magazine which he published from time to time for consenting adults. The Guide contained contact numbers for escort agencies, brothels and prostitutes. There was no charge for listings but it sold for £4.99.

O'Byrne made money from the Guide. It cost less than 50p to put together but around 500 copies were sold every fortnight. It has, he says, since been replaced by *Spice of Life* which is also available on the Internet. It operates free of charge for 'males, females, singles, couples, swingers, bi-sexual, straight, gay, lesbian, transvestite, transexual, gender benders or whatever your sexual orientation may be.'

Men continued to call in and phone during the search. Detective Inspector John McMahon went upstairs and found O'Byrne sitting on the side of the bed in his underpants. He showed his warrant card and told him to get dressed. He was arrested and taken to Kevin Street station where he was questioned for an hour and a quarter. He didn't bother with a solicitor.

During the interviews he told McMahon and Kavanagh lies when he said he owned the house and that he lived alone. But he admitted it was a brothel and that sex was sold there. Again he took full responsibility for it and insisted there was no one else running it with him. It was the second time he took the rap for his partner and she was never charged.

O'Byrne gave the Gardaí the names of the brothels and explained the system whereby he rented the rooms. 'I provided a place for the girls, gave them the use of my exclusive phone numbers and I provided the laundry for them.' he said, 'I used old landline phone numbers from previous places I had on the north-side. I made about £100 a day if it was busy but not as much if it was quiet.' At the end of the interview O'Byrne signed the notes but wouldn't make a statement. He was photographed, fingerpinted and released at 8 p.m.

On 31 December 1999 he was given a month's notice to get out of the house on Synge Street. The landlord got the key back on 2 February 2000. At 2.30 p.m. on 19 May Detective Sergeant John Cribbin arrested O'Byrne on Inchicore Road and took him to Kevin Street where he was charged with two counts of brothel-keeping. He had nothing to say. He was brought before Kilmainham District Court and remanded on his own bail to appear again the following week. Although he didn't know it at the time, it was the beginning of the end of Brian O'Byrne's prostitution business.

The first time he was convicted, O'Byrne considered contesting the case but didn't. This time he decided to fight. On the first day of the trial on 10 July 2001 he pleaded not guilty. The stakes were higher because the case was being heard in the Dublin Circuit Criminal Court and the penalties on conviction were much more severe. O'Byrne had gambled on the Gardaí not being able to convince the customers to give evidence against him. Why should they, he thought, they hadn't committed an offence. But he gambled wrong. After the first day and the evidence of three men who swore they paid for sex in his brothel, Brian O'Byrne changed his plea to guilty. Judge Pat McCartan sentenced him to two years in prison.

O'Byrne was stunned. He couldn't believe it. He never expected to go to jail for an offence which he saw as a victimless crime. He found it hard to understand what had happened to him when the prison officers in Mountjoy Jail clanged the cell door closed on him. The experience affected him deeply. He found his time in prison particularly difficult. He wasn't like the people he was locked up with. Most of them were drug addicts and he refused to take drugs. He was made to feel an outsider and worked out a lot on his own in the prison gym. He lost five stone through a combination of exercise and stress.

But he was also very worried about his own safety in prison and with good reason. One of his customers was out to get him. At 6 p.m. on 30 January 1998 Aiden Byrne from Lower Oriel Street in Dublin went in to Club 6. He was stoned out of his head. The two women on duty were in their 40s. One of them was partially deaf. Byrne handed her £50 but the price was £60. She refused to have sex with him for £10 less. Byrne said he knew Brian O'Byrne.

He said O'Byrne owed him money and told him to go to the brothel where he'd be looked after. He was prepared to offer a reduced rate but he wanted what he came for. The woman again refused and this time Byrne lost his temper.

The 20-year-old started shouting and roaring and then he attacked the woman who refused him. He pushed her down on the bed and raped her. When he had finished, she tried to get away from him but he followed her into another room. She was telling the other woman what happened when he lost it again. This time he smashed a chair and demanded oral sex from the second woman. He pushed her into a chair and forced oral sex on her. The women reported the rapes to the Gardaí but when Byrne was arrested, he couldn't understand what all the fuss was about. 'Sure they were only prostitutes,' he told Detective Sergeant Walter O'Connell. But that wasn't the way Mr Justice Paul Carney saw it and on 10 June 1999 he sentenced Byrne to five years in prison.

Aiden Byrne blamed Brian O'Byrne for his conviction and subsequent incarceration. It was, as he saw it, O'Byrne's fault that his two women made statements and were prepared to give evidence against him. O'Byrne was the reason he was in prison. He was now a convicted sex offender who would have to sign the Sex Offenders register and let the Gardaí know where he was. He, therefore, couldn't believe his luck when he was moved to the Midlands prison and found himself for a time in the same jail as Brian O'Byrne. He wasn't able to get to O'Byrne himself but he was from Dublin's north inner city and he had connections in prison.

There are violent and dangerous people in prison and O'Byrne was attacked on the landing and badly shaken. He didn't feel he was able to protect himself and he had to get out of there. His former business partner approached the Gardaí for help. The prison authorities intervened and Brian O'Byrne was transferred to the open prison at Shelton Abbey. This is a more relaxed, calm, civilised and suitable regime where offenders can receive as much as 50 per cent remission on their sentences. He served the remainder of his time there and, with remission and time off for good behaviour, he was released on 2 November 2002.

Brian O'Byrne was glad to get out. He still regrets fighting the case. He served fifteen months and says he has learned his lesson. He's still in the sex business and runs two sex shops but insists he's no longer in the brothel or prostitution business. He says he's never getting back into it either. From now on, he's strictly legitimate.

He buys and imports sex toys and magazines from Europe and sells them in Shauna's in Dublin and on the website. He also says he replaced the *Dublin Sex Guide* with the *Spice of Life* which is also on the Internet. It carries personal advertisements and listings for free. It also carries notices for women like 'Sexy Suzie', 'Gina from Galway', 'Strict Dom Mistress' and 'Call me and I will cum (*sic*) to you'. Each of these has a mobile contact number beside them.

O'Byrne insists that the magazine and website simply and solely provide a contact service between consenting adults. The *Spice of Life* legal notice states it 'does not knowingly, willingly or otherwise accept ads for massage parlours, escort agencies, brothels, or services connected directly or indirectly with prostitution.'

It goes on to point out that 'all advertisers in the "Spice of Life" are taken at face value and we trust that the ad any person has placed, does not contravene the provisions of the Criminal Justice (Public Order) Act 1994 or similar type legislation.' And then it warns that 'Any ad found to be in breach of such legislation, will be immediately removed and the Offender(s) reported to the relevant Police Authorities.'

Sex shops don't have a great reputation here. In October 2000 a company that ran three in Galway, Limerick and Waterford

was fined £2,400 for having x-rated videos and magazines and dis-
tributing an advertisement for a brothel. 4-play at Buttermilk
Walk, off Shop Street in Galway city centre, was raided twice in
1999. Shardam Trading Company was also convicted of similar
offences at its shop in Waterford.

Brian O'Byrne is now making a good living from the legitimate
sex industry. He doesn't like talking about his past. He wants to
leave it all behind him and move on. He's a family man. He lives
with his partner and children on the northside of Dublin. He says
he's a normal guy who gets up, goes to work, comes home and
plays with the kids.

Only two people have ever been sent to jail for prostitution
offences in this country. Brian O'Byrne is one of them. He still can't
believe it. He feels he should never have been put behind bars.
However, when he was, he made Irish criminal justice history —
he will always be the first person in the history of the State to be
jailed for prostitution offences.

9 *The Publisher*

When Mike Hogan walked out of the Dublin Circuit Criminal Court on 17 October 2000, he refused to talk to the press. This was out of character for the man on a personal and a professional level. Mike Hogan was renowned for his geniality and wit. His good humour and willingness to engage in an open and forthright fashion with people made him well liked and very popular.

From a man who made his living in the media it was unusual and unique of him not even to stop to utter the words 'No comment'. It was also in marked contrast to Hogan's attitude outside the same building the last time he was there the year before. After his victory in the High Court over the Censorship of Publications Board, he spoke to any media organisation that wanted him and posed for any photographs they needed. But this time it was different. Hogan was now a convicted criminal.

Mike Hogan has a story to tell about himself even before he was born. He never knew his father who died of a heart attack at 41 years of age. 'I was literally two months conceived when my Dad died,' he said, 'and he died ironically enough in the Hogan Stand at Croke Park watching the All-Ireland Hurling Finals in 1959. For years I used to think the stand was named after him.'

Hogan was born in Athy in Co. Kildare in 1960. Even as a child he displayed an entrepreneurial flare which he says he learned in the home. His father, a technician for the Post and Telegraphs, had no pension. The family's only income was the widow's allowance. His mother drew the family together. She slept in the same room with him and his two sisters and rented out the other rooms in the house. 'She invented a business as soon as Dad passed away,' he recalls. 'That's how we survived.' Hogan is justifiably proud of his inventive and resourceful mother who no doubt passed on many of her qualities to her only son.

At 14 he was running discos for the local tennis club and later roller discos in Ballybunion. At boarding school he earned money serving on the altar at weddings and funerals. He also sold lines. 'We loved the Dominican Church lines,' he said, 'because they gave you a decent commission. You had 25 lines at a shilling a line and you only had to give back 20 bob so you made five for yourself.'

When he was 17 he opened a record shop, Rainbow Records, with the help of a friend but that didn't work out and he moved to Dublin. He got a job as a lighting technician in RTÉ but left after six months to become involved in Dublin's emerging pirate radio scene. By the time he was 21 he was the top sales representative at Sunshine Radio based at Tamango's Hotel on the northside of Dublin. 'If I got a grand I kept £250,' he said, 'I was doing 85 per cent of the work.'

The owner of Sunshine, Robbie Robinson, fell out with his partner, Chris Carey, a veteran of the 1960s pirate radio scene in Britain. Carey left to set up Radio Nova. Hogan joined him. A new system had been introduced into the sales department at Sunshine whereby he'd have to share his commission with the other sales-people. He wasn't prepared to do that. Three years later he was general manager of Sunshine's biggest competitor and the most profitable and professional pirate radio station in the city.

Nova pioneered most of the new developments in radio in Ireland and pushed the rather staid, stagnant and out-of-date national broadcaster into setting up its own pop music station — Radio 2 — now 2FM. One of the innovations Carey came up with was the idea of doing traffic reports from a helicopter. This was quite a novel and radical approach to 'roadwatch' in the early 1980s in Ireland, and the man who became the voice of 'the eye in the sky' was Mike Hogan.

'He was,' Hogan later said of Carey, 'a hard but dynamic boss, a buccaneer who enjoyed sailing close to the wind.' He could have said the same about himself. He says he learned the discipline of getting up early then and now he goes to bed at 9 p.m. every work night.

It was during this period that Mike Hogan 'arrived' and made some very powerful and influential friends — among them the former Taoiseach, Charles Haughey. Haughey's son, Ciaran, was a partner in Celtic Helicopters. For years he flew Hogan all over Dublin to see where the traffic jams were. The two struck up a friendship which spread to other members of the family, including the boss himself. Twelve years later Haughey turned up in Dingle for Hogan's stag party.

At 36 he married the former model-turned-public-relations executive, Mari O'Leary and the couple now live in a large house in Ranelagh with their three children. The couple were stalwarts of the Dublin social scene mingling with the 'beautiful people'. They were regularly mentioned in the society columns attending fashion and charity balls where the tables cost at least a £1,000. Now Hogan says they're both at home by 5.30 p.m. every evening with the mobile phones turned off. 'It's time for family,' he says. He even broke off negotiations with Vincent Browne while he was buying *Magill* to go home and play with his children.

Hogan moved from Nova to manage its pirate offshoot, Q102. By now he was professionally well-qualified and politically well-connected to legalise his operation. He applied for one of the new radio licences on offer from the newly established Irish Radio and Television Commission. In 1989 he succeeded with the consortium that set up Capital Radio — now FM 104 — in securing one of the two lucrative Dublin licences. Hogan was appointed Capital's chief executive.

The station targeted Dublin's large teenage listenership which Hogan had been adept at attracting in his days with the pirates. He expected to sit back and watch the money pour in. It was the wrong strategy. The advertisers were more impressed with Capital's competitor, 98FM. Its astute focus on the high-spending, twenty- to thirty-somethings as opposed to Capital's concentration on the teenybopper market meant it took most of the advertising spend.

Capital Radio lost a million pounds in the first year and Hogan later admitted it was 'an awful mistake'. He had misjudged what the listeners and, more importantly, what the advertisers, wanted. It was all very different from his days with the pirates. He now had a licence but he wasn't used to dealing with a board of directors and shareholders. He resigned three years later.

Mike Hogan might have been down but he certainly was not out and the wide-eyed Kildare man turned his attention to publishing.

He set up The Hoson Company and began buying up established magazines and publishing others on behalf of several organisations and institutes. At one stage Hosan had nearly 40 publications and an annual turnover of £7m. It published, amongst others, the current affairs magazine *Magill*, the GAA monthly *High Ball*, the official magazine for the band Boyzone, *Banking Ireland*, *Gael Sport*, *The Big Ticket*, *Full Flight*, *dot.ie* which arrived by e-mail and the magazine of the defence forces, *An Cosantóir*. But *In Dublin* was to become the jewel in the crown.

The Hoson company operated from offices in Camden Place, Dublin 2. But from the start *In Dublin* was different from the other horses in the Hoson stable. 'Hoson is a catch-all name used to describe the group of magazines published at Camden Place,' Hogan said. 'I personally own the title *In Dublin*.' In 1992 he relaunched it, and even though he says he was a millionaire before he went into publishing, he set about making some serious money for himself.

The fortnightly listings magazine *In Dublin* was founded in 1976. It prospered on a diet of news and reviews, cinema and theatre listing, books and fashion. At times hard-hitting, investigative and controversial, it also pioneered causes such as divorce, abortion and the legalisation of homosexuality. But by the early 1990s it had become increasingly irrelevant and was surpassed by its Dublin rival *Hot Press* and the British glossy imports. Its trading company 'Hard Facts Ltd' went into liquidation and in 1992 Mike Hogan bought the title from the liquidator for £6,500.

Hogan put the ownership of the magazine into a company called KCD Ltd. The name was conceived after he bumped into the writer Colm Toibin who gave him some financial management advice. The initials stood for Keep Costs Down. The company's registered offices were 3/7 Camden Place, Dublin 2. KCD's sole business was the publication and distribution of *In Dublin*. Mike

Hogan and his wife, Mari O'Leary, were its only two directors. The former model had no active part in publishing the magazine. She ran her own company, O'Leary PR. As the benefactor of the annual profit or the holder of the debt of KCD's annual turnover, Mike Hogan owned *In Dublin*.

There were about 100 pages in each edition of *In Dublin*. Of those, 38 consisted of advertising, more than a third of the magazine. And of that third, twelve pages advertised material of a sexual nature such as telephone chat lines, sex shops, mail order and brothels. Therefore, 32 per cent of the advertising in *In Dublin* was devoted to the sex industry. The most costly form of advertising in the magazine was what the staff referred to as the 'adult ads'. 'I don't know when the adult ads first started,' Hogan said, 'as they were a feature of the publication when I acquired it.' But they were a valuable feature because they were particularly lucrative and Hogan kept a tight rein on them.

The 'adult ads' were advertisements for services described as 'Escort Agencies', 'Massage Parlours' and 'Health Clubs'. Each edition of *In Dublin* carried pages of them at the back. They were in fact advertisements for brothels and prostitutes. They were so tightly controlled that even senior managers at the magazine had nothing to do with them.

The Chief Executive Officer of the Hoson Company was Maeve Kneafsey. She joined as General Manager in 1997 and was promoted in January 1999. While she was a director of all of the trading companies within The Hoson group, KCD was the one exception. It was Hogan's decision to keep *In Dublin*'s holding company separate. 'I am not, nor have I ever been a director of KCD Ltd,' she said.

As Chief Executive, Kneafsey budgeted the cost of producing the magazine against copy sales and adverts in the front. Even though she worked with the *In Dublin* team in all other areas of the publication's production, the management and financial control of the 'adult ad' pages was never part of her brief. The money from the chat lines was included in her budget but the money from brothel adverts was not. 'I never used the income from the ads in the adult section at the rear because I never had the use of it,' she said. Hogan handled the adult advertisements and the income they generated in a very specific and somewhat peculiar way.

Claire Murphy was Mike Hogan's personal assistant and the office manager at *In Dublin*. She worked for KCD since 1993. She was responsible for all Hogan's secretarial work, contract work for various functions and office duties in general. Hogan also made her a director of another company, INK publications. She answered only to him.

In the middle of 1994 her job changed dramatically. Another Hoson employee, Timmy Dooley, had been in charge of the 'adult ads' for *In Dublin* and he called to some of the advertisers to collect the money. A native of Mountshannon in County Clare, Dooley was Business Development Manager for the company. He went on to become a member of the Oireachtas. He was a member of the Fianna Fáil national executive and elected to the Seanad for the party in 2002. At Hoson in the early 1990s he worked on the 'Escort Agency and Health Club' ads. He admitted he suspected some of the advertisements were for the services of prostitutes but insists he didn't know that the places he called to were brothels.

'Some of the places you'd never know, they didn't look seedy or anything,' he said. 'At 22 or 23 you don't give it as much thought as you would at a later stage. I wouldn't know the ads were for brothels. I would have had a suspicion. I'm not denying that you might suspect. I worked in the company. I did some of the work. I didn't have supreme responsibility. I wasn't doing anything illegal.'

Senator Dooley is correct. At that time there was no law against the advertisements. The Criminal Justice (Public Order) Act had not been enacted. When Dooley and Hogan's partner, Michael Dawson, left the company the responsibility for the advertisements landed on Claire Murphy's desk.

'One day the receptionist in our office at 6 Camden Place phoned me and told me there were several queries from people wishing to place ads in the adult section of the *In Dublin* magazine,' she said. 'As office manager and PA to Mr Hogan, I told the receptionist to put any such calls or queries in to me. I got a number of phone calls from these people enquiring as to why had Timmy Dooley not collected their ads. At that stage I had not got a clue as to what type of ads they were on about as I had not got anything to do with that end of the business. I told them that I was Mike Hogan's PA and that if they wished to come in and see me they could.'

And come they did. The brothel owners knew how important the adverts were to their businesses and dealing with another person didn't seem to bother them. They went into the office and handed Claire copies of the advertisements they wanted to put in and the cash to pay for them. Claire passed all this on to Mike Hogan who arranged for the production staff to lay them out for the magazine.

From then on she organised the adverts and Mike took care of the money. They were designed on a Monday for publication the following Wednesday. If a new client came in to place an advertisement or if an existing client wished to change the design of an advertisement, he or she would be taken to the design studio where the advert was drawn up in front of them to their satisfaction. A copy was then printed off and handed to them.

Most of the advertisements once placed continued on every fortnight without any change in design. Most of them were illustrated with a sexy picture. There were beautiful women in lingerie and underwear, which showed off their bare bottoms and plenty of cleavage. There were shady and smouldering illustrations of dark, mysterious temptresses. There were cartoon figures of women dressed as Egyptians or lying by pools sipping cocktails. There were silhouettes of beautiful couples in passionate embraces on exotic strands. Two large-breasted women illustrated the Pleasure Chest Escort Agency.

In Dublin also advertised men as available for escort duty. They were described as 'young, attractive and friendly' and you could order 'Italian and Thai' as if you were choosing from a menu. Like the women, these guys were sculpted out of bronzed, muscled, chiselled and toned bodies. Samson and Delilah illustrated its advertisement for a 'call in/call out service' that 'specialised in couples' with two naked, headless torsos, one on either side of the text.

Playtime, Sins, Stunners, Passions, Heavenly Creatures, Private Temptations — the names conjured up all kinds of erotic, perhaps even spiritual, fantasies. But sex that was seedy, soul-less, impersonal and quick was in reality what the brothels were selling. Behind all the colourful guff, sex for sale was what Mike Hogan was advertising. The men and women in the advertisements bore no resemblance to any of the prostitutes available in Dublin. They didn't work in the brothels. They weren't Irish. They didn't even live here. So how did they end up in Hogan's magazine?

Mike Hogan certainly wasn't going to hire out the huge number of different models that were in the magazine and pay them each the going rate for a shoot. Instead he sourced the pictures in the UK. He paid an English company for the images. They came in to the *In Dublin* offices on a ZIP disc or down the ISDN line. He also ripped off American telephone directories as advertisements for agencies with names like Manhattan, Palm Beach and Nevada started to appear on the back pages of *In Dublin*. Hogan's motto was 'tits and teeth' — sex and a smile. Hogan knew that sex sells and that's what sold his magazine.

On one of his trips to the US, Hogan flicked through the New York phone directories. He saw thousands of advertising displays, personal advertisements and descriptions for what they called escort bureaux and referral services. There were so many other ways to advertise prostitution without actually using the word. He was clearly impressed by what he saw and brought back a chunk of the 1998 Bell Atlantic Yellow Pages. He gave Claire Murphy pages 463 to 506 with the attached hand-written note 'Claire, For Ideas, etc. M'. This was Hogan's trademark initial in place of his signature — the letter M with a tail looping round the top and through the middle with a flourish.

At first Claire Murphy didn't know what to charge the brothel owners. They told her how much the advertisements were. She took the details and the cash and passed it on to Hogan who did the rest. But she had to learn soon enough when she was put in charge. When Timmy Dooley came back from Paris he told Hogan he was setting up a new company. Dooley and Hogan parted company and Hogan told Claire that from then on she was to take over the adult advertisements. As the publisher and her boss, Hogan had the total and final say over what was to be featured in the adverts and printed in the magazine. He proofread them and wrote comments on them before handing them back to her. Claire organised the process and Hogan took the money.

Claire decided early on that she wasn't going to chase that money. She didn't go out to meet the brothel owners or collect the cash. Instead she told them to call in and she would take their advertisements. 'Not all these people initially came in to the office to see me,' she said. 'Some of them decided to wait and speak to Timmy before they would meet me. However, over a period most of them did meet me and I took the ads from them.' She also had a company mobile phone which she used for the business. The brothel-keepers had her number.

The cost of an advertisement covering an eighth of a page went from £300 in 1994, to £400 in December 1998. That was the minimum charge on what the magazine called its premium rate. It was 85 per cent above the normal rates and could perhaps, therefore, be considered extortionate. But Hogan received no complaints. It was a seller's market and he had it cornered. His clients paid up and *In Dublin* became firmly established as the magazine to buy if you wanted to hire a prostitute.

The minimum amount of space the magazine would sell to a brothel advertiser was an eighth of a page. A customer could divide that eighth in half, into two sixteenths, and advertise two numbers for one brothel or two brothels with a different number in each sixteenth. Two women working on their own could also split the cost and take out two advertisements but a customer could not take and pay only for a sixteenth.

'They're not actually sold in half a size,' Claire said, 'those two boxes would be sold to one person.' The brothel customers were, however, granted one concession. They were entitled to a free advertisement in the personal section and a lot of them used it either to publish a second phone number for their brothel or to put in advertisements to recruit new prostitutes.

For the few owners or managers who still wanted to place adverts for their brothels but were not prepared to go near the office or deal with Claire, Hogan made special arrangements. He sent his chauffeur out to pick up the cash. Every fortnight John Farrell called to three brothels. 'One was in Dorset Street,' he said. 'It had a mahogany door. I would say that I was a courier from *In Dublin* "to pick up". A girl would then open the door and hand me an envelope which usually had *In Dublin* or "Claire" written on it. It was hardly ever the same girl who handed me the envelope.' He also called to a brothel with a red door in Temple Bar and to the Academy brothel in Rathmines. It was part of his job for four years.

Another mysterious owner would leave an envelope in the letter box of 6 Camden Place every second Sunday night. It was addressed to Claire Murphy but Hogan usually opened it on Monday morning. She didn't start work until 8.30 a.m. but the boss was at his desk at least an hour earlier. The envelope with the client's instructions was later left on Claire's desk. The money was gone. She only found out what was in it when Hogan went on holidays. 'I would open it and I would see what was in it which was £600 cash for the $\frac{2}{8}$ ads and a note "showgirls" and "women" £600.' It was all very minimalist, clandestine and later illegal.

In Dublin had its own brothel book for a time with the name of each owner and the amount they paid. For the first four years Claire said she wrote all the transactions and the cash amounts for the advertisements in this book and personally handed the money to Mike Hogan. She also gave him a receipt on a compliments slip or on the back of one of the envelopes in which the cash came.

Hogan also kept his own records so he knew how much the adverts were worth to him. He wrote down all the different amounts that various owners paid for the adverts on the back of his filofax and totted up the total. It was informal book-keeping and hardly likely to satisfy the auditor. But then there were no company accounts for the advertisements. That was the sum total of the records he kept of them.

Hogan didn't have to hussle for the business, market the service or offer large discounts to valued customers. He didn't even have to think about what went into the advertisements. 'We never actually pursued advertisers as they made contact with us,' he said, 'and the content of the ads would normally be determined by the advertisers themselves.'

The brothel owners took out the advertisements and paid what they were asked for. There were no negotiations. A small number of long-time customers got a reduction of £50 per advert but that was because for years they advertised in nearly every edition. For the rest of the clients it was a case of take it or leave it. And although the magazine was aimed primarily at middle-class readers in Dublin, it also advertised brothels in Limerick and Galway.

There was no need for any input into the sale of space in the magazine from the advertising staff at *In Dublin*. This type of advertising didn't have to be sold. It was simply bought up. The sales, marketing and advertising managers had nothing to do with the adult advertisements. Similarly the editorial staff had no input or editorial control over their content and the production manager also had very little to do with them. Neither the Chief Executive nor the Financial Director had anything to do with the money brought in.

Hogan said none of these people ever expressed discomfort or uneasiness about the advertisements because they had no involvement with them. Only four people at the office dealt with them — Hogan, his personal assistant Claire Murphy and two graphic designers Jonathan Murphy and Niall Fennessy. Of the four, Hogan was the only one who was happy with the situation. 'I don't hold myself out as being the moral guardian of the nation,' he told *The Irish Times* in 1996.

Claire Murphy was not happy to be in charge of the advertisements but it was now her job and she felt she had to do it. She was under no illusion as to what they were doing. By their demeanour, language and the contents of the adverts she knew that they were selling the services of prostitutes. The word was not mentioned in the office but everybody knew what the adverts were selling. The section dealing with them became known as 'RADS'. It was an acronym for 'Rub a Dubs,' with its obvious sexual connotation.

One of the graphic designers wasn't particularly thrilled with the work either. Jonathan Murphy joined the staff at *In Dublin* after the company he worked for, Ryan Media, was bought over by The Hoson Company. When he was appointed art director, the advertisements became his responsibility. 'I did not enjoy inheriting this part of the work,' he said, 'but it was part of my job and it had to be done. I did not protest about the ads but I was uncomfortable with them.'

Claire Murphy particularly disliked having to deal with the brothel owners but as she put it, 'I had no choice in the matter. They had to be dealt with professionally.' Any suspicions she may have had about the individuals she was dealing with were confirmed when she read articles about them in the tabloid newspapers. She recognised some of her 'famous' customers and said to Hogan they should not be taking advertisements from them. But Hogan didn't care and brushed off her concerns. 'I don't read the newspapers,' he said.

Mike may not have been well up on Dublin's prostitution rackets. Maybe he didn't know the agencies or most of the people who ran them. But then again he didn't need to. As long as the cash kept coming in, Mike didn't ask too many questions. He didn't socialise with the brothel owners who were his biggest customers in the capital's thriving sex business but he did get to know some of them.

'He did know Tom McDonnell who paid for his ads on the off week,' Claire said. 'He also knew Marie Bridgeman, Karen, Martin and Peter who paid for their ads.' Claire kept these people's money separate and did not count it. 'I just gave it to Mike Hogan in the envelope and I would write the amount on it but also the words "not counted".'

McDonnell, Bridgeman, Leahy, and Peter McCormick were long-time clients of In Dublin and, as valued customers, they were treated differently. They paid the reduced rate of £50 less for their adverts but when McCormick started taking out full page advertisements he secured substantial reductions. Hogan said he didn't know Marie Bridgeman but did know a woman called Marie. He admitted he knew McCormick and Martin Morgan 'just to see and say hello to.' Morgan — whose nickname in the tabloid newspapers was 'The Beast' — was from the same town as Hogan, Athy in Co. Kildare. He worked for a time as a doorman in the Westbury Hotel before moving on to become a bouncer for Tom McDonnell. It was there he learned his trade as a pimp.

Hogan also knew McDonnell personally because Tom liked to travel by helicopter. 'I first met him at Celtic Helicopters as he was a regular user of this service and I was a traffic reporter for Radio Q102,' Hogan said. But separate arrangements had to be made for him at In Dublin to allow him come in and pay for his advertisements. This was not because he was a VIP but because Tom McDonnell was trouble. Hogan later played it down. 'It was over some disagreement,' he said, 'but I'm not aware what it was.'

In fact it was Hogan who told McDonnell not to come into the offices on publishing week because he treated Claire Murphy and the staff so badly. It wasn't good to have aggressive criminals swanning in to the offices of a respectable listings magazine and loudly demanding attention in a threatening fashion. It wasn't good for the company's image or the welfare of its employees. All the brothel-keepers' money may have been welcome and good for business but they themselves were not. They were a different breed, prone to be violent, particularly towards women, and used to life in the criminal underworld. Something had to change and in September 1998 it did.

Claire Murphy had just arrived back from her holidays when Hogan called her in to his office. He had sub-let a section of the ground floor of 3, 4 and 5 Camden Place to another publishing company. The brothel owners now had to pass through the offices of Éireann Healthcare Publications to get to where the *In Dublin* designers were. The company objected to people not connected to their business coming in and out of their offices. Hogan had to do something about it.

The criminals were not good for his legitimate business and Hogan devised a way to separate the sheep from the goats — the brothel-keepers from his tenants and other advertisers of legitimate products. He decided to open the office on weekends specially and solely for the adult advertisers. From September they could only come to place, proofread and pay for their advertisements on Saturday. And Hogan told Claire Murphy that she would be there to meet them. 'I was not happy with having to come in on a Saturday but I was told by Mike that I would get a day off in lieu,' she said, 'but it didn't work out because I was also his PA and I had to be there with him every day.'

Claire wasn't the only one told she had to work Saturdays. The two designers, Jonathan Murphy and Niall Fennessy, also had to come in every second weekend to meet the clients and design their advertisements. Initially they got £50 extra but this was later doubled after they complained about the volume of work. But Claire Murphy got nothing. 'I got no commission from Mike Hogan and I got nothing extra for working on the Saturday. It was all part of my job,' she said. Hogan said she was not paid overtime because 'she had a generous package'.

It was an eerie change in the circumstances of her employment. Up until then when she met the brothel-keepers she was in a busy office surrounded by lots of people with access to her controlled by a receptionist. Now when she met them on Saturdays she was often alone. There was one other person in the building, the graphic designer, but he could be anywhere. She was dealing with criminals and taking in large amounts of cash. She was very conscious of the fact that if anything happened she was on her own. There was also a potential danger to her from the fact that, at the end of the day, she now had to move the day's substantial takings, most of it in cash, from one office to another up the road. Out on the street she was vulnerable to attack and robbery.

Hogan didn't work on Saturdays but he devised a new and unique system for keeping the money safe. He told Claire to bring the cash up to his personal filing cabinet in her office. The top three drawers related to his business affairs. He kept details of his properties in the bottom drawer. She was to open that drawer and put the money in the file marked 'Holy Cross'. Hogan named it after the cottage he owned in the Tipperary village. The money was never put in a night safe. Hogan said if it was not left in the office Claire Murphy brought it home.

Hogan counted the money personally. 'I brought over the money and the amounts on complimentary slips,' Claire Murphy said. 'He would return these slips to me having totalled up the amounts along with any other money that would have been put in through the letter box of our offices by people I would not be dealing with.' Hogan didn't use an accounting system and *In Dublin* didn't have a bank account.

Hogan was the sole recipient of the money from the adult advertisements whether he was in or out of the country. He handled it separately from the magazine's other income. The total was made up of the money Claire Murphy put in the filing cabinet, the money his driver John Farrell collected and the cash posted anonymously into the office at night. 'Some of it was lodged to the account of

KCD Ltd,' Hogan said, 'and the balance was handled by myself.'

Hogan made millions from the brothel advertisements. There was a 'rate card' for normal advertising in the magazine but there was none for the adult advertisements. He alone priced them, as he said himself, 'I set the rate'. The official advertising rates for *In Dublin* in 1999 were £1,045 for a full page in mono (black and white) and £1,320 for a page in colour. An eighth of a page for normal advertising cost £220 but for an adult advertisement it was £400 — almost double. A full page of these advertisements could earn Hogan up to £3,200, more than three times the cost of a full-page mono advertisement for normal advertisers.

'The cost of advertising in the adult section of the magazine had always commanded a premium,' he said. This was to say the least an understatement. Even if all eight advertisements on one page were taken up by the few brothel-keepers who as regular long-term advertisers got a £50 discount, Hogan still made £2,800 a page. That was more than double the price of the official rate for a page in colour. In later years he gave his biggest customer, Peter McCormick, a special discount because he was consistently advertising by the page. McCormick was, however, still paying £2,200. There was a lot more money in advertising brothels than legitimate products.

From 1994–97 Claire Murphy estimated that Mike Hogan was taking in around £8,000 per issue, a figure that seems conservative. However, with 26 issues a year this still represented an annual income of £208,000 from this limited, specialised form of advertising. From 1997 on, the figures dramatically increased. More criminals and ex-prostitutes were setting up and advertising brothels. Demand for the advertising space increased along with the cost. By 1999 the advertisements cost £400 each and, with eight advertisements per page and some issues with six and a half pages of adverts, Hogan could and did take in as much as £20,000 in one issue from sex adverts alone. Almost all the money arrived in cash. Hogan ordered Claire to stop taking cheques when some of them bounced although they accepted credit cards because they were traceable.

The brothel owners were not issued with invoices or receipts for the 'RADS'. Most didn't ask for them. Brian O'Byrne did and didn't get any. There was no breakdown of the cost of the advertisements for VAT. Hogan said the £400 cost was inclusive of all prices but he admitted that no VAT was charged on these cash transactions and no VAT invoices were issued. *In Dublin* not only advertised brothels as health clubs and escort agencies, it also carried personal advertisements, chat lines and advertisements for sex shops. In some issues the last ten or twelve pages were filled with these types of sex advertisements.

Hogan was the only one who really knew how much the advertisements were making. His staff didn't know. His personal assistant didn't know. Not even the chief executive of Hoson, which had the licence to publish *In Dublin*, knew how much money was pouring in. 'I did not know how much that income was,' Maeve Kneafsey said. 'It was always clear to me that the income from these adult ads were Mike Hogan's responsibility and he took care of them.' Kneafsey said she didn't even know how much Hogan was charging for the advertisements. When the Gardaí told her she was somewhat surprised. It was, as she put it, 'way above the normal rates'.

Around the beginning of June 1999 Hogan called a meeting with Claire Murphy and the two graphic designers, Jonathan Murphy and Niall Fennessy. He told them there had been a serious complaint from the Censorship Board about the content and presentation of the adult advertisements. The content would have to be toned down considerably. The photos and images of the women had to go. The words 'Escort Agency' were to be changed to 'Health Studio'. In future there was to be no reference to call-outs. The advertisements, however, could still be printed in colour.

Hogan then tried to find out what exactly the Censorship Board was unhappy about and got worried when the Board wouldn't tell him. On Wednesday 7 July he sought advice from his solicitor, Paddy Kennedy, and counsel. The next day he issued a memorandum to staff in which he outlined his concerns.

'The situation appears to be,' he wrote, 'that there is every likelihood that the Censorship of Publications Office will endeavour to close *In Dublin*. In an effort to avoid this we need to put in place some sort of reasonable defence mechanism against claims that we are continuing to run Escort Agencies ads under a different guise.'

He pointed out that some changes had been made but that they didn't go far enough. 'For example,' he wrote, 'when we changed the design lay-outs we kept the same names and telephone numbers so therefore these must change. Similarly the tele lines need to change also, so substantially as to be inoffensive, as in examples provided on *The Star* newspaper.' And he told the staff what he wanted done by specifying a list of 'the rules we need to adhere to:

1. New telephone numbers for all agencies
2. New names for all agencies
3. No obvious sexual connotations in any of the ad copy
4. Signed letters from whatever address by whomever stating that the business is a Health Studio.

There is no guarantee that this will work but we have to try and we have to do it immediately.' He signed the memo Michael.

The staff, however, didn't seem to get the message quickly enough for Michael. The half-naked women were replaced with inoffensive images — insects, birds and flowers — but he still wasn't happy. He called a second meeting and this time he was angry. He believed he'd told the staff that all emblems had to go.

The two designers were not privy to the original memo but he left them in no doubt as to his feelings at that second meeting. 'He stated that he wanted name changes for most of the ads previously published and they were to revert to black and white from colour,' Jonathan said. 'This was done in the next publication. This gave rise to considerable problems with the advertisers.'

Some of the brothel owners were not happy but most, if not all, accepted the changes. All suggestive text was dropped as the wording, descriptions and layouts of their advertisements were changed. Those who refused to change their names and numbers were told their advertisements would be dropped. 'On his (Hogan's) instructions to me,' Claire said, 'only names and wording approved by the company lawyers would be passed.' The advertisers might have been annoyed but there was nothing they could do about it. Hogan's instructions were a *fait accompli*. If the owners didn't like it, they could lump it. There was no magazine better than *In Dublin* in which to advertise their brothels.

A list of new names for the brothels was drawn up to make the advertisements acceptable to Hogan's lawyers and the Censorship Board. Now anodyne and sanitised, the brothels were given names such as Maples, The Premier Club, The Studio and Beverley Hills. All overt sexual references had been removed. The brothel owners were then given the choice of a new name from the list. If they weren't fussy, the magazine picked one for them. By the time *Ireland On Sunday* decided to advertise, 'Essentials' was one of the few names left.

In spite of the name changes, the services the brothels provided remained the same and the same people continued to place the same advertisements. Samson and Delilah was renamed French Connection 'because you're worth it'. Ascots, designed to conjure up the images of the 'aristocratic and well-heeled horny horsey set' lost its tattooed red-headed lady and became The Ambassador. Under a 'New Owner' it offered sauna, massage and showers. 'Staff required' was also printed in very small, discreet text on the bottom left-hand corner.

Towards the end of June Hogan became more conscious of the need to completely reform the 'adult ads' pages so he personally checked over the proofs before they went to print. Beside an advertisement for French Connection he wrote 'No Health Studio'. That description was also missing from a number of other advertisements and he wanted it included.

He ruled that the name 'Showgirls' for one of the 'Health Studios' was unacceptable. He also noticed a number of silhouettes and cartoon drawings of women, beside which he wrote one word, 'why?' Beside another advertisement he wrote 'No massage' and in the advertisement for Ultra he crossed out the words 'Phone Brenda Now' and wrote 'No' in large capital letters beside it.

After he had examined the pages for one of the last issues to be published with the advertisements, he wrote in the covering note to Claire, 'These are just my comments, I shudder to think what counsel will say.' Hogan was still trying to publish as much as he could without breaking the law or getting into trouble with the Censorship Board. The changes he ordered were designed to avoid a prosecution while at the same time ensuring that he continued to milk millions from this fat cash cow.

It was a fine line he was walking. Hogan later said he ordered the changes because 'I thought the ads were offensive,' but he also admitted the real reason why he made them. 'I ordered the changes in an attempt to appease the Censorship of Publications Board.' His efforts were in vain. By the time all the changes appeared in the magazine, it was too late. The Board had already decided to ban *In Dublin* and force it off the shelves.

10 *The Man Who Didn't Know*

The Censorship of Publications Board met on 18 April 1999 and three out of four of its members voted to ban *In Dublin* for six months. A member of the public had made a complaint about the adult advertisements in the magazine. 'There was,' he wrote, 'a good deal of objectionable textual matter to be found in each issue.' A photograph of a naked woman sitting astride a chair turned backwards à la Christine Keeler had also caused offence. 'The Board may be interested to know,' he informed them, 'that an enlargement of this cover appeared on a poster on two sites in Dublin.'

The Board took the complaint very seriously and examined at least three recent issues of *In Dublin*. It wrote to Hogan saying it had no wish to have to consider prohibition of his 'eminent pub-lication' but it had to consider the complaint with care. Hogan was also concerned and he made a number of genuine attempts to find out what the problem was and solve it.

He wrote back to the Board to say it had been his 'considered opinion for some time that a number of adverts which have appeared in the Personals section of *In Dublin* have exceeded what I would believe to be the acceptable norms for personal advertising.' He then asked for confirmation that the Board was only concerned with advertising. He even submitted examples of suggested changes to the advertisements and asked for comments and recommend-ations. But the Censorship of Publications Board ignored him.

Hogan, therefore, continued to publish the advertisements and the Board was not impressed. At its meeting on 15 May the members expressed concern that — shock, horror — certain advertisements might be taken to be for prostitution services. Hogan didn't know it then but the Board had already made its decision. It found that the advertisements 'have usually or frequently been indecent or obscene and for that reason the sale and distribution in the State of the said issues and further issues of the said periodical publication should be prohibited.'

The Board had the power to do this under legislation that curiously enough also dealt with contraception and abortion — Section 9 of the Censorship of Publications Act 1946 as amended by the Health (Family Planning) Act of 1979 and the Regulation of Information (Services outside the State for the Termination of Pregnancies) Act 1995. The order was made on 31 July 1999 that *In Dublin* was to be pulled from the shelves and was not to go on sale after 10 August.

The ban was serious for Hogan. His magazine had been censored by a State body which had ruled it was breaking the law.

His biggest source of income had, with the stroke of a pen, been capped. The immediate problem he faced was what to do about the next issue of *In Dublin*. It was due to hit the streets two days after the ban came into effect. Hogan had the right to appeal to an appeal's board but that would not solve his immediate cash and distribution problems.

There were six full pages of adult advertisements planned for *In Dublin* on 12 August and another 3 advertisements on the seventh page. It didn't say it in the magazine but all except one of those advertisements were for brothels which offered sex for between £60 and £120 per visit. Fifty-one advertisements at £400 each represented as much as £20,400 for Hogan in adult advertising revenue alone. Even allowing for the maximum discount on every advertisement he still stood to lose £17,850 on that one issue and he was not about to just let that go.

The Hoson Company issued a statement saying that the ban was 'a matter of great concern to the company and its customers.' It continued; 'It is the management's intention to respond vigorously to any unfounded allegations. It is also their intention to enter into discussions with the relevant authorities to enable publication to resume as soon as possible so as to ensure customers are not disappointed.' But Hogan had no intention of awaiting the outcome of those discussions. To do so would disappoint his most profitable customers, the brothel owners who relied on *In Dublin* to advertise their prostitutes.

Hogan came up with a brainwave. The Board's order specifically stated under the section 'Name of Publication' that *In Dublin* was the magazine that was banned. That was all it said. It didn't qualify, elaborate, expand or explain that any similar, new or renamed publication was also banned. This allowed Hogan to circumvent the ban.

He got rid of the 'In' from the title of his magazine and Vol. 1 No. 1 of a supposedly new magazine *Dublin* went on sale for the fortnight spanning 12–25 August for £1.95/€2.48. It was exactly the same as the planned and largely printed issue of *In Dublin* with the same design, price, typography and editorial flavour. It even carried the same catch phrase, 'the definitive guide to the fortnight'. Ironically *Dublin* sold more copies than *In Dublin* had the fortnight before.

Hogan had some heavy hitters on his side. The Irish Council of Civil Liberties, The National Union of Journalists and the Vienna-based International Press Institute all condemned the ban. The NUJ said it was 'an attempt to drag Ireland back to the dark ages.' The ICCL said the procedures adapted by the Censorship Board were 'from another era'. The Press Institute was far more scathing in its criticism. It was dismayed to find 'that a progressive and democratic country like Ireland still maintains an institution such as the Censorship of Publications Board, the mere existence of which runs contrary to the democratic principles of freedom of expression.'

But the Board had its supporters and defenders. The Chairman of the Fianna Fáil Parliamentary Party, Dr Rory O'Hanlon, said it was 'absolutely correct' and that it would be 'very good work' if *In Dublin* had to 'disappear'. And the editor of Hoson's most influential publication, *Magill*, resigned because she said she was greatly disturbed by the adult advertisements in its sister publication. 'There are levels of knowing and levels of awareness,' Emily O'Reilly said, 'and what has come out over the last few days has disturbed me greatly.' The Government appointed her Ombudsman and Information Commissioner in March 2003.

But this was really a minor setback. Hogan was winning the public relations battle hands down. He was seen to be defending the reputation of a 'flagship' publication, protecting the jobs of its 37 employees and preserving freedom of expression, literature and speech. It didn't look good for the part-time, five-member Censorship Board. Its ignominious history was recalled in the press and on the airwaves, and Hogan found himself in the esteemed company of James Joyce, John McGahern, Samuel Beckett, Seán Ó Faoláin, and Edna O'Brien. And it got worse for the Censorship Board when Hogan went to court.

Hogan said the Board refused to tell him where his company was going wrong when it found parts of In Dublin to be indecent and obscene. His lawyer, Senior Counsel Joe Finnegan, told the High Court that the Censorship Board wrote to Hogan and told him there had been a complaint about the magazine. But it did not tell him whether that complaint was about the adult advertisements, the editorial content, or the main advertisements such as a full page promotion for Durex condoms.

Hogan said he was in the dark as to which adverts were objectionable and wrote back asking for more details and seeking a meeting. He had no wish to wage an ongoing feud with the Board. He certainly had no intention of becoming Ireland's answer to Larry Flint, the US publisher of the pornographic magazine Hustler. His attitude was that if the Board identified specifically where the company was breaking the law then it would comply with its views. He even offered to publish a 'sanitised version' of In Dublin until the court determined the rights and wrongs of the prohibition order. But by that time it was too late for such a compromise. The Board could not revoke, amend or withdraw its prohibition order.

Lawyers for the Censorship Board said the sex advertisements were at the heart of the complaint. The complainant was offended by the pages of advertisements for health clubs, escort agencies, adult shops, chat lines and the personal advertisements with sexual connotations. Senior Counsel Diarmuid McGuinness also said Hogan's attitude to the Board's prohibition was made clear by the publication of the new magazine *Dublin*. This he described as a contempt of court which should not be tolerated.

The High Court judge, however, didn't see it that way. Mr Justice Diarmuid O'Donovan said he deplored the fact that Hogan had circumvented the ban by publishing *Dublin*. But while it may have been contrary to the spirit of the law, it was not unlawful and therefore not a contempt of court. On the other hand, he said the behaviour of the Censorship of Publications Board was 'incredible and reprehensible'.

The judge found the Board had been unfair to Hogan in two ways. Firstly by refusing to meet him and secondly by not telling him that it had already determined the fate of the magazine while continuing to conduct a correspondence with him as to its future. The Board decided to ban *In Dublin* on 18 April but didn't tell Hogan until 3 August. He was pointlessly still trying to sort out the problem three and a half months after they had decided on the ban. The judge overturned the ban and cleared the way for *In Dublin* to go back on the streets until the court could decide on the validity of the ban. There was, however, a sting in the tail. He directed that it was not to carry any more advertisements for health clubs or escort agencies.

Outside the court, Hogan professed himself delighted and relieved. 'The ban would have closed us down,' he said. 'It is like saying *The Irish Times* could come back in six months time — it could not; business is about continuity.' He said if reason had reigned, if the Board had met him and discussed the problem, perhaps it could all have been sorted out and never have ended up in the courts. 'I would like to think I am a fair and reasonable person to sit down and have a discussion with,' he said. He refused, however, to make any long-term decision about dropping the advertisements until the High Court ruled on the matter.

By this time in 1999 Hogan had published sixteen issues of *In Dublin*. Taking an average figure between maximum and minimum earnings, the Gardaí estimated he had a trading income of nearly a £$\frac{1}{4}$m (£244,500) for the eight months of the year and over £400,000 for a full trading year (26 issues). They believe he took in over £2m for the adult advertisements alone from the time he took over *In Dublin* in 1992. Most of the money came in cash and the only apparent record that was kept of it was in the back of Hogan's filofax. It was an extremely lucrative source of income on which no VAT or tax of any sort was paid.

'It has been a very trying 10–12 days,' Hogan said of that time. This was in many ways an understatement. He had one of his most profitable publications banned and had launched another one to replace it. The editor of the most prestigious magazine in his company had resigned over the issue but Hogan took the case to court to defend his position and won. However, little did he know then that more trying times lay ahead.

The day before the court case began Operation Gladiator was set up to tackle those profiteering from prostitution. 'While this would include the activities of pimps, brothel owners and the criminal gangs which operate brothels,' a Garda Press Officer Inspector Simon O'Connor said, 'it would also take in the publishers.' The Censorship Board's ban was one of those incidents which prompted the Garda Commissioner to take action. Another was the revelations which appeared in a Sunday newspaper three days before.

On Sunday, 15 August 1999, *Ireland On Sunday* ran a story headlined '*In Dublin* refers girls to brothels'. Written by John Mooney, the paper's crime correspondent, the article was the result of a two-month undercover investigation into the 'Vice Trade' in Dublin. Mooney taped conversations which ran to fifteen pages and he also kept his own notes and documentation, such as a fax from *In Dublin*. The second part of his investigation ran the following Sunday after Hogan's victory in the High Court.

Mooney said he was told by 'contacts in the vice world' that *In Dublin* was actively organising the advertising of brothels and meeting the brothel owners and managers. One Saturday afternoon he stood outside the magazine's offices at Camden Street and watched for two hours. He noticed a pattern of people calling every half hour and recognised some of the faces, including Peter McCormick. The newspaper decided to investigate further.

Mooney got hold of an untraceable mobile phone number and rang *In Dublin* around noon on 5 July 1999. He asked about placing an advertisement for an escort agency and was put through to Claire Murphy. Mooney told her he was acting for a man who wanted to place an advert for a brothel. 'We don't actually run ads for brothels here, believe it or not,' she replied, 'we only do ads for health studios.' Mooney ended the call.

Claire Murphy said later the call annoyed her. 'In my seven years working there nobody had ever asked to place an ad like that i.e. an ad for a brothel.' Mooney had mentioned the unmentionable. Clearly he didn't have the subtlety of a genuine brothel owner but that didn't stop him.

Five minutes later he rang Claire Murphy back and told her an advertisement for a health studio would be fine. He was told to call in on Saturday afternoon. They'd design an advertisement for him and he could sit with the designer until he was happy with it. He was quoted £400 for an eighth of a page, £800 for a quarter page or a two-eighth strip across the top. Even though the proposed advertisement was for a health studio, Mooney had already said he wanted to advertise a brothel. *In Dublin* agreed to design the page and logo. All it needed was a telephone number.

'We do everything,' Claire Murphy told him. 'We can even think up the name.' She did this because Hogan, on legal advice, told her to rename the brothels. On Saturday 10 July, Mooney met a man in a white t-shirt and black leather trousers. Claire Murphy had sent the designer Niall Fennessy out to meet him after Mooney pretended he couldn't find the *In Dublin* offices. He was afraid of being recognised as a journalist, but ironically Fennessy thought he recognised Mooney as someone who had been behind him in school. He didn't say anything at the time but was surprised because he didn't believe Mooney was the kind of guy who would be in the brothel business. He was right.

Murphy and Fennessy had earlier been out on the street looking for Mooney to direct him to the office. 'I recall a further phone call on my mobile from Johnny,' Claire said, 'asking me to go out and sit into his van but I refused and Niall offered to go out.' Fennessy saw Mooney's jeep and waved. Mooney drove over, rolled down the passenger window and handed him an envelope with £400 cash for Claire. The following Monday Claire faxed a copy of the advertisement to Mooney from Hogan's office. It was on a piece of paper marked 'Mike Hogan, personal' and was signed by Claire.

In Dublin named the brothel 'Essentials' and advertised it as a health studio. It was illustrated with a butterfly motif. The staff dealing with the advertisements had been under pressure to satisfy the lawyers. All the pages of brothel advertisements in that issue were sent to them for approval before the magazine went to print.

'On that Saturday things were hectic due to all the changes in names, phone numbers, etc. and the name Essentials was one of the last names available,' Claire said. When Mooney rang to ask her why 'Staff wanted' was not on the advertisement, Claire told him she didn't recommend putting it in because it could give the wrong impression. She didn't mention the legal advice the boss had received or the problems he was having with the Censorship Board. 'You don't want everyone to know you've no staff,' she said to him.

Claire suggested instead that he put the advertisement looking for staff in the magazine's personal column. When Mooney asked how much it would cost, she replied, 'It's free, we're not that bad.' But nothing was really free in Mike Hogan's business and for this free advertisement there was also a catch. The personal advertisement was only free if a customer took out a £400 advertisement in the adult section.

The advertisement for 'Essentials' Health Studio was published in the edition of *In Dublin* of 15–28 July. The first day *Ireland On Sunday* received 70 calls from men looking for sex — asking where the brothel was and how much it cost. Mooney took the calls. He knew what to say. He had phoned other brothels to find out what they were offering and at what price. Over the next few days he dealt with another 120 inquiries for sex.

The following week Mooney rang again to ask about placing the advertisement a second time. He told Claire they had been inundated with customers and would need more staff. He said Claire offered to help. 'We would know here if there are girls looking for work,' she said, 'so what we could tell them is that yours is the place to ring. You know you get a lot of girls coming through here and they might say "do you know any new place or nice place", you know this sort of thing where there are certain places that they don't want to go near. Think about it and come back to me.'

'We're looking for someone in the don section,' Mooney said, 'Domination and all that.' 'Well, we don't get into any of that,' Claire replied. 'If any of them literally just say do you know of any place looking for staff we just give out the name.' Mooney recorded Claire Murphy as she said this and kept the tape. But Claire Murphy categorically denied ever referring women to 'health studios' when she was subsequently questioned about it by the Gardaí. She also said she didn't know of any other In Dublin staff member having done so. 'If I said the words attributed to me, I probably did so in order to get rid of him,' she said. 'If I said that then I did not mean it and I had no intention of doing so. As far as I recall John Mooney phoned me several times that day and was pestering me and I was under pressure and I would have told him anything in order to get him off the phone.'

The statistics support this version of events. Out of twenty prostitutes interviewed as part of Operation Gladiator, eleven or 55 per cent found work by ringing the numbers advertised in the adult section of In Dublin. The other nine were long-term practitioners who were either poached or got work through the grapevine. But not one of them ever contacted the offices of In Dublin to look for work. Nor were they aware of any other prostitute in Dublin having been referred by staff at In Dublin to any brothel. None the less, these and other figures do show that the magazine played a central role in the prostitution business. Of 89 men questioned leaving brothels, 61 or just over 68 per cent said they got the phone numbers from In Dublin. The other 28 couldn't or wouldn't say how they got the numbers.

When Mooney asked Claire if he could put a picture of a naked woman on the second advert, he was told no.

'We're under the kibosh from the Censorship Board,' Claire said. 'There is a big clampdown on all this sort of advertising so no women can go in.'

'It's just that we wanted sort of a topless girl or something like that if that was possible?' Mooney said.

'But don't you know you're living in Ireland, in Dublin. You'd have to be putting that sort of crap into *Penthouse*, a top-shelf magazine.'

'Yeah, yeah, yeah.'

'Ah sure, there's no point in causing trouble. Do you know what I mean?'

'Yeah, fair enough.'

'No. You can put anything you like on it but it can't be a woman because we have been told to tone things down here for a while. We're under the kibosh if you know what I mean.'

'I'm with you.'

'You have to play ball because if you don't play ball there's no ad.'

Mooney then offered to pay £200 for an advertisement for staff wanted in the personal section. He spun her another yarn. The first advertisement had been so successful he said the man he was acting for was reluctant to put another one in until he got the staff problem sorted out first. But that suggestion was also ruled out because of the clampdown.

Mooney offered to pay by cheque but *In Dublin* preferred a credit card. 'Do you not have a Visa card,' Claire asked him. 'A Visa would be better because you have to lodge (a cheque) and it's traced back, even for your own identification, do you know what I mean? You'd be better off not lodging the cheque.' Another advantage of paying by credit card was the brothel owner didn't have to make an appointment or queue up to pay on Saturday afternoon. It could all be done over the phone.

Two weeks after he last spoke to Claire Murphy, the first part of the investigation was published. She heard about it when she came back from her holidays. 'The person who wrote that article has been selective in what he wrote,' she said. Claire Murphy had been caught in the frontline of the newspaper's sting. She had been tricked and humiliated but Mike Hogan's humiliation was to come. At the time he didn't pay much attention to the article. He didn't realise its significance. But it marked the beginning of the end of what was for him an extremely profitable enterprise.

Ireland On Sunday made a number of serious allegations. The newspaper accused *In Dublin* of offering to refer prostitutes to pimps. It said that well-known pimps and criminals, some with connections to the drugs trade, settled their accounts in cash outside of office hours on Saturday. It also claimed that *In Dublin* was commercially pivotal to the prostitution trade in Dublin and other parts of the country. These were serious criminal allegations which the Gardaí could not ignore.

Mike Hogan was now the focus of a criminal investigation but one that was very different to the other inquiries into prostitution in Dublin. There was no surveillance or interviews with punters and women. There was no need for search warrants or unexpected raids. There were no messy finds of used condoms and bags of smelly towels. The Gardaí knew the advertisements were for brothels and already had proof through their targeting of brothel owners. Club Elite, Flamingos, The Academy, Maples, Fleur de Lis, Body Harmony, Tropical Paradise, Palm Beach, Angels and The Advantage — all of whom advertised in *In Dublin* — had all been investigated and/or raided.

This was an investigation into white collar crime — clean, crisp, shirt and tie stuff. There was no call for muscle or restraint, handcuffs or arrests. Probing interviews in unfamiliar Garda stations were replaced by determined inquiries in pursuit of the facts in comfortable homes and city centre offices. It was all very civilised and polite and all those caught up in it co-operated fully. The lawyers, however, were on standby at all times. They were present at interviews on behalf of and on the instructions of their clients and they kept a legal eagle eye on the whole procedure.

The Hogan investigation was also different because it was trying to establish whether a different law had been broken, in this case the Criminal Justice (Public Order Act) 1994. This law prohibits the publication of advertisements for brothels and prostitution. Hogan was also being investigated to see if he had broken the Criminal Law Sexual Offences Act of 1993 by organising prostitution like the brothel owners and managers had. They broke only one law but Hogan was being investigated because he might have broken two.

The first person to be approached was the source of the allegations of criminality, the journalist John Mooney. On 3 September 1999, Detective Inspector John McMahon met him and he agreed to co-operate. He made a statement reiterating the allegations he'd made in the newspaper and offered corroborative evidence. Two weeks later he gave McMahon the fax Claire Murphy sent to him confirming that *Ireland On Sunday* had advertised a brothel called 'Essentials'.

Mooney also gave McMahon a fifteen-page transcript of the audiotapes he'd recorded of his telephone conversations with Claire Murphy. When they listened to them, the Gardaí felt there was a line of questioning apparent throughout that could irritate and illicit a 'get rid of him at any cost' response. Claire Murphy did say that John Mooney had been pestering her.

Mooney made the calls to obtain material for the article and the Gardaí felt some of the questions endeavoured to draw out specific answers favourable to the newspaper's investigation. There was a possibility, therefore, the conversations could be interpreted in a very broad sense as leading to entrapment.

McMahon stressed, however, that they were looking at Mooney's methods from the point of view of a criminal investigation and their views were not meant as a criticism of methods used from a journalistic point of view. 'The requirements,' he said, 'are fundamentally different in each case.' Anyway the Gardaí would obviously have to conduct their own interviews with Claire Murphy.

Two weeks later McMahon and Detective Sergeant Mark Kavanagh visited her at her home in Raheny. Her solicitor, Anthony Harris, was also there. Claire Murphy told the Gardaí she knew she was mentioned in the article but vehemently denied the allegations of criminality. She agreed to help in any way she could. She agreed to be interviewed but broke down in the middle of the first one and it was stopped. It was not easy for an innocent person to find herself being questioned about possible criminal activity.

The interview was continued two days later at the Garda's Dublin headquarters in Harcourt Square. When it was over, Claire Murphy signed the notes. Two months later she made a statement to the Gardaí without her solicitor being present. She also gave them whatever documentation she could including memos, notes and the copies of the pages of the US telephone directories that Hogan had given her.

The investigation was neither complicated nor protracted. There were only seven people that needed to be spoken to. Along with Claire Murphy, four other *In Dublin* or Hoson staff members were interviewed — Jonathan Murphy, Niall Fennessy, John Farrell and Maeve Kneafsey. Both graphic designers said the word prostitution was never mentioned in the office but Murphy said he had his own interpretation of what the advertisements were selling. Fennessy said everyone in the office understood they referred to prostitution.

Maeve Kneafsey presented the Gardaí with a one-page, prepared statement but made a second one in response to questions during the interview. She said she was happy not to have any involvement with the adult advertisements and that she never directed that the brothel advertisers should only be dealt with on a Saturday. Hogan's driver, John Farrell, also made a short statement at first but in a second, more comprehensive one admitted collecting envelopes from three known brothels.

The last person to be questioned was the boss. Once Operation Gladiator was established, Hogan knew the Gardaí would come looking to talk to him so he approached them first. He told his solicitor, Patrick Kennedy, to contact the special investigation unit at Harcourt Square and unofficially state that he was taking full responsibility for the adult advertisements in the magazine. If any breach of the law was found, he was 'putting his hands up' and stating that no one else was responsible for the advertisements. He also let it be known that he would co-operate with the enquiry in any way he could.

It was clear to the Gardaí that they had to see Hogan. He had questions to answer and he agreed to meet them. On 9 December 1999 Hogan and his solicitor Patrick Kennedy, Detective Inspector John McMahon and Detective Garda Michael Mahon sat down in an interview room at the headquarters of the National Bureau of Criminal Investigation in Harcourt Square. McMahon cautioned him and explained in detail that they were trying to find out if the adult advertisements in *In Dublin* advertised brothels or prostitution. They also wanted to know what his involvement with them was and what he knew about them to find out whether or not he had broken the law.

Hogan declined to make a statement — 'not at this stage' he said — so the detectives put 74 prepared questions to him. He answered each one but gave few detailed responses and gave away as little as possible. During the interview he left the room a number of times to consult privately with his solicitor. When asked what his instructions were to Claire Murphy when she took over the adult advertisements, his answer was 'I don't recall precisely'. When asked did he call a meeting and instruct that the content of the adult advertisements be toned down, he replied 'Quite likely'. And when asked whether he ever issued a written instruction regarding the content of the advertisements, his reply was 'quite possibly yes'.

When he was asked about high profile articles in the *Sunday World* naming Tom McDonnell, Marie Bridgeman and Peter McCormick as major players in the prostitution business, his reply was 'I don't recall them. I don't personally buy the *Sunday World*.' He also said he didn't remember a member of staff bringing the articles to his attention and expressing concern at the company taking advertisements from these people. Other non-committal replies included 'I don't recall this', 'Not to my knowledge', and 'I have no knowledge of this matter'.

He said he was aware of the *Ireland On Sunday* articles but wouldn't accept the allegation as true that *In Dublin* was commercially pivotal to the prostitution trade in Dublin and other parts of the country. He also said he didn't know if well-known pimps or criminals with links to the drugs trade settled their accounts in cash at his offices on Saturday afternoons. And he said he didn't use his driver John Farrell to go out and collect money and advertisements for the adult section even though Farrell himself had admitted he had.

When it was put to him that he changed the content of the advertisements so that he could continue running them even though he must have known that some of them were for the prostitution business, he still protested his innocence. 'I never knew for a fact that any of the advertising was involved in the prostitution business,' he said. 'I changed the adverts in an attempt to appease the Censorship Board.' When the Gardaí continued to press him on this, the heart of the matter, he stopped giving explanations and confined himself to one-word answers:

Q. I have to put to you that in all the circumstances you were aware that the adult ads were in fact advertising prostitutes or brothels.

A. No.

Q. I have to put to you that members of the staff at *In Dublin* were all aware that the ads were advertising prostitution or brothels.

A. No.

Q. I have to put to you that members of the staff at *In Dublin* were all aware that the ads were advertising prostitution or brothels and that they made this known to you but you continued to publish them because they were an extremely lucrative source of personal wealth to you and your wife.

A. No.

Q. Do you accept full responsibility for publishing the adult section of the magazine in so far as the adult ads were concerned?

A. Yes.

Q. Do you accept full responsibility as publisher of the magazine for the content of the adult ads.

A. Yes.

Q. I have read over to you, Michael Hogan, and your solicitor, Paddy Kennedy, the memo of the interview. Do you agree that it is a true and accurate account of the questions put to you and the answers given?

A. Yes.

And that was it. John McMahon read the record back to him and Hogan initialled each page and signed the interview notes. It marked the end of the investigation and the beginning of the prosecution. On 18 January 2000 Detective Inspector John McMahon sent the file to the Director of Public Prosecutions with the recommendation that Hogan be prosecuted for offences contrary to Section 23 of the Criminal Justice (Public Order) Act 1994 which prohibits the advertising of brothels and prostitution.

The offence in law is committed by the person who publishes or causes to be published, distributes or causes to be distributed, an advertisement for a brothel or the services of a prostitute in the State. The investigation team concluded that since Hogan cleared the advertisements before publication it was hard to see how anyone could believe they were advertising anything other than brothels and prostitutes.

'The explicit female images leave little to the imagination and it would be difficult to visualise what therapeutic assistance the staff from the escort agencies/health clubs advertised would provide other than sexual,' John McMahon wrote. 'In addition to the content it would appear that Hogan was the only one at *In Dublin* concerned with the ads that did not realise that they were advertising prostitution.' Hogan was the man who didn't know!

McMahon concluded: 'The foregoing I believe proves beyond any doubt that Hogan knew exactly what the ads represented and what lengths he was prepared to go to maintain the publication of the ads. It is not unreasonable to suggest that the ads were in fact a "black market" operation by Hogan.'

McMahon's boss, Detective Superintendent Martin Donnellan, agreed with him that the case should be tried on indictment. The charges were too serious for the lowest court, the District Court, and he recommended they be heard in the Circuit Court where the penalties on conviction are more severe.

'There is sufficient evidence to bring charges against Hogan in respect of the adult ads in *In Dublin* magazine,' Donnellan wrote.

'He was not an absent company director or publisher who was not aware of the content of the ads or what they advertised. He was the person at the magazine who controlled the ads and profited very handsomely from them. He charged a premium of 85 per cent on the ads yet his advertisers still remained with him.'

Claire Murphy's position was, however, very different and the Gardaí felt she didn't have a case to answer. She accepted the advertisements as part of her normal working day but she was unhappy about them and got no extra money for doing them. Therefore, she really couldn't be prosecuted for living on the earnings of prostitution or advertising the services of brothels. 'The case against Claire Murphy is less clear,' Donnellan wrote. 'In all the circumstances there does not appear to be an answerable charge against Ms Murphy established.'

No charges were ever brought against Claire Murphy but the DPP didn't take long to decide that Mike Hogan had a case to answer. Four months later, on 18 May 2000, he met the Gardaí by appointment and was charged with 53 counts of advertising brothels and prostitution. He was brought before Kilmainham District Court and remanded on bail to appear there again in July. It was all handled very quickly and quietly, and there was no journalist in court to report the proceedings. But at 6.20 p.m. that evening RTÉ News got wind of it and it was broadcast on the Six One news twenty minutes later.

On 7 July the case was returned for trial to the Circuit Criminal Court. There was some delay in the proceedings when Hogan discovered he didn't have enough cash on him to post the higher deposit required for bail. It had been doubled to £6,000 and he was short a £1,000. His counsel, Vincent Heneghan, said Hogan was facing 'a matter where no custodial sentence can be imposed.' Hogan had to wait around the court to organise the money, and within an hour he handed it over and signed the bail bond.

His next appearance was to be his last, five months to the day after he was charged. On 18 October 2000, Mike Hogan pleaded guilty to ten sample charges between 19 June 1997 and 12 August 1999. He admitted advertising the brothels Flamingos, Tropical Paradise, New Imperial, Angels, Emmanuelles, Personal Services, Tiger Lillies, Secrets of Seduction, Leather and Lace, and Xclusive. Xclusive advertised for staff and offered homosexual services.

Judge Kevin Haugh said that Hogan was entitled to benefit from his co-operation with the Gardaí, the manner in which he had conducted himself since being charged and his plea of guilty. But the judge said he had attempted 'to play ducks and drakes' with the Censorship of Publications Board and the advertisements made no attempt to disguise the services they offered.

In his defence Hogan's lawyer pointed out that the advertisements were already being carried in the magazine when Hogan bought it in 1992. The legislation he was being prosecuted under was not introduced until 1994. Hogan, he said, accepted that ignorance of the law is no defence but he didn't know it was illegal until the Censorship Board contacted him in August 1999.

'It was very embarrassing for Mr Hogan,' Vincent Heneghan said, 'and will no doubt affect his business dealings in the future.' Hogan couldn't have been sent to jail but on the 53 charges could have been fined over half a million pounds. The maximum sentence was £10,000 on each charge but the judge said he felt the appropriate penalty was half that, £5,000 on each of the sample charges. Mike Hogan became the first person in Ireland to be convicted of advertising brothels and was fined a total of £50,000.

Claire Murphy felt hurt and used. She was always uncomfortable with the advertisements but if she had known they were illegal she wouldn't have had anything to do with them. For all her extra work she never got paid an extra penny. She didn't even get the day off in lieu she was promised for working on Saturdays. The whole episode left her severely traumatised and she needed medical help for at least three months after it. She never went back to work at *In Dublin* after the *Ireland On Sunday* articles were published. Even though she was on a substantial salary, she took a principled stand and resigned from the company.

Mike Hogan, on the other hand bounced back — if ever he was down. He was back in the papers, pictured at social events, giving interviews about his latest business venture and selling off his magazine titles. Hosan Ltd and KCD Ltd failed to file accounts and were struck off the Companies Register. At least seven of Mike's other companies went the same way — Ryanho Publishing Ltd, Where Publications Ltd, Irish Theatre Publications Ltd, Gael Sport Publications Teo, Inflight Publications Ltd, The Musical Lottery Company Ltd and Message on Hold Ltd, which was set up to supply equipment that plays messages on telephone systems.

Hogan said there was a valid reason for the closure of the companies. He pointed out that Inflight Publications was the trading company that published the CityJet inflight magazine and when the airline was taken over by another airline with its own magazine, the Cityjet magazine was no longer needed. 'Where Publications and Ryanho also closed for similar valid reasons,' he said. In June 2002 Hogan bought the magazine *Gay Ireland* for what he said was 'a substantial sum'.

In Dublin has also had its share of problems. By the end of 2001 Ink Publishing, the company which publishes the magazine, had lost over £1.3m. Three of its subsidiary companies — Rathgar Publishing, Grosvenor Publishing and Lifestyle and Leisure Publications — owed it more than £600,000. In August 2002

Hogan put six of his titles, including *Magill* and *In Dublin*, up for sale.

Mike Hogan was perhaps lucky the Criminal Assets Bureau didn't come after him. He went into negotiations with the Revenue Commissioners with a view to settling his tax problems. They wanted £1m from him. He wanted to pay substantially less. Not surprisingly, Hogan would not comment on the matter. 'My tax affairs are a private matter like everybody else,' he said.

He was, however, prepared to comment not on the detail but on the outcome of the investigation. 'I have been convicted. I made a mistake. I paid a substantial fine. I'm sorry that I did it and I have no further involvement in it whatsoever. It's not something I'm particularly proud of but you can't live in the past,' he said. And in his typically colourful and good-humoured manner to illustrate the point, he quoted his friend, 'As Charlie Haughey says you can't take to the bed!'

11 Hooker with a Heart

Justine Reilly was different. At 29 years of age she realised there was more money to be made selling other women's bodies than selling her own. She didn't go to secondary school. She was not married and didn't have any children. She had no skills or qualifications. She had worked in low-paid jobs as a cleaner and in pubs before becoming a prostitute. 'The only reason I got into this business was financial,' she said.

Justine worked for pimps for years but had little to show for it. She knew what it was like for the women and was not impressed with the way the other brothel-keepers, male or female, ran their businesses. 'The jobs I worked in before paid very little. I worked for very unsavoury characters in the business,' she said, 'but I do not wish to name them.' She didn't have to, they were already well known.

Originally from Blessington in Co. Wicklow, Justine moved to Dublin and ended up living in White Oaks in Clonskeagh. Her younger brother John became better known because he made legal history in the most tragic fashion. He was an army ranger and completed two tours in the Lebanon. He left the defence forces in 1993 to work as a UN sanctions inspector in Iraq. While he was home on leave in June 2001, he stayed over the bank holiday weekend at his cousin's house in Tallaght. He arrived at 11.30 p.m. on Sunday 4 June, played cards and drank a lot of alcohol — cider, beer, whiskey and a glass of poitín.

At 3 a.m. Gráinne Murphy, who was also staying over with Thomas Reilly and their baby Oisín, put her baby down for the night. She left him on a makeshift bed on the sitting room sofa and went upstairs to sleep. When she came back down at 8.30 a.m. on Monday morning, she saw John Reilly asleep on the armchair and baby Oisín lying face down on his right-hand side.

She picked up Oisín but he felt cold. She noticed dried blood near one of his ears and on his face. She then saw a silver fold-up Leatherman knife on the floor. There was blood on John Reilly's left hand and jeans. When the Gardaí arrived, they found him sitting on the stairs sobbing. He didn't know what happened. He couldn't remember.

It was three years before this horrific incident that Justine Reilly changed her life and established herself as a brothel-keeper. She began, like everyone else, by advertising in *In Dublin*. She went in to the office where they created the advertisement and a logo for her on a screen in front of her. Once she was happy with it, she paid £400 and another £400 every fortnight until the magazine stopped taking the brothel advertisements. Justine then moved on to the Internet.

Justine advertised on escortireland.com. Clients found her

brothels on the link page 'Dublin escorts'. 'Body Harmonies' and 'Tropical Paradise' and the mobile numbers for contacting them were listed. 'I found it on the Internet,' Derek said. 'I put in the words, "Dublin, Escorts", into the Yahoo search engine. There is a place which came up and it had a phone number for a place called "Body Harmonies".' Justine also advertised in the *Dublin Sex Guide* and the magazines *Deviate* and *Consenting Adults*.

The advertisements in *Consenting Adults* were designed to be stimulating and enticing and advertised the women as opposed to the brothel. 'Donna' was an attractive brunette who was adventurous and full of fun; 'Sophie' was blonde, busty, beautiful and waiting to hear from YOU! There was 'Barbie by name and Barbie by nature, I am an absolute doll, blonde and sexy' while Jade was a 'slim, sexy blonde who just loves giving and getting a good time'. Fun and games were Laura's middle names; if you were man enough for a passionate redhead then Brooke was the woman for you while Mandy, a sexy redhead, was dying to meet guys.

Justine advertised the services of at least eight women but not all of them were available at the one time. Two prostitutes and two mobiles could cater for all comers. Brooke, Mandy, Laura and Barbie could all be contacted on one number while Sophie, Kasey, and Jade shared the other. Justine also had business cards printed for the women to hand out so the customers would remember to return and avail of the 'Body Harmony Exclusive Service'.

Like most things in life, the reality for both the woman and the customer in the sex business was very different to the dreamworld of the advertiser. Justine's prostitutes were expensive, not exclusive. At the beginning she charged the same as every other brothel in town, £60 for half an hour. She took £20 and the woman got £40 but she also always took £30 from the first £60 each woman got per shift. The extra £10 went towards advertising costs.

However, when business got good the prices went up. 'Here in Tropical Paradise,' the sales pitch went, 'we charge £80 a half hour including sexual intercourse.' The split was now £50 for the woman, £30 for Justine. The hourly charge was £120 and Justine took £50 of that.

The business details were written into a characteristically feminine pink, sparkly A4-sized brothel book. The money was left between the pages for Justine to collect. She wrote 'taken' in the book after she picked up the cash. If she didn't call in, it was left in an envelope in a drawer under the TV or under a cushion on the sofa.

The women opened up the brothel in the morning and locked up at night. Toiletries and towels were provided but the women had to wash and dry them. Justine also left instructions, or as she called them 'suggestions', on what had to be done in the brothel. Everyone had to do their part to keep the place tidy and chores like hoovering or cleaning the bathroom were assigned to a different woman each day.

The brothels that Justine ran under the names Body Harmonies, Tropical Paradise and Club Tropical were, by and large, clean and comfortable. One operated in Parnell Street, an area earmarked for urban regeneration on the northside of Dublin, the other at Portobello on the southside of the city. They were fully furnished and heated, and when they weren't busy the girls could sit around and watch the television, which Justine bought for them. She paid the ESB, phone and cable TV bills. She also ensured the women in one brothel told the clients about the services of the other so when they phoned they could be sent to the nearest one. Kelly, who worked in Club Tropical, said, 'We were always told if clients couldn't make it that we were to refer them to Body Harmonies on the southside.'

Justine's approach to prostitution was different in that as a former prostitute she cared about the women who worked for her. She spoke as if there was a mission statement underlying her operation. 'I decided to set up my own agency where girls worked equally and without fear,' she said, 'so I got together with about five other girls and set up this agency called Body Harmony. The other girls worked for me.'

But this was no women's collective where all were equal, the profits were shared and women empowered women. Justine saw herself as a businesswoman and a boss. She was very professional in her approach to her work. It was making her a lot of money. She dressed well, used bank accounts and laser cards, and drove a brand new small car, a 99-D registered Ford Ka. She carried a number of mobile phones and kept records in filofaxes and notebooks. Business details such as lists of the names of girls looking for work were also kept in her 'Management 2000' book which she kept in her handbag.

The women agree she treated them well. Mandy worked as a chef in Dublin for two years for very low wages. She couldn't survive after paying the bills and the exorbitant rents in the city. 'On average I was coming out with £120 a week after tax,' she said. 'I am staying at a house with a friend. We are paying £115 a week between us for the house.' The remaining £60 wasn't enough for heat, light, transport, food and entertainment so she decided to become a prostitute. She bought a copy of *In Dublin*, rang a few of the brothels and started in Body Harmonies the next day. She had high praise for Justine whom she knew as Jade.

'Jade runs the brothel. She doesn't work as a prostitute on the premises. She just pops in and pops out,' she said. 'If we wanted milk or a video, we would ring Jade. If any of the girls were sick, Jade would make them go to a doctor. She gives the girls lifts home. She gave all the girls her number and if we have any problem we would ring her. Jade would ring each of the girls who were working about once a tour to make sure everybody was all right. She would ask if we were busy. She would always ask to make sure we were all right. If we had a bad week, she would give us money and we would pay her back.'

Justine hired a lot of women from the country, from counties like Waterford and Kerry, who perhaps, unlike women from the cities, did not have a tradition of working as prostitutes. Justine was sympathetic to the novices. Chantelle came to Dublin in September 1999 to try to earn enough money to afford a place to live. As soon as she had one, she was going to bring her 5-year-old son up from the south-east to live with her. A friend gave her the number of Tropical Paradise. She said she believed it was an escort agency. 'I thought you'd just go out for dinner and that,' she said. 'I didn't think it would be a place like this.'

But Justine knew from personal experience what it was like for a woman the first time. She didn't force anybody to do anything they didn't want to. 'She said whatever you want to do in the room is up to you,' Chantelle said. She eased her way into the capital's sex industry and continued to work as a prostitute for Justine even after she had enough money for the deposit on her flat. She was happy with Justine and, when she closed one brothel, Chantelle moved with her to the next one and changed her name to Toni. 'I have always made sure that the girls that work for me are well looked after and insist that they visit the Woman's Health Centre regularly,' Justine said. 'The girls just don't work for me. They are my friends.'

Twenty-three-year-old Brooke from Ballybough in Dublin also needed the money to look after her child. 'When I first found out I was pregnant I bought the *In Dublin* 'cos I wanted to work,' she said, 'but I chickened out. I had my baby. I still didn't want to do it but he needed stuff and I hadn't a penny.'

She rang a couple of brothels but Justine was the first to ring her back. On her first day, two women explained the system and showed her around. 'I told them I was new but they knew. I didn't have to tell them,' she said. 'They didn't have to tell me what to do. No one tells you what to do. You do what you want. I was here as a prostitute. Everyone knows what's involved.'

Tropical Paradise was anything but what its name suggested. It started life as 'Club Tropical' and operated out of Stuart Hall in Parnell Street, one of the tax-incentive apartment blocks built in the 1990s in some of the more run-down areas of Dublin city centre. The clients phoned one of the two house mobile phones and when they arrived were buzzed in at street level. They could choose either Eve, Nicole, Sharon, Jade, Martina, Kelly or Shanty to bring them into the apartment and have sex with them.

Michael was in Dublin for the day. He bought a copy of *In Dublin* and rang the number in the advertisement. He had special requirements. 'On the phone I told the girl I wanted to give the girl a light spanking,' he said, 'and she said that was fine.' And that's exactly what he did to Eve and he was quite happy to hand her £60 for the pleasure of it.

Twenty-two-year-old Eve became a prostitute because she needed a career change. With clients like Michael, life may have been strange but it was never dull. 'I worked in an office full-time,' she said. 'I was bored and underpaid, and I needed the money so I left.' Justine interviewed her for the job at Eddie Rockets in O'Connell Street and offered her work during the hours she wanted. Eve found it quiet and wanted more work.

Justine ran Club Tropical in partnership with another woman, Simone. Her brother was a well-known armed robber and he briefed her on how to handle the Gardaí. She was to get a lawyer and tell the Gardaí nothing. As well as helping Justine to run the place, Simone also worked morning shifts as a prostitute. 'She had her own regular customers,' 19-year-old Nicole said, 'and she said she was going to Australia.' Simone didn't need to act on her brother's advice immediately. She was abroad when the raid took place.

The Gardaí had Club Tropical under surveillance for the previous week. When they walked in at 6.45 p.m. on 16 October 1999, Eve and Nicole were there. Pat arrived fifteen minutes later expecting to have sex with one of them. He was, to say the least, a bit taken aback. 'I have been in brothels about twice this year,' he said 'and I never thought that something like this could happen.' His reaction was an indication of just how much the brothels had become an established part of Irish life. The clients didn't even consider the possibility that one day the Gardaí would turn up.

Half an hour later Justine rang Eve to make sure everything was all right only to be told the brothel was being raided. She handed the phone to Detective Inspector John McMahon. First Justine told him she was on her way down. Then she changed her mind and hung up. McMahon knew Justine ran the brothel and rang her back on her mobile. When he asked her whether she was coming down or not, she told him if he called again she would sue him for harassment and hung up again.

The phones in the flat rang constantly during the search. The Gardaí found the usual stuff — KY jelly, Kleenex, baby powder and baby oil. There were over 70 condoms, the brothel book, rosters, envelopes — one with £200 in it. There was also a copy of In Dublin and a copy of a brothel advertisement for Tropical Island with 'Staff required' and 'New location' on it. The brothel needed a new location now. The raid closed down Parnell Street but not

Justine's operation. Body Harmonies was still in business and the clients from Tropical Island, Tropical Paradise and Club Tropical were re-directed to the southside.

Body Harmonies had been operating out of a two-bedroomed house beside the Grand Canal in Portobello for over a year. It was, by the standards of most brothels, firmly established and well known. It had a strong, loyal, recidivous customer base. The women who worked there had their own regular customers who returned to them again and again. Some just wanted company. 'Clients would vary with what they want,' Tara said, 'about 55 per cent want full sexual intercourse, others hand, some oral. Some clients would just come in and talk and wouldn't have any sex.'

On 28 November 1998 Justine rented the apartment in Rathmines from a man from Co. Mayo. 'I let it to two females, one by the name of Beth Kelly, who was in her late twenties with short blonde, bleached, straight hair and about five foot five in height,' the landlord said. 'She spoke with a north Dublin accent.' Justine told him she was a self-employed hairdresser just back from England. She even had a business card to prove it — 'Beth Kelly, professional stylist, serving the entire Dublin area. Evening appointments available on request.' Her mobile number was on the card.

Justine told the landlord she had a friend, Jack Connor. He was still in England, she said, but was coming back to rent the place with her. The owner never met Jack. He always dealt with Justine. 'I only gave a second name because it was a big house and he wanted someone else to share it,' she said. 'He had no idea what went on.' She signed a lease and paid the security deposit and the first month's rent in cash, a total of £1,450. From then on she lodged the rent directly to his bank account. The telephone and the ESB were put in her false name, Beth Kelly.

Body Harmonies opened at 11 a.m. and closed sometime between 1 a.m. and 4 a.m. the following morning. There were two shifts, 11 a.m.–7 p.m. and 7 p.m.–close. The last woman out took the keys with her and therefore had to be first in the next morning to open up.

After midnight the brothel catered for the men who staggered home to the flats and bedsits of Rathmines, Rathgar and Ranelagh. It satisfied those who hadn't managed to meet a woman in the city's late night pubs and clubs. It offered a release to those frustrated individuals who had spent much of their evening, but not all their money, in the wine bars or lap-dancing clubs on nearby Leeson Street.

Most of the clients were sent to the brothel after they called one of Justine's mobile phones, the so-called agency phone. The women in the brothel wouldn't have spoken to them and therefore wouldn't know they were coming. Justine usually answered the phone but, as it got busier, she got a second phone and hired 'a friend', to answer it. Both of the phones were ready-to-go. Justine paid her friend £5 for every call she took.

The punters could chose from eight women — Chantelle, Donna, Leesa, Tara from Scotland, Sophie, Kasey, Laura or Mandy from Kerry. The usual services were provided to a sometimes unusual array of clients. For example, one of Kasey's customers was a freak for cleanliness. 'I have a towel in my bag,' he told her 'because I am conscious of hygiene, as I am a medic.' The health risks inherent in having sex with a prostitute, however, didn't seem to have crossed his mind.

The women only got paid if they worked. There were some, therefore, who earned less than others because the punters didn't pick them as often. On Sunday Justine usually made out the roster for the week and sometimes the women had to book the shifts they wanted or they wouldn't get them.

With only two girls working a shift, there were times when some of the women were left without work for the week. They could be called in quickly if someone didn't show up. All the women's mobile numbers were written in the roster book. Justine penalised slackers while putting the most reliable women on the most lucrative shifts.

Security at the brothel was paramount and Justine insisted on strict adherence to safety procedures. The women never opened the door without first going upstairs and looking out the window to check who was there; the key was thrown down for each woman to let herself in; clients got in only after they were scrutinised.

This was the way the system worked for everybody and Justine even stuck rigidly to it herself. One day she met a client at the door of the brothel as she was coming out. She told him she couldn't let him in; it was club policy. She closed the door and he had to ring the bell so one of the women inside could check him out before admitting him.

This security check was also designed to prevent the brothel being robbed or raided. 'We would never open the door immediately,' Mandy said. 'We would go upstairs and look out for security reasons so that two men couldn't force their way in and rob us. We were also keeping a look out for the Gardaí.' It worked for the former but failed for the latter. On 4 November the Gardaí knocked on the door with a search warrant and had to be admitted.

Justine hadn't heeded the warning three weeks earlier. Following the raid on the Parnell Street brothel, she closed Portobello but only for a few days. She rang the women and told them not to go to work. It was only a temporary measure. Justine was making around £3,000 a week and she was not prepared to forego that for long.

Within a week it was business as usual at Body Harmonies. The Gardaí targeted her again and in the three days before the raid they took statements from ten men who admitted they'd been to the brothel and paid for sex. This time they made sure Justine was there before they went in.

At 1.40 p.m. Justine opened the door to the small search party of four detectives — two women and two men. Mandy and Chantelle were the two women working. There was only one customer there and he suddenly realised that he had an urgent appointment when the Gardaí walked in. 'I was just about to leave when you arrived,' he told them. The exhibits officer, John Cribben, bagged and tagged the usual paraphernalia — baby powder, bottles of baby oils, incense sticks, boxes of condoms, a peni-vib, tubes of KY, letters addressed to Beth Kelly, copies of *Consenting Adults*, Body Harmonies business cards, a cane, a roster, laundry receipts and lodgment records for rent and bank deposits.

Justine admitted managing the brothel and went upstairs with John McMahon and Mary Delmar and made a statement. She told them she called in every day 'for a couple of hours' to collect the money and make sure everything was all right. 'I don't take clients myself,' she said.

She admitted that she was the woman McMahon had spoken to on the phone three weeks earlier when they raided Parnell Street but insisted she was only looking after that brothel for her friend. She claimed she didn't go down to speak to him that day because the brothel wasn't hers. 'I was afraid to get involved,' she said, 'and didn't want to come forward for that reason.'

Justine wasn't arrested or questioned. She was given another chance. She made and signed a voluntary statement and this time she heeded the warning for a little longer — two months. But for Justine, brothel-keeping was now an old habit and one which died hard. She had developed a pattern of closing down one apartment, once discovered, only to open up another while retaining the same numbers and names. By February 2000, Club Tropical and Body Harmonies were both back in business again and had to be shut down a third time.

This time the brothel apartment was in a block on New Row Square in the shadow of St Patrick's Cathedral. 'Beth Kelly' rented it for £800 a month from an antiques dealer in Francis Street. She told him that she and her friend were working as mobile hairdressers in hospices and old people's homes. They had no references, she said, because they had just come back from England. He was conned and agreed to rent to them. On 21 February he met Beth and her old brothel-keeping business partner, 'Simone', in the apartment. He took her car registration number for the carpark and handed her the keys.

Body Harmonies 2 was hard to find. This time there was a phone in the apartment and the directions were kept beside it. The women, like air-traffic controllers, guided the punters in. They sat on two couches in the sitting room while the men landed, sized them up and took off with one of them.

The less popular women passed the time smoking, watching TV, answering the phones and washing the towels in the machine in the kitchen. Most of the women here had worked for Justine in the other brothels. They simply changed their names and took up their old jobs in the new apartment. Their regulars followed them.

Five days after re-opening Justine hired a new prostitute. 'Cinamon' was a black woman in her late 30s who had a husband and two children at home in England. She had worked in Scotland but couldn't make enough money there so in January she came to where the business was booming. At £80 a half-hour or £120 an hour, the money was far better in Dublin than in Edinburgh. A taxi driver gave her an old copy of *In Dublin*. She rang up Club Tropical, spoke to Justine and was hired straight away.

On her first day she met one of Justine's long-service employees, Chantelle, now Toni, and moved in with her. *In Dublin* had by now stopped advertising brothels so the new clients found out about the brothel on the Internet. When it was searched, Gardaí found part of an A4 refill pad with seven pages of Internet reviews of prostitutes working in Body Harmonies, under one of the armchair cushions.

Internet reviews are supposed to be customers' comments where they offered their own opinions and rated the women and the brothels. But Justine didn't canvass her customers. She simply reviewed her own brothel and all the reviews were positive. She wasn't alone. The other brothel owners did it as well. There was, therefore, never a bad review of an Irish brothel or a comment from a dissatisfied customer on the website.

Every few weeks Cinamon went home to England for a few days to see her children before coming back to Ireland to prostitute herself again. She worked whatever shifts she could get. 'Because I was only here temporary and I am black it was like I wasn't stepping on anyone's toes,' she said, 'I just fitted in and worked any shift.' She didn't ask too many questions either. 'I don't know who runs the place and I don't want to know. However, I did enquire if a man or woman ran it and I was told a woman. I would not work for a man in this business.'

Again two women worked each shift. Each had three, maybe four clients and made an average of about £200 a day but it varied. 'I hadn't any clients today,' Tammy said on the day of the raid, 'but I had four yesterday. There were about fourteen here altogether yesterday.' On 1 March, Justine made £370. The following day she had made £90 by the time the Gardaí arrived.

Over the two days of the surveillance operation, fourteen men called in two four-hour periods. Not all agreed to co-operate with the Gardaí but seven made statements and that was enough. One of them was sitting on the bed with a towel around his waist when the raid took place. It was 2.25 p.m. on 2 March 2000. At £80 it was the most expensive shower he'd ever had.

The minute Simone, Justine's partner, saw the Gardaí she got up off the couch and walked over to the other girls. She put her finger to her lips and shook her head signalling to them to be quiet. When Mary Delmar asked her what she was doing, she walked back across the room, sat down and said nothing. She did what her brother, the armed robber, had told her to do and tried to make sure the others did the same.

At first Justine tried to cover for at least one of the women by saying she was there to get her hair done. When it became clear how ludicrous that suggestion was, she took the rap for herself and Simone. Both were arrested but on the way to the station Justine insisted Simone had nothing to do with the brothel. It wasn't true but without Justine there wasn't going to be enough for a prosecution against her.

There was some evidence that Simone was managing the brothel with her. Her phone records showed that in the last two weeks in February she had phoned Body Harmonies or Tropical Paradise 75 times, nearly five times a day. She had also phoned Justine 48 times while Justine phoned her 72 times. Simone also called the women on their mobiles but Justine cleared her. 'She was just visiting,' she told Mark Kavanagh, 'having a cup of coffee. She had nothing to do with the lease.' Kavanagh wrote this in his notebook and Justine signed it.

Justine had also been listening to the advice of Simone's brother about how to deal with the Gardaí because that was all she said or signed. At 3 p.m. she spoke to her solicitor and on legal advice she said nothing of any substance. She admitted leasing the flat under the false names of Beth Kelly and Colleen McCann: 'I usually use the name Beth Kelly and I just made up the other name,' she said.

She also accepted she was known as Jade but said she didn't remember how much the rent was and couldn't say how it was paid. She also said she didn't know who lived in the apartment and didn't know the girls who were there when it was raided. Later she admitted the working girls provided full body massage and she got a percentage. But she insisted she knew nothing about statements the men made admitting paying for a variety of sexual services there.

After that Justine had nothing to say and when the interviews were over, she refused to sign the notes. She was fingerprinted, photographed and given tea, biscuits, buns and cigarettes. At 9.45 p.m. she was released without charge. It took the Director of Public Prosecutions less than four months to direct the Gardaí to proceed with the case against her. On 21 June 2000 she was arrested and charged with twelve counts of brothel-keeping and brought before Kilmainham District Court.

The case was sent forward to the Circuit Criminal Court and Justine pleaded guilty to four sample charges of brothel-keeping and one of managing a brothel from October 1999 to March 2000. She went in and out of court with a big, red wig on her head to disguise herself from the photographers. Her lawyer alluded to the incident where her brother had stabbed her cousin's son when he said the family had suffered a great tragedy in the past year. On 4 March 2001 Judge Yvonne Murphy gave her a twelve-month suspended sentence and fined her a total of £11,500 — £1,500 for Parnell Street, and £5,000 each for Portobello and New Row.

Six weeks later her brother John pleaded not guilty at the Central Criminal Court to the murder of the 18-month-old child. Baby Oisín Reilly-Murphy's neck had been so forcibly slashed his cervical bone was cut. 'Have you accepted with certainty that you killed Oisín?' John Reilly was asked during the thirteen-day trial. 'Yes,' he replied.

His defence, however, was that of sane automatism, whereby a person with no history of psychiatric disturbance commits a purposeless act of which there is no memory. A specialist in parasomnia and other sleep disorders, Dr Caitríona Crowe, told the court that sleepwalking, night terrors or a combination of both may have caused John Reilly to stab the child. The sleep disorders could have been triggered by large amounts of alcohol.

It took the jury of six men and six women seven and a half hours over two days to find John Reilly not guilty of murder but guilty of manslaughter. Mr Justice Paul Carney said the case had been 'unique in the criminal law of this country'. A relatively small quantity of poitín had, he said, a unique, inexplicable and extraordinary effect on John Reilly and 'he had no control over his body or his actions.' He was, the judge said, functioning like an epileptic or a diabetic 'in a bad state of hypno or hyper'.

The judge said he was satisfied a jail sentence would serve no purpose. He sentenced John Reilly to five years in prison suspended on his own bond of €1,000 provided he kept the peace for five years and did not carry a multi-tool Leatherman knife or any other similar device. As the sentence was passed, John Reilly showed no emotion. He left the court quickly without making any comment.

After her brothel-keeping conviction, Justine Reilly fell out with her family. 'I made a mistake and lost my family and contact with them through the shame and the humiliation I received,' she said. 'I am not a criminal and I am going on 36 years of age and all

I want to do is get on with my life and re-correct what is wrong.' Before that, however, there was the problem of the £11,500 fine. She wasn't jailed for brothel-keeping in March 2001 but in order to remain free she had to pay the fine before March 2004. If she didn't, she would spend a year in prison.

Justine said she tried to earn the money through manual work such as cleaning and working in bars and restaurants but she wasn't making enough money to support herself and save for the fine. With little education and no qualifications, she had few options open to her and decided to look for a job as a taxi driver. She applied to the Carriage Office for a licence but didn't state on the application form that she had a criminal conviction. But the Gardaí checked and when they found it, they refused to allow her drive a taxi. She appealed the rejection to the courts.

The case came before Judge Seán McBride on Wednesday 9 October 2002. Justine Reilly took the stand to fight for her right to repay her debt to society.

Judge: Since your conviction, you feel you have paid the penalty.

Reilly: It was not just the humiliation. I have lost practically everything and I need another chance. I received a large fine, I don't have a high level of education and the only kind of work where I could make the money in that sort of time would be with a taxi.

Judge: Are you prepared to give an undertaking not to engage in the former activity and you will be a law-abiding citizen for the rest of your life?

Reilly: Yes.

Judge: Was there any question of drugs being involved, inspector?

Inspector: I read the file and it is not indicated.

Solicitor for Reilly, Catherine Staines: From a very early stage, this was something that was being run by a number of women rather than others.

Reilly: I had worked for some very unsavoury characters myself, and myself and a few other girls decided we would get an apartment. When the situation arose and the police came in, some of the other girls had husbands and children and I did not. I went forward and said I was responsible, not realising the seriousness of the situation.

Judge: Why did you not disclose your conviction in the first place?

Reilly: I was called into the place. I had never been involved with the law and my perception of a conviction was a prison term and all I received was a fine. I did not see it as important.

The judge thought about it for a while before over-ruling the Gardaí and allowing her to become a taxi driver. He said it was a difficult case but decided to grant her a PSV licence if she promised not to 're-engage in her former activities and be law-abiding for the rest of her life'. He also said if she broke the law the Gardaí could come back to the court and apply to revoke the licence within seven days. Justine Reilly hasn't been in trouble since. She drives a new saloon car and at the time of writing was apparently working to pay off her fine.

But one question remains unanswered. What happened to all her money? At £80 for half an hour the rates in Justine's brothels were among the most expensive in Dublin. The Criminal Assets Bureau carried out an analysis of her income and estimated she was making over £5,000 a week, giving her an annual turnover of around £284,000.

The report also noted Justine's and her partner's 'complete disregard for the Criminal Law (Sexual Offences) Act 1993 as they continued to operate brothels, despite having been shut down on three occasions'. Justine and her partner may not be off the hook just yet. CAB has yet to decide whether the financial side of their brothel business requires further investigation.

12 Professionals, Pretenders and Part-timers

Arlene Hunt was 26 years old in 1999 when she decided to go into the brothel business for herself. The mother of a 4-year-old child, she lived with her boyfriend in her own house on the South Circular Road in Dublin. She'd been working as a prostitute in the city for four years but had never been in trouble with the law and had no previous convictions.

A stunning looking, well-educated woman she was not forced into prostitution through the usual routes of poverty or drug addiction. She went into it voluntarily with her eyes as well as her legs open. She saw it as a legitimate business and saw herself as a businesswoman. She drove a brand new Toyota RAV4 jeep. She bought her house the year before from the money she made as a prostitute. She felt this was the time to make a lot more and invest it in more property.

Since 1995 Arlene had worked in at least five brothels for three of the city's biggest operators. 'I worked in the Arches, Thomas Street, The Fantasy Club, in Stephen's Street and Mayfairs in South William Street for Tom McDonnell,' she said. 'Then I worked in Palm Beach in Camden Court for Peter McCoy. McCoy's girlfriend is from the north.'

Arlene left Palm Beach to work for Marie Bridgeman in La Mirage, Tiffany's, Flamingos, and the Emerald. They were all based at Wexford Street in Dublin. She stayed there for two years until July 1999 but left after she had a row with the Bridgemans. Paul Bridgeman had bugged the brothel and was listening outside in the car to the women giving out about him. When he confronted Arlene about it, she realised what he had done. Marie sided with her son and fired her. Arlene's friend, Antonella Gallen, backed her up and left with her.

Antonella Gallen, or Antonia as she was known, was a 36-year-old Spanish woman who had worked as a prostitute for the past eight years. Originally from Valencia in the south of Spain she worked all over Europe before coming to Ireland in April 1998. She lived in a hostel in Camden Place and worked only for Marie Bridgeman for the year and a half she was in Dublin.

Antonia had a similar background to Arlene and the same outlook on life. She too was educated and like Arlene saw prostitution as a legitimate business. She was also a determined businesswoman who wanted to put her money into property. The two like-minded women became good friends. It was, therefore, no surprise to

Marie Bridgeman when she sent Arlene packing that Antonia went with her. 'We both decided we didn't want to work for anyone else,' Antonia said.

Even before the row the two women had already begun the process of setting up on their own. They had had enough of handing over a third of what they earned to a pimp. They started telling their regular customers and the men they saw in the last few weeks in La Mirage that they were moving on. Like true entrepreneurs, they brought their client base with them when they left their old jobs. They told the men where they could be found in the future. They were still working in Wexford Street but they had already rented an apartment opposite St James's Hospital. It was the base for their new business. It was ironic that they leased it from Lowe and Associates on Lower Rathmines Road.

Lowe and Associates are the estate agents for the Criminal Assets Bureau. They have sold most of the multi-million euro properties that the Bureau has seized. They got over €2m for a luxury flat and country estate belonging to the international criminal Mickey Green. They sold an apartment and retail complex at Smithfield in Dublin for over €4m. Eagle House was owned by the cigarettes smuggler, 'Mr Kingsize' Noel Duggan and another criminal Christy Dunne. Lowe and Associates also sold the Academy brothel in Rathmines for the CAB. But unbeknownst to themselves, the company had rented an apartment to the type of people being targeted by the Bureau, one of its most valued and prestigious clients.

Lowe and Associates were conned by the women. They leased the apartment in their own names and paid the rent in full and on time, £675 every month. They produced false references on headed notepaper showing they had jobs in companies they didn't work for. 'I made up my own reference and maintained I worked in the *Sunday Business Post*,' Arlene said, 'Antonia made up a reference that she worked in the POD.' They said they got the notepaper from friends who worked in the newspaper and the night-club.

Both women were experienced prostitutes. Arlene used the name Chelsea. Antonia was Marina. They worked for themselves. They didn't hire anyone else. They were the only two working in the apartment. They didn't live there. It was used solely to sell sex. 'We leased the premises for the purpose of operating a brothel,' Arlene said.

Both women were smart. In four years Arlene had learned a lot about how to run a brothel in Dublin. She knew how the system worked here. Antonia brought in ideas from the continent. Arlene put the ESB in her name and paid that bill. Antonia did the same with the phone. The women split the cost of everything. 'We pay all the bills half and half,' Antonia said. They put money for the bills in a kitty which they kept in a Bank of Ireland bag in the apartment. There was £75 in it the day the Gardaí raided the apartment.

The apartment on James's Street was christened 'Fleur de Lis'. In the American novel by Elmore Leonard and movie of the same name *LA Confidential*, 'Fleur de Lis' was the name of a call-out service which employed women who had face-lifts. They were 'hookers cut to look like movie stars'. In the pimp Pearce Patchett's Los Angeles, 'Fleur de Lis' offered 'whatever you desire'. In Arlene and Antonia's Dublin, it offered pretty much the same.

The two women adapted a logo which is often used in France to refer to a prostitute. 'Fleur de Lis' was advertised in *Penthouse* and *In Dublin*. The women paid £750 for an advertisement for their 'health studio' in *In Dublin*. 'It was a large ad across the top of the page,' Arlene said. 'This was a provisional measure as we were only starting up.' They paid £350 sterling for the advertisement in the Irish edition of *Penthouse*. They put the landline telephone number for the apartment in each.

They also had business cards printed up, one for the business and one each for themselves. It was either 'Chelsea. . .' or 'Marina Valet Service, Best Service in Town' with the landline or mobile number on it. Arlene knew the value of the business cards. They got more clients in and kept the old ones coming back. They would also cut down advertising costs once a regular clientele had been established.

The women worked from 10.30 a.m. to 10 p.m. everyday except Sundays. They were their own bosses and their hours were their own. 'Some days I would finish at 5 p.m.,' Arlene said. 'Tuesdays and Thursdays I might work late.' They charged £60 for half an hour, £100 for an hour and they supplied the condoms. Arlene didn't do call-outs. Antonia did the odd one. Arlene only gave her mobile number to her regular clients because she used it mainly for family, friends and her child-minder.

The women buzzed the men into the brothel and claimed they only saw an average of four a day each. The Gardaí believe they saw a lot more. In fact, Fleur de Lis was so busy that within six weeks of it starting up the buzzer broke. Arlene or Antonia had to go down the three floors to let the men in to the apartment complex.

'On a good day I could make up to £300 a day but the average would be £180,' Arlene said. 'When we worked in Wexford Street we got from our clients £60 and we had to give £20 to Marie and Paul Bridgeman.' 'Whereas any money we earn here we keep for ourselves,' Antonia added.

Arlene and Antonia catered for almost all sexual tastes. As experienced prostitutes they had few inhibitions. They'd seen it all before. They weren't shy or prudish and were prepared to cater for almost all demands. They developed a reputation and carved out a niche for themselves in the strange and deviant part of the market. They were popular with cross-dressers, submissives, bondage freaks and fetishists.

There were three televisions in the apartment, one in the sitting room and one in each of the bedrooms. The video in the sitting room was connected to all three TVs so the same tape could be played simultaneously all over the apartment. The videos weren't the sort you might pick up for a Friday night in with the family. *Wild Bill Fat*, *Hungry 200*, *Filthy Fuckers* and *Extreme Special 5* were among the favourites.

Sometimes the customers arrived with their own extreme videos and the women let them put them on. *Bizarre Sex*, *Piss Action* and *Piss Parade 7* were amongst the blockbusters that were shown at Fleur de Lis. As is evident from the titles, these are tapes for people who find the notion of they themselves or others being defecated or urinated on sexually exciting. Hard-core, triple-x pornographic magazines were also available for perusal on the sitting room coffee-table. 'I provide everything,' Arlene said. 'The whole works. A full sexual service.'

The women also supplied their own accessories. Both had the standard baby oils, lotions and talcs but Arlene had, over the years, built up a wide and varied collection of sex clothes and toys. She kept them in the bedroom wardrobe. There were French-maid stockings, a fish-net dress, a PVC skirt with peep-hole, a dress with peep-hole, a rubber mask, PVC underwear, skirts, tops, dildos, handcuffs, heavy leather straps, a strap-on dildo, a body brace, thigh-high PVC boots, restraints for wrists, specialist underwear, a pair of rubber pants, a cage and three whips.

The Gardaí had Fleur de Lis under surveillance for five days and took statements from six men before they raided it. When they searched it on 28 October 1999, there were three clients inside. One was a transvestite, another masturbated while Antonia rolled around the floor and when the Gardaí arrived Arlene was straddling the third dressed in a furry bra and black thigh-high boots. He was a regular who normally paid £70 for full sex.

'You're in the wrong room,' Arlene said when they walked in on her in full stride. Seán McAvinchey took a drag from his cigarette. 'No,' he said, 'we're in the right room.' 'No,' she replied, 'you're in the room next door.' 'No,' McAvinchey said again, 'we're the police.' 'Ah, fuck youse anyway,' Arlene replied.

It was a run-of-the-mill, civil and good-humoured search until the Gardaí opened the wardrobe and found a soother, a baby's bottle and a nappy. 'What's going on? Is there a child here?' an angry Mark Kavanagh asked. Prostitution is one thing. Paedophilia is very different. The nappy turned out to be a constipation pad. It was too big for a baby and could only fit an adult. 'A particular client wears the baby's pants,' Arlene explained, ' and uses the baby's bottle and soother.'

The two women knew they were caught red-handed and admitted their guilt. On 23 March 2000 both were convicted at Kilmainham District Court of two counts of brothel-keeping and fined £450 and £950 on each charge, a total of £1,400 each. It was a small fine for them. Detectives estimated that on a very conservative calculation they were making between £1,500 and £2,000 each a week. 'The reason why we set ourselves up,' Arlene said, 'is because we're sick to death of working for scumbags, in particular Marie and Paul Bridgeman and Martin and Peter McCormick.

But not every brothel-keeper was a scumbag and some prostitutes, particularly the older ones, were quite happy to remain with the same madam for years. Their approach was more discreet than their younger, more ambitious colleagues. They'd been in the business a long time and a lot of the women they'd worked with were now diseased, damaged or dead. Some like Margaret Helly even got promoted to positions of responsibility.

Margaret Helly decided to become a prostitute late in life. She was 41 when she began working at the Academy brothel. 'I have been working on the premises for the past three years as a prostitute,' she said when she was questioned by the Gardaí in 1999. It was a strange career choice for the married mother-of-four who lived in Co. Kildare. At 21, 18, 16 and 15, her children were almost reared but she still needed the money. Her husband was unemployed and in receipt of a disability pension.

The Academy Health Studio and its 'sister studio', the Advantage, were two of Dublin's longest established and busiest brothels. The Academy was open for nine years, the Advantage for fifteen years. Both operated out of the same buildings between 1981 and 1999. Teresa Behan owned them both.

Teresa Bartollo was born in Malta. She spent the early 1970s moving between England, Northern Ireland and Ireland. At one time she had homes in each place. She married in England on 12 September 1973 but divorced in Northern Ireland nine years later. On 10 January 1995 she married again. Her husband is Irish. The two marriages gave her a total of three aliases to use in connection with her brothel business. She was at various times Teresa Behan, Teresa Byrne and Teresa Bartollo.

Teresa Bartollo set up her first brothel in Dublin on 19 December 1980. She paid £3,000 for the lease on a property just off Dame Street and turned it into the Advantage Relaxation Studio. She advertised it as a health studio/massage parlour in the *Golden Pages* for five years, from January 1984 to May 1989. The advertisement said it offered sauna, baths, massage and solarium. It offered sex for cash too. She also advertised the Advantage in a pornographic magazine which was banned in Ireland. On 27 July 1995 she sold the lease to a South African woman for £19,000 and concentrated on her main earner, The Academy.

Teresa realised in 1989 that a property on Lower Rathmines Road had great potential for prostitution. With three floors, a basement and an annex, there was plenty of space and scope for development. It was a high street location in the centre of one of the busiest suburbs in Dublin. It was also a high-density rental area and had a ready-made market in tenants and students. She bought the property for £36,000 and applied to Dublin Corporation for permission to convert it to a health and leisure club.

Teresa put in showers, benches, a Jacuzzi and a sauna and two doors at the front of the building. The outside one was always open. The other door, six feet inside, had the name written on it. The renovations cost her £25,000 but she only had £16,000 of her own. On 30 October she took out a mortgage for £45,000 with the UDT Bank. Four years later she decided to hide the fact that she owned the Academy and registered it in the name of her sister, who lived in England. The title deed stated that Carmen Petrie held the property in trust for her sister Teresa 'for her absolute use and benefit'.

And benefit she did. Brothel-keeping made Teresa Behan a wealthy woman. On 10 January 1990 the Academy brothel in Dublin opened for business. For almost six years she ran the two brothels, the Advantage and the Academy, simultaneously. In four hours over two days in November 1999 for example, 28 men went in to the Academy for sex. Each spent a minimum of £60. During that short time it took £1,700 and the Academy was open twelve hours a day from Monday to Saturday and eight hours on Sunday. Four of the seven women working there had keys to open and lock up. At its height it was earning between £2,000 and £2,500 a day.

Teresa operated the same system in both brothels. The customer arrived and paid £20 house money before he was shown into a room and offered a shower. The Academy was a little more exclusive. It offered a Jacuzzi or a sauna for an extra £20. There was a bell under the mantelpiece and the customer pressed it when he was ready for service. The woman came back, gave him a massage for a few minutes and then asked him if he wanted anything else. If he did he paid the remaining £40 there and then.

The prostitutes who worked in the Academy dressed in white coats like nurses or beauty therapists. 'The purpose of the white coats,' Margaret Helly said, 'is to make the girls look a bit more respectable. I am not trained and do not have any qualifications as a masseur and as far as I know none of the other girls working here do.' Underneath the coats the women were topless and wore only knickers, stockings and high-heeled shoes.

In 1997 Teresa Behan's parents got sick and she returned to Malta to look after them. She also became ill herself and was diagnosed with cancer. She offered Margaret the opportunity to move into management and gave her the chance to run the brothel while she was away.

Margaret leaped at the chance to make extra money. At first she looked after the brothel with another woman but went on to become the sole manager. She struck a deal with Teresa whereby she was paid by commission — £5 for every customer in addition to the money she earned on her own. 'It's my share for running the brothel,' she said. 'I also work as a prostitute. My stage name is Emma.'

Teresa Behan was now the absentee landlord. Margaret Helly was her agent. She looked after the maintenance and cleaning of the building. She watched the door, collected the post, kept the books and made out the rosters. There were 2 shifts each day,

10.30 a.m.–4 p.m. and 4 p.m.–10.30 p.m. She also bought the talc and baby oils.

The women paid for their own condoms and disposed of them outside to cut down on cleaning. The Academy was self-financing and Teresa only came back to check on it once a year. The last time she was in Dublin was for a week in September 1999. She checked out the brothel twice and was happy that the business was running smoothly.

Teresa Behan left Margaret Helly two bank account numbers — one in the Bank of Ireland, the other in the Irish Permanent. She ran the business through her Bank of Ireland account. Margaret lodged £300 from the takings every week and the money in it was used to pay the brothel's bills and other expenses.

The phone and cablelink were in Teresa's name but Margaret paid them. The phone was a public coin box so the women paid for their own calls. Margaret emptied it when the bill arrived. The other bills such as ESB were paid directly through the bank. All Margaret had to do was lodge the money to ensure there was enough in the account.

Margaret also brought the towels to the laundry a few doors up the street. She placed the advertisements in *In Dublin* and hired new women. 'If we were looking for new staff, I would speak to the new girls and tell them to come in and either I or one of the other girls would speak to them,' she said.

The advertisements always stated 'full-time staff required' and cost £350 a fortnight. 'A man from *In Dublin* came every two weeks to collect the money,' she said. When he stopped calling, the brothel was advertised on the Internet but ironically the publicity generated by the *In Dublin* controversy brought the brothels to wider public attention and this brought in more customers to the Academy. Margaret deducted the cost of advertising from the takings.

The £300 she lodged every week was usually enough to cover the brothel's running costs. The account had a turnover of more than £15,000 a year. The profits from the business were put in to the Irish Permanent account to keep them separate from the costs account. Margaret lodged around £700 or £800 to that account every week. 'I have nothing to do with this money,' Margaret said. 'It's Terry's own money.' Margaret called Teresa Terry and this money was allowed to accumulate. Then it was withdrawn in large quantities. In October 1999, for example £8,000 was taken out.

Amazingly Teresa Behan paid tax on the business. She paid £760 a month for eight months of the year to the Revenue Commissioners in the name of the Academy Health Studio. She gave Margaret a chequebook and she wrote the cheques and signed Teresa's name. The tax came out of the money in the Bank of Ireland account. Teresa also employed an accountant to manage her business affairs here and Margaret had her number in Malta if there were any problems.

Margaret Helly was paid well for her work. She took £40 from every one of her own clients as well as the manager's commission on her own and everyone else's clients. The client paid the first £20 at the door and £40 for sex in the room. It was a case of hard luck if once inside he got cold feet or changed his mind. The £20 was the non-refundable entrance fee. Teresa got £15 and Margaret got the other £5 whether the man did anything or not. The women might lose a customer but the owner and the manager always got paid the minute a man walked in the door. 'On a good week I would make between £400–£500 from my £5 per client commission,' Margaret said. She no longer had to scrimp and save and was able to go on luxury holidays. In 1999 she brought her family on a two-week, all-expenses-paid trip to Las Vegas.

But the gravy train came to a sudden halt at 2.45 p.m. on

2 December 1999. A team from Operation Gladiator raided the Academy and found Margaret and Rebecca there with two men. One of them was face down on a bench with a topless Rebecca massaging his back. She was wearing the Academy uniform — white coat, black stockings, knickers and high-heeled shoes.

The second man was sitting in a room reading a magazine. He refused to make a statement and made his excuses and left. A few men called during the search and the phone kept ringing. Margaret Helly admitted running the place for Teresa Behan and three months later was convicted of managing a brothel. She was fined £500 at Kilmainham District Court.

Eileen O'Reilly was another outwardly respectable woman who saw little harm in setting up a brothel. The 50-year-old bought the lease on a basement in Richmond Street in Dublin and was operating for seven years before she was caught in October 1999. Using the name Geraldine Murray she paid £750 a month rent and ran her business quietly and discreetly.

She drove in from her south Dublin home every day in her brand new Renault Laguna arriving with her little dog on a lead — the epitome of aristocratic respectability. However, she wasn't afraid of a little hard work. She took out the black bags full of towels, swept the steps leading down to the brothel and ensured there were fresh flowers at the door on the street. She paid the ESB and phone bills and hired staff. The women knew her as Geraldine or Ger. They charged between £50 and £70 and gave her £20 for each customer.

Three women were working when the brothel was raided at 8 p.m. on 1 October 1999. One of them was in the process of 'servicing' the one man there. At the same time two detectives called to Eileen's home on Loretto Avenue in Rathfarnham. She was surprised, uncomfortable and, to say the least, a bit flustered.

She immediately admitted running the brothel but was embarrassed to have the Gardaí on her doorstep. She was also afraid that neighbours might see them, her friends might call or her family might come home. She asked if she could speak to them somewhere else — anywhere but at her home. She agreed to drive to Harcourt Terrace Garda station to be formally interviewed.

An hour later Eileen O'Reilly told the Gardaí everything. She co-operated fully and agreed to plead guilty. She was renovating her house in Wexford and John McMahon and Mark Kavanagh drove down one Saturday morning at 6 a.m. and brought her back to court in Dublin. She had no previous convictions and the case was dealt with by 'summary disposal', that is at District Court level where the penalties are less severe. She was convicted of running a brothel on 18 October 2001 at Kilmainham District Court and fined a total of £1,150.

The Criminal Assets Bureau estimated that Eileen O'Reilly made over £87,000 a year from brothel-keeping, a total of around £600,000. She used some of the money to pay off the mortgage on the house in Loretto Avenue and paid £27,500 for the house at Camolin near Enniscorthy in 1996. CAB is examining whether her properties, savings, investments or other assets require further investigation.

It's highly unlikely that CAB will end up investigating Michelle Bailey's finances. She was 27 when she was convicted of helping to maintain a brothel called Sandra's Health Studio on Dorset Street in Dublin. A mother of two from the country, she had fallen on hard times and got involved in prostitution to support her family. Her partner didn't know what she was doing and the revelation had, as her solicitor so eloquently put it, 'caused problems' for them. Even the Gardaí felt sorry for her. They found £95 on her when they searched her. They only took £50 and later gave that back to her for what Detective Sergeant Gerard McDonnell called 'humanitarian reasons'. Bailey was fined £100 in the Dublin District Court.

Ironically the woman accused of running that brothel walked free from court after it ruled the search warrant was invalid. The charge was dismissed against Rita McLoughlin, née Adhekwa, a 32-year-old Nigerian asylum-seeker who lived at Ashington Heath on the Navan Road. The court heard that a Detective Garda searched 'Sandra's' with a warrant issued by a District Court judge. The defence solicitor submitted that the warrant could not be issued to a Garda officer below the rank of inspector. The Gardaí learned not to make that mistake again.

Two other foreign women accused of running a brothel in one of the more prestigious areas of Dundalk in November 2002 were never even prosecuted. When Gardaí raided the luxury apartment in the Kilgar complex off Jocelyn Street, they found a farmer from the Cooley Peninsula coming out of one of the rooms with his trousers around his ankles. The apartment had been under surveillance the previous week and customers had come from all over Louth, Cavan, Monaghan and Northern Ireland.

The women were in their 30s and from Moldova and the Ukraine. Both spoke English very well and had been living in Ireland for some time. Both had addresses in Dublin. They ran the brothel on a part-time basis for three days a week. They advertised on the Internet and charged clients £100 a half-hour. They leased the apartment from the owner who didn't know what was going on. The brothel was closed down after complaints from neighbours. The two women were never charged. The farmer complained to the Gardaí afterwards that it was the most expensive fifteen minutes of his life and 'definitely not worth the money'.

Gardaí believe that Russian, Albanian and Chinese criminals are all trying to establish a foothold in the Dublin vice scene. When detectives raided an apartment complex in Dublin's south inner city, they found over €10,000 hidden in small amounts throughout one apartment. They suspect a number of Albanian men were running a brothel there.

A fight among two Chinese gangs armed with knives and machetes in Dublin city centre in the summer of 2001 was over an unpaid brothel bill. The brothel on the southside was owned and operated by a triad gang and staffed with Chinese women. Zhang Da Wei and one his friends visited the brothel but left without paying the €300 bill for the sexual services they received.

Twenty-three-year-old Chen Long was given the job of collecting the debt but Zhang and his friends refused to pay and one of them was attacked. The scene was set for a violent showdown when the two gangs met on O'Connell Street in the early hours of 10 July 2001. One man died, another was stabbed in the neck but Gardaí who got to the scene saved his life, while another man had to have part of his scalp surgically reattached to his head in hospital.

Another sinister development was the arrival in Dublin in 2001 of a Belfast drug-trafficker-turned-people-trafficker. The 51-year-old was involved in drug smuggling and served time in the UK for attempting to bring in £2.5m sterling worth of heroin. He had connections with loyalist paramilitaries and convictions for burglary, theft and assault. However, he was making frequent trips to Moscow and Gardaí believe he was recruiting Eastern European women to work as prostitutes here.

Detectives first came across this man when they called into the city centre flat of a 33-year-old American prostitute. Tonja Marshall was running a brothel in the apartment she lived in on Castle Street in Dublin 2. The Gardaí called in and she promised to stop. However, she then got the Belfast man to lease an apartment for her in Camden Street and she set up her operation there. He was her business partner and it was his job to source properties for her. 'I would never go along with him to view the premises,' she said. 'I would just tell him the type of place I would require.'

The Belfast man rented the apartment because he was able to provide references. He told the estate agent that he was a Northern Ireland businessman working in Dublin who needed a place to stay three or four nights a week. He said he required at least two bedrooms because his wife and children might want to stay over. As soon as he got the keys, he handed them to Tonja who started working there as a prostitute with three other women — one Irish, one English and one Albanian.

The brothel opened for business in April 2001 under a variety of names — Pleasure Chest, Nevada, Bottoms Up and Calendar Girls. The contact numbers were all 'ready-to-go' mobiles. Tonja designed the advertisements and paid £800 to advertise on the websites Irishescorts and escortireland. Tonja, or Vicky, Diamond or Alisha as she called herself, charged £100 for half an hour, £150 for an hour and £200 for the executive service. 'This was to attract an out-of-town clientele,' she said. She hired the other women and took a 40/60 split of their money along with her own.

The first sign of trouble for Tonja came within six weeks when some of the shops on Camden Street noticed the large numbers of men streaming in and out of the apartment at all hours of the day and night. The following month the landlord and his wife told the Gardaí they thought their apartment was being used as a brothel. Then the ceiling in the kitchen fell in. There were too many customers using the shower and the pressure got too much on the ceiling below. It cost her £6,000 to get it fixed. And as if that wasn't enough, Tonja had a blazing row with her business partner.

'He was not treating the girls with respect,' she said 'and he didn't pay the previous month's rent.' They had a fight and the Belfast man left the country. But he cleaned out the bank account and took most of the earnings from the brothel with him. Tonja had to hand over the rest of her savings to the landlord. She paid him £1,400 which was the balance of the money owed by her partner and another £6,000 for three months' rent, two in advance. She wanted to remain in business in Camden Street but, alas, it was not to be.

Tonja knew the Gardaí were on to her. They watched the brothel for six days in late October and early November 2001 and interviewed ten customers. They searched it on 5 November. It was sheer coincidence that as they were just about to walk out the door of Pearse Street Garda station to raid the Pleasure Chest, Tonja walked in to try and sort the problem out. 'It was basically a get-rich scheme gone wrong,' she said. She went back up to Camden Street with them and uniquely became the only brothel-keeper to raid her own brothel.

Her behaviour in the Dublin District Court on Thursday 25 April 2002 was also unique and instead of being sent to prison she was commended for trying to change her life. 'You are a wonderful judge,' she said to Judge James McNulty after he fined her €500 and gave her a month to pay. 'I wish you would come to America. We need more like you. Going through life will take you to some strange places. At the moment I'm just a degenerate but hopefully in the next couple of years I will be a productive member of society.' The judge, however, felt she was being 'a bit hard' on herself by calling herself a degenerate. 'We all make mistakes,' he said. She left the court promising to start a new life as a tarot card reader.

But it was not just the women who made mistakes and got caught operating brothels in a ham-fisted fashion. Thirty-four-year-old Stuart Haddow was caught after his flat was raided for drugs. He had just opened and hadn't made enough money to recoup his investment before he was caught and closed down. Gardaí went to the flat at Custom House Dock with a warrant under the Misuse of Drugs Act and discovered it was a brothel. They seized the usual paraphernalia as well as a couple of televisions, video recorders, leather straps, £120 cheque and £150 cash. Haddow had no previous convictions and Judge William Hamill fined him £500 in the Dublin District Court.

Keith Thompson was a little more successful in his venture. The 23-year-old ran Club 59 in Jervis Lane between Parnell Street and Mary Street in one of the capital's busiest shopping districts. The brothel was also busy. Open six days a week, an average of ten men called each day. The clientele included students, professionals, farmers and labourers. It advertised its showers and massages in *In Dublin* and guaranteed personal service.

Thompson drove up in his black Mitsubishi Lancer and opened up at around 10.30 a.m. each morning. The women began arriving half an hour later. He provided the two-bedroom building and clean towels and charged them £20 house money per client. He was making around £1,200 a week in cash, an annual tax-free income of over £60,000.

Like Stuart Haddow, Keith Thompson was a target of the local district detective unit before the establishment of Operation Gladiator. He was arrested and charged in the summer of 1998 but he continued to advertise and operate the brothel while out on bail. RTÉ secretly filmed him over a number of days and six months after it was raided, Club 59 was still open for business. On 13 January 1999 Thompson was convicted in the Dublin District Court, fined a total of £500 and given a six-month suspended sentence. In his defence he claimed an older person introduced him to prostitution.

But there were also the brothel-keepers that got away. The so-called 'Queen of Tarts' Marion Murphy was on the target list but the team from Gladiator simply never got to her on time. By then their work was well known in Dublin's vice circles. The 49-year-old from Monaghan worked in the sex business in Dublin for over 25 years, first as a prostitute then as a brothel-keeper. She has convictions going back to 1977 when the fine for a woman caught selling her body was £2.00.

In the early 1990s the two biggest brothel-keepers in Dublin were Tom McDonnell on the southside and Marion Murphy on the northside. She ran two brothels within spitting distance of Fitzgibbon Street Garda station, Laura's Studio at Belvedere Place and The Kasbah Health Studio on Mountjoy Square. There were seven operating within a half mile of the station which, when it became known, was a major source of embarrassment to the Gardaí. Once they moved in, most of the brothels shut down and moved on. They kept their numbers and set up in other parts of the city. But business was good for Marion Murphy and she wasn't prepared to jeopardise that. She decided to stay and fight.

The investigation into Marion Murphy's operation began after a disgruntled customer sent a series of letters to the Minister for Justice and the Garda Commissioner. The man, a former post office clerk, managed to spend £12,000 in eight months on one of the Kasbah women, Margaret 'Poppy' Healy. The affair is well documented in Dave Mullin's book *Ladies of the Kasbah*. When the money ran out, so did Margaret's love and the spurned clerk began his letter-writing campaign which led to the investigation.

Between 5 July and 20 August 1991, 123 men were filmed going in and out of Laura's and the Kasbah. Marion Murphy drew up an imaginative price list. She charged £5 for hand relief, £10 for hand relief while topless, £15 for hand relief while fully naked,

£20 for 'Swedish', £25 for oral sex and £30 for full sex. The brothel was raided on 5 September 1991 and the case came to court on 3 February 1993.

Marion gambled on the punters being too ashamed to turn up and give evidence in court. It was a gamble she lost. The men arrived in the Dublin Circuit Criminal Court wearing crash-helmets and coats over their heads to avoid being recognised or photographed. Some even continued to wear them inside the building and had to be told to take them off. Marion threatened to name some of her high-profile customers she referred to as the Fine Gael client, the schoolboy, the churchmen, the lawyers, her police clients and the high flyer in the GAA. She later complained she had been prevented from doing so. 'That's not justice,' she said, 'that's not fair.'

On Friday 5 February 1993 a jury of eight men and four women unanimously convicted Marion Murphy of keeping a brothel. She was fined £100 and given a six-month suspended sentence. Judge Gerard Buchanan warned her that if she was to be convicted again for the same offence she faced five years in prison. But like McDonnell and Bridgeman, the other major players convicted before Gladiator, it didn't deter her.

Marion continued to run brothels and was spoken to by detectives seeking information during the investigation into the murder of Belinda Pereira. When two of them went to see her at her brothel in the north city, they found their way blocked inside by a steel gate. Marion opened it. When they asked to speak to Marion Murphy, she told them Marion wasn't there but invited them in. During the conversation that followed they realised they were talking to her. Two pimps from Marion's home county Monaghan remain the prime suspects today for the Sri Lankan woman's murder. Marion later paid a woman £500 a week to run her brothel in James's Street. It was making around £2,000 a week for her.

Marion is also renowned for running prostitution operations in Cork, Limerick and Galway. She rented apartments or booked hotel rooms on a short-term basis to cater for demand. She advertised mobile numbers and when customers called them they pressed a number for a woman in a particular part of the country, say 1 for Cork, 2 for Limerick etc. She also got hold of an old Bank of Ireland van which she turned into a mobile brothel by removing the bank's logo from the side. The van was at the Galway Races and the Clarinbridge Oyster Festival. Marion Murphy has also had her share of tragedy. Her partner Jim McLoughlin was found dead in his car. She has four children and lives in a luxury house in Castleknock.

Teresa Behan is another well off 'madam' who also quite literally got away and stayed away, out of the country. On 4 December 1999, two days after the Academy was raided, she rang Dublin from Malta. She spoke to Mark Kavanagh at the headquarters of the National Bureau of Criminal Investigation. She admitted she was the owner of the property on Lower Rathmines Road and said she had been running a massage parlour there for the past ten years. It was a legitimate business she said; she paid tax on her earnings.

However, when he started to ask a few questions and put a few facts to her, she admitted she knew it was a brothel. She insisted she was not doing any harm and pointed out that prostitution was legal in other countries. She also told him her parents were ill and she would not be coming back to Ireland. She was going to live permanently in Malta.

Like Marion Murphy, she has also had her fair share of tragedy. Her father, whom she went home to look after, died. Her mother developed Alzheimer's and she herself has cancer. She promised to close down the Academy but she didn't get the chance. On

26 January 2001 officers from the Criminal Assets Bureau walked in and took possession of her property on Lower Rathmines Road. It was the first brothel seized by CAB. Any hopes she might have had of earning more money by selling it off were scuppered. It was put up for auction and sold for £265,000 on 10 May 2001.

Teresa Behan, Byrne or Bartollo didn't try to stop the sale. She didn't even contest the seizure. The state cannot collect the proceeds of that sale for seven years. Teresa Behan has until 2008 to come back and try to claim the money. She doesn't need it and almost certainly won't. For nearly twenty years she ran two of the most profitable brothels in the city. CAB got some of her money but she made a lot before the Bureau was even set up. In her case crime has paid. She got most of it out of the country before CAB could get to it and she herself got out just in time. It's unlikely that she'll ever come back to Ireland. If she does, she's liable to be prosecuted.

13 The Policeman and The Beast

The headline said it all: Police Raids — What To Do. Brothels all over Dublin were being raided. The punters and prostitutes were making statements and admissions to the Gardaí. The owners and managers were being prosecuted and put out of business. The Criminal Assets Bureau was even trying to bankrupt them. The anonymous article on the Escorts Ireland website (www.escortireland.com) was the start of the fightback. 'We have decided to post a few hints on how to cope with these raids,' it boldly declared, 'should this happen to you!'

The piece warned the woman in the brothel that, if she was going to make a statement, she was to make sure she didn't incriminate herself or others. 'If you are stupid enough to say your boss is called Joe Bloggs and he has been your boss for six years, you will almost certainly find yourself and Mr Bloggs with a court date,' it said. She was told there was no need to be rude to the police officers. She was to give her name and address and check the search warrant. A sample statement was published so she would know what to say. The first golden rule for those in the vice business was 'Think before you write. Study before you sign.'

The 'masseuse' was also warned that if she admitted that any sexual act took place for money, her statement would 'probably be read out in a court of law'. She was to say she gained her experience by massaging friends, boyfriends and people. Sample scenarios, questions and answers were outlined. If, for example, she was asked had she done any exams she was to say she hadn't because she was too nervous. The precise words she could use were spelled out for her. 'Under no circumstances would I accept cash or any goods for sex,' she was advised to say, 'I would consider this morally wrong. I get paid for the time I spend with the client, that's all. The money is for my time and not for sex.'

Gardaí suspected that the website and the advice sheet were the work of a former part-time policeman-turned-brothel-keeper. He saw what was happening and tried to warn others of the dangers by advising them how to stay one step ahead of the law. Ironically, his own advice couldn't save him. He was the last person to be convicted under Operation Gladiator more than three and a half years after it began.

Peter McCormick had watched as almost all his colleagues and competitors were caught and closed down. He wanted to stop the rot before his turn came around. He changed his operating system and tried to distance himself from his business. He used his police training to dodge surveillance and avoid answering incriminating questions. He nurtured and developed advertising on the Internet. He hid the vast sums of money he made through a web of financial transactions in four jurisdictions. He did everything to try to operate above and beyond the law. He nearly succeeded.

Peter McCormick was born on 6 May 1959. His family was involved in the hotel business and ran the Kings Arms Hotel in Larne, Co. Antrim. He still uses his home address on the Old Glenarm Road on his passport and receives mail there. He married Denise at nineteen years of age and they lived in Newcastle, Co. Down. They had two sons before they separated. McCormick then met and married another Northern woman, Elizabeth (Heather) Troughton, and they now have a young daughter. Elizabeth also used his home address in Larne on a number of her bank accounts.

McCormick was formerly a part-time policeman in Northern Ireland. He was a member of the RUC reserve for nine months but left around 1982. He and Elizabeth both worked in the hotel business in Longford for almost a year and a half in 1989 and 1990 before going back across the border to open a pub in south Armagh. They bought The Trap in Keady in November 1990 and spent a lot of money on entertainment and promotions, trying to get it off the ground. It didn't work. The pub was slow to develop a loyal and lucrative customer base, and the business was put into receivership. It was sold at a loss of nearly £50,000 sterling on 16 May 1992.

The affair is, however, indicative of the character of the man because, if not foolhardy, Peter McCormick was certainly brave. It took real courage for an ex-RUC man to run a pub in the heart of IRA bandit country two years before the first ceasefire was announced. McCormick and Troughton were declared bankrupt and a bankruptcy order was made against them on 16 September 1994. The order was lifted on 17 September 1997 because it appears that in Northern Ireland bankruptcy orders are routinely lifted after three years. McCormick stayed in the north for another six months and worked at a hotel before once again heading south.

McCormick arrived in Dublin in 1995 and lived in two flats in Dublin 7, one on the Navan Road until December 1995, and the other on the New Cabra Road until the summer of 1996. He told the landlord he was a financial adviser. Elizabeth joined him and in July 1996 they moved to a rented house in Whiteoaks, Clonskeagh. They stayed there until she bought a house in Stillorgan a year later.

McCormick paid the £550 a month rent and said he had a job at The Leather Studio, Westbury Mall, Grafton Street. His future business partner, Martin Morgan aka 'The Beast', also worked in the Westbury Mall. McCormick stated on the Clonskeagh lease he had worked there 'for the past two years in the capacity as security consultant'. By that time, however, he was already in the business which was to make him rich and, at least in certain circles in the capital, famous.

Peter McCormick was involved with prostitutes in Dublin since 1995 and even opened an account with one who worked for him in April of that year. However, while she may have been able to lodge money to that account, McCormick made sure that he was the only one who could withdraw it. He was the only authorised signatory.

The woman stayed and worked for him at the brothel he opened at Camden Court on 27 May 1996. He leased it from a property company, Linkyard Ltd, using a false name, Peter McCoy. He put the ESB in that name and gave the company director, John Lowe, a mobile number also registered under Peter McCoy. He agreed to pay £600 a month rent which increased over the years to £900 and paid it in to the company's bank account. McCormick said he was unemployed but with the amount of money he was making the high rent was no problem.

Pretty Woman, or The Palm Beach Massage Club as it was also known, was based in the three-bedroom apartment at Camden Court for the next four years. The brothel opened every day from 10.30 a.m. to midnight. It operated two shifts, an early and a late each day, which were staffed by between two and five women depending on the time. The average number of clients per girl was six a shift. The women charged £60 for half an hour and McCormick's 'house money' cut was £20 — the standard third.

McCormick set it up and ran it with Martin Morgan. It was one of the busiest brothels in Dublin. From Monday 10 April to Friday 14 April 2000 for example, 187 men called, an average of 37 a day. The pair took in £7,480 in cash for those five days and that didn't include their earnings over the weekend, their busiest time. The average weekly turnover at Camden Court was not less than £16,800 a week. McCormick's cut was £5,600 a week.

It wasn't long before the landlords found out that McCormick was running a brothel in the house. It would be a lot longer before they could get him out. Linkyard's John Lowe asked him to leave but business was booming and McCormick wouldn't go. He wasn't going to walk away from an address that was now so firmly established in the minds of many as a place in Dublin where sex was for sale.

McCormick claimed they had spent money renovating the house and he demanded £18,000 compensation. In March 2000 Lowe instructed his solicitor to serve a notice to quit on McCormick but it was the Garda raid the following month that persuaded him it was time to go. It was his longest-running and most lucrative brothel.

In July 1996, two months after Palm Beach was up and running, McCormick again used the name Peter McCoy and for his second brothel he rented a basement flat in Leeson Street. He passed himself off as the pinnacle of respectability. He told the landlord he was involved in the provision of 'catering services' and that his son was studying accountancy at Queen's University. For a man from Northern Ireland and an ex-RUC man, the opening date had special significance. The twelfth of July is the anniversary of the Battle of the Boyne and the day of the Orange parades all over the North.

McCormick paid £1,100 rent a month for 'Cleopatra's'. It may seem expensive but it was well worth it. The brothel was turning over £2,400 a week with McCormick and Morgan sharing £1,200 of that. It was in business for nine months before it was first raided.

On 20 March 1997 detectives from Pearse Street found four women and two men there and all admitted they were either buying or selling sex. Morgan was also there and even though he was identified as 'The Boss' he kept his mouth shut and said nothing incriminating. He was not prosecuted and, although he is one of Dublin's biggest brothel-keepers and pimps, he has never been caught and continues to operate.

Four months later, Cleopatra's was raided again. This time there were seven women there, six of whom admitted they were prostitutes. McCormick arrived at the back door of the apartment in the middle of the search. He had the keys on him but said a friend he was visiting in the flat gave them to him. He wouldn't name the friend and said he knew nothing about the lease. But two raids were enough for him and so later that month he closed Leeson Street and moved Cleopatra's on. New Cleopatra's was later set up at Pleasant Place.

In the meantime, however, another of McCormick's brothels was up and running at Lower Mount Pleasant Avenue in Rathmines. This was a four-bedroom house which he rented from 3 June 1997 to 29 June 1998. Again he used the name Peter McCoy. He got it relatively cheap — £300 a month cheaper than Cleopatra's and he paid the landlord £8,500 for the year.

Three months later he opened the Garden of Eden brothel in a two-bedroom apartment at Grattan Hall in Dublin 2. He paid £500 a month for that and it ran for the next nine months. He also had another brothel in a one-bedroom apartment in Rathmines.

In just over a year, therefore, Peter McCormick along with Martin Morgan had set up six brothels and established themselves as the biggest operators in the city. But McCormick's false name, Peter McCoy, was on too many leases. The estate agents were becoming suspicious. It was time to diversify and bring in a manager. Enter the beautiful and beguiling Belfast prostitute who used the false name Sarah Moran. For McCormick this system had the added advantage of distancing himself and Morgan from the prostitution operation and made it more difficult for the Gardaí to prosecute them.

McCormick adapted this practice at Pembroke Square in Dublin 2. He first rented it under the name of Peter McCoy on 31 October 1997 and paid £850 rent a month in cash. However, as soon as the two-bedroom apartment was run as a brothel, the complaints started flooding in to the management company and the owner. She saw the articles in the *Sunday World* about the prostitution business being run in Dublin by 'Baldy' and 'The Beast'. She realised that 'Baldy' was her tenant Peter McCormick and that 'The Beast' Martin Morgan had not only been going in and out of the apartment, he was often with McCormick when he paid the rent.

The landlord decided not to renew McCormick's lease but that didn't stop him running his brothel in her apartment. He collected some of his mail there and used it as his address when he registered as a director of a company called Olympic Security Services Ltd. He was not prepared to let go of this prestigious location that easily. Besides, business in the brothel business was always better if there was consistency.

Unknown to the landlord, her next tenant was also working for her previous one. Sarah Moran took up the lease at the end of October 1998. She paid the increased rent of £900 in cash every month and the brothel operation ran from her apartment for another year. Sarah and another woman, a black lady from England, also worked there as prostitutes.

The scam was so successful that McCormick's next four brothels were rented by Sarah Moran. The first one 'Playmates', or 'Playgirls', opened at Leeson Court on 30 April 1998. Sarah registered the ESB in her false name and on the form said she was self-employed at Pembroke Square. This was, of course, true. After all she was a prostitute working out of that apartment.

'Playmates' or 'Playgirls' operated for less than two months when the neighbours realised it was a brothel and called the Gardaí. It was raided and four women admitted they worked there while two men admitted paying them for sex. It was also the first time the Gardaí had come across another of McCormick's employees. Herbie McHenry was the minder for his women.

Herbie worked as a taxi driver but gave it up after a drug addict stabbed him with a syringe in Dolphin's Barn. He lived with his family in Templeogue but left after a row. He then lived in a van for a time before moving into one of McCormick's apartments at Bishopmeade on Clanbrassil Street. He was employed by April, one of the prostitutes who was very close to McCormick. She used to go into the coffee shop where he worked and one day she offered him the job. He may have been protecting McCormick's employees but it was the women who paid him out of their own money to mind them. 'Each client that comes in I get £10,' he said. 'I'm just a minder for the girls. I don't know what goes on in the rooms.'

McCormick's next brothel also opened in Sarah's name on 1 May 1998, the day after Playmates began. The two-bedroom apartment at Parliament Square was rented for a year initially for a £1,000 a month but that was reduced to £850 at Christmas. The landlord received a complaint from the management committee that his apartment was being run as a brothel but when he confronted Sarah about it, she denied it completely. He went to the Gardaí but they couldn't catch her in the act so nothing could be done until the lease was up. Needless to say, it wasn't renewed but in the meantime the steady stream of men looking for the 'massage parlour' regularly approached the other tenants in the block.

Brothels number ten and eleven were by now also up and running at prestigious addresses in Dublin 4 and Dublin 2. Number twelve started up on 6 November 1998 when Sarah leased a two-bedroom apartment on Burlington Road for £900 a month. Within six months the landlord knew it was being run as a brothel and when the rent wasn't paid on 1 June 1999, he changed the locks and used it as an excuse to terminate the lease.

The landlord waited for Sarah to return to tell her he had re-let the apartment. However, instead he watched as McCormick arrived and tried but failed to get in. Three days later Sarah rang demanding to know why she'd been locked out. The following day the landlord's wife received an abusive call from a man with a Northern Ireland accent. It was time to call in the Gardaí. When the landlord let them into the apartment, it was obvious that McCormick had been running it as a brothel.

Sarah Moran used the same mobile telephone number as a contact for the ESB at Burlington Road as she did for the next brothel at Drury Hall. She paid £1,500 cash to the landlord for the deposit and the first month's rent. It opened for business on 2 December 1998. It wasn't long, however, before the landlord there also began to suspect that 'something was not right'. He also confronted Sarah Moran but she told him 'there was nothing going on in the apartment'. Sarah knew, however, they'd been rumbled and didn't bother paying the rent the following month. The landlord called around to the apartment, took the keys off the two English women there and threw them out.

McCormick was making a fortune from his prostitution operation but there were problems. Complaining neighbours, inquisitive Gardaí, active management committees and awkward landlords who just wouldn't take the money and turn a blind eye were all hampering the smooth and successful running of the business. He knew he had to run it in a more discreet yet efficient fashion. He decided to streamline the operation and devised a system which he hoped would stop the punters bothering the neighbours and drawing attention to the brothels.

He set up a control centre which processed the calls from the men and made appointments for them with the women. They could either have sex with a prostitute in one of his many brothels around the city or they could avail of his call-out service and have sex in the privacy of their hotel room or home. The system centralised his operation and made it easier for him to keep track of what was going in. It was also designed to further distance him and Martin Morgan from the criminal activity and make it much harder for the Gardaí to get them.

McCormick established the control centre in a south city apartment in the Bishopmeade complex on Clanbrassil Street. He had one of his Portuguese prostitutes take out the lease on 4 May 1999. She paid a month's rent and a month's deposit in advance, a total of £1,500 in cash. She put the ESB in her name and said McCormick's company, Olympic Security Services, employed her.

She gave a reference on headed notepaper from a company called 'On Course Catering'. It had an address at Aungier Street, from where convicted brothel-keeper Brian O'Byrne operated a sex shop. When the landlord called three months later to collect the rent, Herbie met him and handed him the cash. Herbie had moved in and he paid him the rent every month for the next year until April 2000 when the landlord discovered what was going on and asked him to leave.

Bishopmeade was a two-bedroom apartment with a kitchen and a living room at the front. It was the call centre for, amongst others, Playtime, International Health Studios, Sculptures, Secrets, Blondes, Executive Services, Cleopatra's, Pretty Woman and Lady Jane's. The mobile number for 'Blondes' was registered to McCormick's false name Peter McCoy. At least fourteen brothel mobile phone numbers operated from the apartment. They were advertised in *In Dublin*.

McCormick ran so many brothels he took out full-page advertisements in the magazine and got the highest discount of any brothel-keeper, £1,000 per page. Each advert cost £400 for an eighth of a page but McCormick put a different name and number in each slot and instead of paying £3,200 he got it for £2,200. He had advertised consistently since August 1995 and within three years he was buying advertisements by the page.

The call centre system was simple. The punter rang or texted one of the mobile numbers, 'What girls are available today, any redheads?' and 'hv u a Nicole Kidman on yr bk' were two of the less obscene. The women waited in the apartment to take the calls.

There were three women on the early, and four on the late shift.

At first the caller was told the address and apartment number of the brothel to go to but as the Gladiator raids on other brothel-keepers continued McCormick tightened up the procedure for security reasons. The client was directed to a designated meeting place. If it was the La Rochelle brothel in Lamb Alley, then he was told to wait at the Spar on Thomas Street. If it was the Temple Bar brothel at Fownes Street, then he was to wait at the Globe in front of the Central Bank.

The call centre then dispatched the prostitute to meet him from the nearest apartment or from one of the functioning call-in brothels, such as Palm Beach. She was given a description of the man to look for. To the casual observer the meeting looked like a casual date. Indeed that's what it was supposed to look like. The women were instructed in some cases to take the client for a walk around the Central Bank before taking him to the bedroom just in case the Gardaí were watching. There was also the other golden rule when dealing with clients — get the money up front.

When Palm Beach closed at midnight some of the prostitutes came around to Bishopmeade and carried on working from there until the early hours. Punters could also call in there for sex. The women were in the kitchen, Herbie had one bedroom but the second one was usually available. The call centre ensured continuity of business. If one brothel was shut down, the call centre could react immediately. The next time the client rang he could be re-directed to another brothel or to a prostitute waiting in another apartment.

McCormick was the consummate pimp. He was both charming and tough. He didn't drink and kept himself fit and lean by boxing and working out five days a week. But he was also popular with the women who worked for him. He wasn't violent or abusive. He was personable and attentive to their needs and, when he or Morgan weren't driving them to and from call-outs, he got Herbie to look after them. While his partner and child were at home in bed, McCormick was out in the early hours of the morning chauffeuring and cruising around, minding, cajoling and checking up on his women, as well as reminding them what he expected of them. He even organised mortgages for some of them.

He was particularly close to one of the prostitutes, April. He could be seen walking around hand-in-hand with her at 1 a.m. and 2 a.m. He brought her for meals to a Chinese restaurant on George's Street after she finished work in the Palm Beach brothel. They called and texted each other incessantly with adolescent messages like 'head wrecker', 'freakazoid' or 'I love you'.

He also continued to drive her to meet clients, have sex with them and earn money for him. In the four months from January to April 2000, McCormick rang her 294 times, nearly three times a day every day, while she called him more — 441 times. He also called the Palm Beach brothel another 300 times. During the same period he called Elizabeth at home on his mobile only 24 times.

McCormick was a hands-on operator. The system at Bishopmeade may have been set up to distance him from the operation but he still called in there every night. He also did the rounds of the other brothels to collect his money and ensure the business ran properly. He was a proponent of the 'tough love' philosophy and he insisted the women kept themselves and the brothels tidy. He put up cleaning rosters and wouldn't tolerate them being late. He had no time for drugs and wouldn't employ junkies. They were not only anathema to his way of life, they were also bad for business.

The women had to notify him in writing if they wanted to take holidays. 'Jocasta', for example, wrote him a letter to tell him she was finishing work on 16 April 2000 but would be back after her two-week break. And even though the women could be working until 4 a.m. and 5 a.m., sleeping on the job was not permitted. McCormick was a strict taskmaster and he fined the women if they broke any of his rules.

McCormick's prostitutes were also among the most expensive in Dublin. They could afford to be. The other brothels were being shut down. It was a seller's market and by 1999 he dominated it. He could charge what he liked. For 'call-ins' to the brothels it was £80 for half an hour, £150 for an hour, but in January 2000 the half-hour 'call-in' charge went up to £100. For 'call-outs' it was £100 a half-hour and £160 an hour, but again the half-hour charge was subsequently increased to £120.

In fact McCormick pioneered the half-hour call-out. It had never been done in Dublin in that short a time before. He was able to ensure the women were in and out and paid within 30 minutes because he drove them to the meeting place and waited outside to pick them up. The women felt safe and McCormick doubled productivity. He only took a third of the women's money on call-ins, but on some of the call-outs he took half.

On a busy day and night there could be up to twenty call-outs so McCormick and Morgan, his business partner, were busy driving women all over the city. They could take in as much as £1,600 a night from Bishopmeade alone. For example, between 3.12 p.m. and 5.20 a.m. on 8 April 2000, McCormick and Morgan split £1,780 that the women took in from 22 clients. The £10 advertising charge and the £10 paid to Herbie the minder were taken from the women's share.

Bishopmeade also controlled much of the business that went through the six other brothels he had set up after the call centre. Maximum Services and High Society were based at Custom Hall on Gardiner Street. Again on 17 January 2000 one of his women rented it out and paid a £600 deposit and £600 for the first month. There were usually two women on each shift there and each one saw between two and five men a day. With *In Dublin* no longer doing the advertisements Maximum Services was advertised in *Loaded* magazine and on the Internet. It was also called Ex-Models and Hi-Society.

McCormick kept three types of records — rosters, dockets and envelopes. These enabled him to watch the women and the money. The roster, like those kept by other brothel-keepers, detailed the time of arrival, the name of the prostitute seen, whether it was a call-in or call-out and the time spent with the client. The women used symbols. A Δ represented a half-hour visit, an O stood for an hour. The roster sheet was used in the brothel or apartment.

The booking dockets were used in the Bishopmeade call centre. These were sheets from a receipt book kept by the phone. When the call came in, one of the women recorded the client's details and duration of stay. These dockets recorded details of call-ins and call-outs, and by counting them McCormick knew how many men had been seen and how much he was owed. However, by comparing the dockets with what was written in the roster sheets, he could also make sure his prostitutes weren't fiddling him.

McCormick also used envelopes to control and monitor the money. While the house money from all the women in a brothel was kept in one envelope, there was a separate one for each call-out. The woman put the money in it, wrote on the outside the length of the call-out and what McCormick was due. She also noted down any expenses that may have been incurred such as advertising costs, taxi fares or disciplinary fines. The women had to show taxi receipts. These records could also be cross-checked against the booking dockets and rosters but once everything tallied the paper work was supposed to be destroyed. McCormick was conscious of not leaving behind an evidential paper trail.

The next apartment was leased in February 2000, the month after Maximum Services. The same woman rented it but this time with a man. They took one on Fownes Street in Temple Bar for £1,000 a month and turned it into 'Ex Models — Ireland's No. 1 Escort Agency'. The advertisement invited the clients to 'Relax in our luxury apartment with our large selection of beautiful and friendly model-like girls.' It was a place where the women brought the men for sex.

The mobile number the man gave the landlords as a contact rang in to the 'High Society Escort Agency'. It was advertised as a health club in a magazine called *Miss Behaviour*, which was available in sex shops. The calls came in to the call centre and the women who worked out of the apartment were phoned. They were told to meet their client at the Central Bank and walk him around before bringing him back. If this 'call-in' business was quiet then the prostitutes were sent from Fownes Street to Bishopmeade to do 'call-outs' from there instead.

Fownes Street operated into the early hours. McCormick didn't have to visit it too often because of his minder and his system of records and checks. Herbie had a set of keys for Fownes Street and kept an eye on it and the women. They in turn also had to check in with the call centre when they were finished with a client. They were given a mobile number at Bishopmeade to call. When they rang it, 'Jocasta' logged the details of the sexual transactions. It was also the number for New Cleopatra's at Pleasant Place. If a woman rang, it was one of the prostitutes. If a man rang, it was customer.

Herbie also kept an eye on the women in two of McCormick's other brothels which operated in early 2000, La Rochelle near

Christchurch Cathedral and Executive Services at Christchurch Place. La Rochelle was set up to look like a massage parlour with muscle charts and price lists on the wall. The neighbours became suspicious, however, and reported it to the Gardaí.

Two detectives called on 7 February 2000. First they spoke to a man who had just come out. Then they knocked on the door of the apartment. Herbie answered and let them in, and they saw two women and another man in the bedroom. The neighbours' suspicions were confirmed but in true McCormick style, La Rochelle was closed down. The brothel moved on to the next apartment which was already rented. 'Sweet Convenience' was selling sex at Pleasant Place while 'Playtime' was based at Blessington Street.

McCormick was a forward thinking, energetic and ambitious brothel-keeper. He had firmly established his business in Ireland and now planned to expand his empire and set up in England. He leased a place on the Seven Sisters Road in north London for twenty years beginning on Christmas Day 1999. He agreed to pay an annual rent of £26,000 sterling but this was to be reviewed every five years.

The place was perfect for a brothel. The lease allowed for the building to be used as a sauna and massage parlour and this was specified on it. McCormick paid £6,500 of the rent with a draft from the TSB in Stillorgan. Unfortunately for him, the venture never got off the ground. When the Vice Squad in London heard about it, they objected to his proposed development. Another attempt to open 'a special beauty treatment centre' on Gale Street in Dagenham also failed. McCormick was refused planning permission for that on 21 March 2000.

Peter McCormick was making a lot of money but the State didn't know about it and wasn't getting any of it. He didn't have a regular job and therefore appeared to be unemployed. However, he never drew the dole in Dublin and wasn't registered for tax with the Revenue Commissioners.

The Department of Social Community and Family Affairs had no record of either him or his wife claiming social welfare for themselves. They did receive some State benefits from Northern Ireland between November 1992 and March 1998 using an address at Cecil Street in Portadown. They also claimed the children's allowance here for their daughter who was born in September 1998 but €117 a month would not be enough for all three to live on.

McCormick didn't pay tax although his wife paid a small amount. Elizabeth Troughton said she ran a B&B at 155/156 Upper Leeson Street. As a director of the Leeson Lodge Ltd, she registered for income tax on 29 August 1997. The company was registered for PAYE, PRSI, VAT and Corporation Tax.

Revenue records show that Leeson Lodge Ltd filed its first tax returns for the fourteen months up to the end of 1998. They showed a turnover of just over £69,000. But with operating costs of nearly £66,000, Elizabeth claimed she was only making a net profit of just over £3,000.

For the tax year 1998/1999 she said she earned £19,200 and paid only £4,290 tax. It was a surprise that a guesthouse in one of the most sought-after areas of Dublin within walking distance of the city centre, Lansdowne Road and the RDS didn't appear to be doing all that well.

The Leeson Lodge Bed and Breakfast started off in July 1996 with four bedrooms on the top floor of the two-storey building at 156 Leeson Street. At the time Peter McCormick was renting the basement but Elizabeth said she didn't know him, in spite of the fact that they had been in south Armagh, Longford and Clonskeagh together. When the house next door at 155 became available in September 1997, Elizabeth incorporated the six bedrooms there into her business.

Olympic Security Services Ltd also used the top floor of 156 Leeson Street as its registered address. The company provided security services to building sites, nightclubs, hotels and shops. Peter McCormick and Martin Morgan were two of its directors. It was stated on the VAT registration application form that the company was paying £50 a week rent. However, the landlord never got any rent from Olympic. In fact he never rented to the company in the first place. His agreement was with Elizabeth Troughton. The company only lasted just over two years. It didn't file any returns and was dissolved on 16 June 2000.

On 11 September 2000 the landlord at Leeson Street told McCormick and Troughton he wanted them out. But McCormick told him they would not go easily and would resist any attempt to evict them. He told the landlord he could tie him up in litigation for another year and a half and gave him two choices — six months rent-free or £50,000 compensation. McCormick was offered £5,000, but he said he regarded that as an insult. He told the landlord's representative that he would have to improve on the offer or there would be problems. He also told him that, while he didn't threaten people, he had not always been a good boy.

The landlord managed to get McCormick out and the Leeson Lodge moved on from 155/156 Leeson Street, but McCormick wasn't joking when he said he hadn't always been a good boy. He was a highly intelligent and successful criminal. In less than five years he had opened at least eighteen brothels in Dublin. He very quickly went from being a bankrupt to a millionaire. His success didn't go un-noticed and he was identified as a target for both the National Bureau of Criminal Investigation and the Criminal Assets Bureau. But McCormick had already moved to distance himself from his money and his prostitution business. Detectives were to spend the next nine months re-connecting him to both.

14 The Last CAB and Gladiator Targets

The time had come to spend some of that hard-earned cash. Peter McCormick needed some stability in his life. He had been a nomad for far too long. Dublin had been good to him. It was home to his longest-lasting and most successful business enterprise. He was making more money than he had ever made before. It didn't really matter if he was breaking the law. After all he was, on the face of it, a successful company director and his girlfriend ran a successful guesthouse. They could mix in respectable social circles. No one was any the wiser. For the last five years they'd been living in rented accommodation and now was the time to put down some roots. Now was the time to invest in bricks and mortar.

In 1997 Peter McCormick and his partner Elizabeth Troughton moved into a house at Lawnswood Park in Stillorgan, Co. Dublin. It was bought in Elizabeth's name on 29 August 1997 for £184,000. She was given a loan of £169,000 after she declared on her mortgage application pre-tax profits of over £161,000 from 1995 to 1997.

When the Revenue Commissioners looked at the figures, they immediately spotted the discrepancy. On the one hand she told them she made only £19,200 in 1998/99. But on the other hand she told the building society she made £71,000 in 1997 and had a turnover of £69,000 by the end of 1998.

She was also able to find an extra £33,000 when she bought the house. This was to pay a £15,000 deposit and £18,000 in stamp duty and other expenses. So where did all the extra money come from and why did she declare so little of it? With McCormick making so much from prostitution, it wasn't difficult to figure that one out.

There were other discrepancies. Elizabeth Troughton told the Criminal Assets Bureau that Peter McCormick had no financial interest in the house. In fact, she said, she bought it before she even started to go out with him. This just didn't add up for a number of reasons. First of all, she had been living and working with him for the previous seven years. Secondly, he went with her to view the house on 7 July, six weeks before she bought it. And thirdly, she might have made the first offer of £183,000 on it but it was McCormick's mobile number that was given to the auctioneer. It was he who made the improved and final offer of £184,000 that secured the house, even though it was put in her name.

Ten days before the deal was sealed, the couple took out a life assurance protection plan together. This is a normal thing for a couple to do who have just bought a house together, but a bit strange for people who say they don't know each other. The sum assured was £169,000 — exactly the same amount as the mortgage on the house. The policy, therefore, appears to have been principally a mortgage protection policy. McCormick and Troughton moved in to the Lawnswood house.

As well as the substantial monthly mortgage repayments of over £1,000 a month, Elizabeth could also afford to pay another £241.65 a month mortgage protection, although she changed to a cheaper policy in September 2000 which cost £54 less a month. She was also paying another £100 a month, £50 each into two other policies — one for herself and one for their daughter. Eleven months later Peter and Elizabeth made a will in which they named each other as their sole beneficiary.

The couple made costly and substantial improvements to the Stillorgan house. They spent £38,000 on renovations between December 1997 and February 1999. They converted one room into an office and fitted it out in oak. They paid a company in Belfast £16,000 sterling for the work. They also put in a fitted kitchen and spent £1,400 at a home store in Magherafelt in Derry and £2,400 at a furniture shop in Belfast. They spent over £1,000 on re-wiring and £1,400 on radiator covers. In the garden they spent another £3,300 on ornate bricks and £2,400 on garden furniture. They bought two fountains and a trellis and paid £4,500 to a gardener to put it all in. The total cost of bringing the house and garden up to the standard of luxury they required was over £65,000.

The house was also adorned with a valuable art collection. They liked Mildred Ann Butler and had three of her works — 'A Happy Family' cost £7,200, 'Peacocks' cost £2,100 and 'The Lake' cost £3,000. They were all bought in May 1999. They also bought Percy French's 'The West of Ireland' for £3,500 sterling and a painting by Gwladys McCabe. They paid £900 sterling for her 'Punch and Judy'. The 50 cm x 60 cm signed oil on board work was sold in May 2003 by James Adam Fine Art Auctioneer in St Stephen's Green for over €3,000. Ten paintings in the house were worth in total over £18,500.

McCormick wore a £4,900 Gucci watch. Elizabeth's engagement ring was worth £4,250. In September 1998 they spent £4,700 on a diamond and sapphire ring in Appleby's of Grafton Street. Her jewellery collection included diamond and sapphire earrings and a matching bracelet; gold and diamond chains and pendants; and a 2oz gold nugget which they picked up in Dubai. It was all worth over £24,000. McCormick also had two Northern Ireland registered cars — a BMW first registered in 1998 worth £26,500 sterling and a Rover 216SI valued at £10,000 sterling.

But, ironically, one of the country's most successful criminals was to become a victim of violent crime. In August 2000 a gang of cruel, ruthless and dangerous criminals broke into the house. They held a knife to the hand of the couple's baby daughter and threatened to cut off her fingers if they weren't told where the money was. The gang got away with around £40,000 in cash and jewellery. Afterwards McCormick vowed his home and his family would never be so violated again. He installed an expensive state-of-the-art security system with electronic gates, cameras and television monitors which had the capacity to record and freeze pictures and print out hard copies. He also brought two dogs into the house.

The attack on his family affected Peter McCormick the most. He could easily handle the loss of money. There was plenty more where that came from. He had at least twelve bank accounts in

Ireland, Northern Ireland, England and the Isle of Man. He used addresses in Dublin, Belfast, Larne and London. He had sterling and non-resident accounts in Irish Nationwide Grafton Street as well as other loan and company accounts. He also had an account with Nat West in London which Gardaí believe he set up to run a brothel there.

Thousands of pounds went through the accounts. On 10 October 1999, for example, £10,000 was put into his TSB account in Grafton Street. Six weeks later another £10,000 was lodged but this time in the form of a draft drawn on the Ulster Bank in the Isle of Man. McCormick also had an account there. He denied trying to set up an offshore company on the islands of St Kitts-Nevis. 'That was just a fact-finding mission,' he said. 'I have no accounts in any tax haven outside of the Isle of Man.'

Elizabeth had almost twice as many accounts as her husband. She had 23 accounts — savings, current, loan, credit card, sterling, company, credit union, share, non-resident and foreign. She also had accounts in Dublin, Larne, Belfast, the Isle of Man and the UK. Some were dormant, others were for relatives and three were for the guest-house business.

She lodged nearly £80,000 into one of her Irish Permanent accounts between 1997 and early 2000 but by October of that year there was only £416.76 left in it. She set up a quarterly share account by lodging £10,000 to it from another account. At one stage her non-resident investment account with First Active had over £25,000 in it. The balance on her Ulster Bank/Isle of Man account on 1 March 2000 was £10,684.34.

There is, however, little information available about her three Isle of Man accounts except to say that there was a lien or a charge over two of them, one for £7,000, the other for £8,000. A lien on an account usually means there's more money in it than the amount of the lien. The lien usually represents three-quarters of the full amount. Therefore it's likely there was at least £9,300 in one Isle of Man account and £10,600 in the other. CAB could not get any details about another overseas account she had with the Alliance and Leicester.

Peter and Elizabeth also held a number of joint accounts. One of those was with AIB Finance and Leasing in Belfast where they borrowed £140,000 for the pub in Keady. When it was sold at a loss for £92,000 the bank was left short by £48,000. This is believed to have been written off when the couple were bankrupted.

Elizabeth told the Criminal Assets Bureau that they knew the business was going downhill and they took cash and stock from it before the liquidator was appointed. She said they had to hide this money from the creditors because they were bankrupts. She wouldn't say how much it was but admitted it was 'a nice sum'. They also invested some of that money in another pub run by a friend in Northern Ireland.

Elizabeth admitted they used at least three accounts in Dublin for the money they took out of Northern Ireland. They collected it in dribs and drabs and lodged it in two of her accounts and in their joint sterling account with Irish Nationwide. The figures tend to substantiate this. In 1996 she put £5,610 in her Irish Nationwide deposit account, the following year she lodged £14,778. She also lodged £9,850 in her EBS account in 1997. However, within four years most of the money was gone out of these accounts. There was over £13,000 in their joint Irish Nationwide sterling deposit account in 1996 but by the year 2000 there was only £1,794 left.

It wasn't surprising, therefore, that the investigation into such a complex and sophisticated financial and prostitution network was to prove long, difficult and expensive for the Gardaí. McCormick was a very clever criminal. He had some inside knowledge on the workings of police procedures from his days in the RUC. He was clearly not going to be an easy man to catch.

The nine-month investigation into his activities was two-fold. On the one hand there was the clean, complicated, white-collar work led by the head of the Criminal Assets Bureau, Detective Chief Superintendent Felix McKenna. Gardaí and Revenue Officials from CAB tracked the money trail from Belfast to Dublin, to London to the Isle of Man. It involved untangling the web of financial transactions, property deals, company business, fine art and jewellery purchases and payments or, as in McCormick's case, non-payments to the Revenue Commissioners.

On the other hand there was the dirty prostitution work led by another Chief Superintendent, Seán Camon. Teams of detectives from Operation Gladiator were out all hours of the day and night crouched in cars, gathering evidence, stopping men coming out of the brothels. They followed the women to some of the city's plushest hotels and wealthiest suburbs. They watched as McCormick visited his brothels and prostitutes all over the city to check on his business and collect his cash.

The surveillance began in September 1999 and focussed on two locations — the Palm Beach brothel at Camden Court and the control centre at the Bishopmeade apartment. The teams monitoring the brothel were static. They watched the men going in and took statements from them when they came out. These detailed the usual routine of showers, talcum powder, massage and sex and the usual array of prices for service.

McCormick had made an attempt to disguise Palm Beach as a genuine massage parlour by putting medical and anatomical charts on the walls and making the women dress in white nurses' tops. Each of the three bedrooms had mirrors on the wall and a bench in the middle. The doors were labelled KI, Reflex and Aroma. It fooled at least one dissatisfied customer with a back problem or at least that's what he told the Gardaí.

Tom said; 'I gave her £50 and lay on my stomach while she started to massage my back. I saw charts on the wall in the room with human bones and muscles on them. The room was made up to look like it was a medical centre but take it from me it's no medical centre. She took off her blouse. She offered me full service but I declined her offer. I now believe that Camden Court is a fucking whorehouse. I got dressed and left. I will never be back in that place again. I was afraid of my life.'

Over at Bishopmeade the detectives had to be mobile to hear some of the equally-colourful stories from the customers there. The centre was a hive of activity with women taking off like bees in all directions, all over Dublin, to mate with a variety of the city's drones. The Gardaí followed them on their call-outs to luxury houses in Donnybrook and Lucan. They tailed them to hotels like the Shelbourne, the Ormonde, the Airport Great Southern and Wynn's.

On 5 January 2000 they interviewed a religious brother from the west of Ireland who was in Dublin to break his vow of chastity. The man behind the collar told them he'd travelled up with a copy of *In Dublin* that day. He rang 'Secrets of Seduction' and left the hotel phone number and his room number. A woman rang him back and told him his 'date' would be with him in 30 minutes. The charge was £160.

'We introduced ourselves and talked for about ten minutes and she asked me for the £160 which I gave her,' he said. 'After, I invited her to stay for a drink but she declined. I saw her drive off in a smallish car.' Sandra had no time for small talk. Her boss wouldn't allow it. She had other men to see and money to make.

Religious life can be extremely lonely and this man yearned for companionship, warmth and company but Peter McCormick wasn't in the comfort or friendship business. All he had to offer was sex at a high price and ultimately emptiness.

At 3.08 a.m. on 7 January 2000 McCormick dropped one of his women off at the Spar in Thomas Street to meet a man who paid her £100 for 20 minutes in the La Rochelle apartment. He told the Gardaí it was his first time but, if it was, it wasn't to be his last. Two days later he booked into Wynn's Hotel and rang one of McCormick's numbers for a red-haired girl. When she arrived he bought her a gin and 7-Up in the bar and they went upstairs. She made sure she took the money off him first, and after sex she called base on her mobile. 'I'm checking out now,' she said, 'make sure you tell Peter.' She knew McCormick would not have been happy that she had a drink with the punter and was now running late.

McCormick knew the Gardaí were on to him and that he was being followed. He adapted basic anti-surveillance techniques such as driving off in one direction only to do a sharp U-turn and head off in the other. He also pulled up beside some of the detectives in their car and stopped and stared at them. He was aware the Gardaí would ring the brothel numbers to gather evidence against him so he introduced basic security checks for the women on the phones.

He told them to get a number from the punters so they could call him back and check him out. Some of the brothels were on voicemail so if the men were serious about wanting sex they had to leave their number anyway. Sometimes the men would call one number only to be told to call another and maybe even a third before they could get a woman.

But overall the investigation didn't frighten McCormick or drive him underground. He still ferried the women around the city and the Gardaí watched him as he continued to call into the brothels to collect his money. McCormick's business partner had, however, a very different attitude to the Garda investigation. When the pressure came on, Martin Morgan went to London for a while. He wasn't in the country on 15 April 2000 when the Gardaí made their move.

Detectives from the National Bureau of Criminal Investigations and the Criminal Assets Bureau raided five places that night. First was the call centre at Bishopmeade where they waited until McCormick was inside before going in. 'Do what the fuck you like,' he said to them. They arrested him at 1.20 a.m. They took his mobile phone from his belt and seized the other nine on the table. Three women were sitting there waiting for the calls. Detective Garda Mick Moran had a list of ten numbers for McCormick's brothels and prostitute services and, as he rang each one, another phone rang on the table.

McCormick was questioned all night. He wasn't worried. He was well versed in police investigation and interview techniques. He asked for a solicitor, refused to suspend questioning and said nothing of any evidential value. He was courteous but not co-operative. He made no admissions of criminality during his eight hours of detention.

When he was shown items seized in the course of the searches, he had 'no comment'. When he was asked about the brothels, he replied 'nothing to say'. He knew he didn't have to say anything. The burden of proof was on the State. However, it didn't really matter that he wouldn't explain his complex financial and criminal activities. He would be taking a fall. He was fingerprinted and photographed and released at 9.05 a.m.

Three other brothels were also searched that morning. At 3 a.m. Herbie was arrested at Executive Services in Christchurch Place. At 10 a.m. detectives went into the brothel at Camden Court and an hour later they searched the apartment at Fownes Street. They found boxes of business cards, rosters, cash and the usual prostitution paraphernalia.

They found similar material two days later when they raided Maximum Services at the Custom Hall apartments in Gardiner Street. They also found rosters, directions for call-outs to homes in Castleknock and Ballsbridge and a black strap-on penis. The two women caught there admitted they were prostitutes and the man admitted he'd paid for sex with one of them.

In Store Street Garda station Herbie admitted he was paid by the women to mind them but denied he was running the brothels. 'The girls let the clients into the apartment,' he said. 'I don't know what goes on in the rooms.' Herbie insisted he did nothing else. He didn't collect the money or do the rosters. He lived in a room in Bishopmeade and kept a motorcycle helmet and a commercially sponsored leather suit in the wardrobe.

He said he was given McCormick's number when he started in the job but claimed he had never met him. When his mobile was checked, there were 185 calls from it to McCormick in four months. There were also 343 calls to the numbers for Palm Beach, Cleopatra's and Executive Services. From then on Herbie had 'nothing to say'. He was released and a file was sent to the DPP but Herbie McHenry was never charged with any offence.

The one place the Gardaí raided in the early hours of 15 April that wasn't a brothel was McCormick's home in Lawnswood Park, Stillorgan. The CAB found documents there which linked him to at least six of the brothels. There were lodgment slips which paid the rent for Camden Court, Parliament Street, Burlington Road, Drury Hall, La Rochelle and Christchurch Place.

They also found details on McCormick's alias Peter McCoy's mobile phone number. However, the most interesting documentation they discovered confirmed what they had long believed. McCormick had taken over from Hogan as the country's number one advertiser of brothels and was the driving force behind the new 'sex for sale on the Internet' phenomenon.

Escortireland.com marketed itself as 'Ireland's No. 1 Adult Entertainment Directory'. In fact it took over much of the advertising of brothels in Ireland after *In Dublin* stopped taking the advertisements. It may claim it didn't know but as many as thirty prostitutes and brothel-keepers were paying £200 a month to have their numbers posted on the site. The Gardaí found a box with thousands of Escortireland business cards in the office at Lawnswood Park. The number on the card rang one of McCormick's mobiles.

There were pages about advertising with Escortireland.com and more pages about escort agencies in Dublin, Cork, Galway, Limerick and Belfast. Over 60 agencies were on the site including McCormick's brothels — Palm Beach, Hi-Society and Pretty Woman. There were also computer printouts about purchasing fifty domain names and the cost of maintaining an Internet site.

But Escortireland was also selective about what kind of person it allowed to advertise on its website. While it welcomed business from prostitutes and Irish brothel-keepers, it didn't take advertisements from those it felt might threaten the status quo and introduce a more violent, sinister and dangerous element into the illicit sex industry.

Russian, Albanian and Moldovan brothel-keepers trying to set up here found they were unable to advertise their businesses on the most important noticeboard in the country. The inability of the East Europeans to advertise the services of their brothels is one of the main reasons why they have so far not been able to establish a strong foothold in the Irish vice industry. They have been starved of the oxygen of publicity.

When Garda technical experts examined the computer seized from McCormick's house they found it had been used in the operation and maintenance of the website. However, they couldn't prove that had been done in this country so they couldn't charge him in connection with it.

They also suspected he was behind a number of Internet addresses designed to give the two fingers to those who were investigating him. Criminalassetsbureau.com and Barrygalvin. com were just two directed at CAB and its personnel. Galvin was the Bureau's Legal Officer at the time and one of a small number of civilians licensed to carry a hand-gun for his own protection.

There was another reason why the Gardaí believe McCormick was behind the website. One detective wrote a stinging review of one of his brothels and sent it in to be posted on the website. He said the women were ugly, the sex was awful, the prices were too high and the whole experience was dreadful. Needless to say, the review never appeared on 'Ireland's No. 1 Adult Entertainment Directory'. However, a copy of it was found in the house in Stillorgan during the raid.

McCormick was clearly a sophisticated and technologically-proficient criminal who was at ease in cyber space. But he said someone else owned the website and that he was only going to work for the company. 'The Escortireland cards were in my possession,' he told the CAB. 'I was going to act as an agent for Escortireland and distribute them around the sex shops. I was getting £100 a week for this. I never got any money for this. I was working a week behind.'

The Gardaí couldn't get enough evidence to show to the level of the criminal standard of proof that McCormick was running the website. They couldn't get him before a court on advertising prostitution and he was never charged with that offence. He was, however, charged with organising prostitution and allowing his place at Camden Court to be used as a brothel.

On 3 March 2003 Peter McCormick pleaded guilty to the first charge at the Dublin Circuit Criminal Court and the second one was taken into account. He was remanded on bail for sentencing on 6 May. But McCormick didn't sit at home worrying about whether he was going to be heavily fined and sent to jail. Instead he headed for Hawaii to marry and honeymoon with his new bride Elizabeth Troughton.

Elizabeth had been through a traumatic time. The CAB had also been after her. They had searched her home as part of the criminal investigation into Peter's activities but they believed she was not totally divorced from those. The 'babes in the wood' routine just wouldn't wash. As far as CAB was concerned, it was clear that she had benefited from the money he had earned from prostitution and that she had questions to answer about her income and lifestyle.

She tried to give CAB officers the run-around. She said she would call them and make herself available for interview in June 2000 but she didn't. When they called to see her three months later, she wouldn't speak to them. She told them she had to go to work. When they offered to go with her and speak to her there, she told them she had suppliers calling. She told them she didn't know when she'd be available and when they tried to make an arrangement with her she told them she had a baby to feed and shut the door.

She couldn't hide forever, however, and in November 2000 the Bureau decided to move on the happy couple. It calculated that McCormick had earned over £637,000 between 1996 and 1999 on which he could be assessed for tax. It then sent him a bill for £128,000 for 1996/97, £116,000 for 1997/98 and £91,000 for

1998/99, a total bill for three years unpaid tax of over £335,000. His partner, Martin Morgan, was also sent a bill for just two years of nearly £¼m.

In Elizabeth's case the assessment was for four years. Bureau officers found she earned over £231,000 between 1995 and 1999 but she only declared earnings of £19,200 for one of those years. CAB sent her a bill for unpaid tax of £18,000 for 1995/96, £24,000 for 1996/97, £30,000 for 1997/98 and £34,000 for 1998/99. Elizabeth knew she was caught and decided to settle. Even though the total bill was only for £106,000, she actually agreed to pay more. Seven months later in July 2001 she settled with the Criminal Assets Bureau for over £150,000.

Elizabeth and Peter were newly-weds, less than three months married on the day he was sentenced. However, the woman by his side in the Circuit Criminal Court on his 44th birthday, 6 May 2003, was not his bride but one of his prostitutes. April sat with him in the hall outside and on the bench inside court number 8.

April stuck by him and helped him to avoid the waiting photographers. They wouldn't get a picture of Peter McCormick for the television news that night or the following morning's newspapers. The wily ex-policeman gave the cameramen the slip when he and April calmly walked into an area reserved exclusively for barristers. He ignored the wigs and gowns and disappeared down the stairs and out through the kitchen.

Senior Counsel Hugh Hartnett did a first-class job defending his client. The man he described to Judge Desmond Hogan bore only a superficial resemblance to the biggest brothel-keeper in Dublin. McCormick, he said, was a family man with children. He had a long-term partner whom he had recently married. He had no previous convictions and was now settled and hardworking. He was a partner with his wife in a bed-and-breakfast business in the city.

McCormick was portrayed as a man who was easily led and made a mistake. The court was told that he had worked as a hotel and bar manager for a number of years but had been introduced to the prostitution business by another man who had been arrested but was not brought before the court or prosecuted.

His counsel asked the judge to take his plea of guilty into consideration. It not only saved considerable time and expense for the State, it also saved the punters like the religious brother and the student the embarrassment of having to come to court and give evidence in public. He also pointed out that McCormick was one of those charged as part of Operation Gladiator and that none of the other targets who had pleaded guilty had been sent to jail. There was Garda evidence of this in court but that evidence was in fact wrong. Tom McDonnell and Brian O'Byrne were both jailed in spite of their guilty pleas.

The defence also pointed out that the plea of guilty was made at an early stage. This was also true but Detective Sergeant Seán Cullen had already told the court that when he was arrested and questioned McCormick made no admissions to help the investigation. But his lawyer finished with a flourish when pleading with the judge on McCormick's behalf not to impose a custodial sentence. 'He has for most of his life led a blameless life,' Hugh Hartnett said, 'I ask your Lordship to see it as an isolated blip in his career.'

And that's exactly how Judge Desmond Hogan saw it. 'He does appear to have now ceased and gone into business with his wife,' he said. 'While I do not intend to impose a custodial sentence I do have to mark the seriousness of the crime. The fact is he was running this as a business involving a number of girls and he certainly seems to have been running this business in an organised way. I intend to deal with it by way of a fine.'

Peter McCormick was fined €3,000 and given three months to pay. He would serve four months in prison if he didn't. He was also given a two-year suspended sentence that will be activated if he gets involved in pimping or prostitution again in the next five years. Dressed in blue slacks and a blue short-sleeved shirt he looked more like a busman than a brothel-keeper. He's only the second person in the history of the State, along with Samantha Blandford Hutton, to be convicted of organising prostitution.

Afterwards he was relaxed, affable and approachable and when asked how he felt, he smiled and in his soft Northern accent said 'No comment'. In spite of the fact that the photographers and an RTÉ television camera crew followed him again up and down the halls of the Four Courts and watched and waited for him to come outside, McCormick didn't panic. He knew the cameramen wouldn't get him and they didn't. He simply melted away …

Conclusion

The brothel-keepers all operated similar systems. They leased, bought or rented apartments and houses, and fitted them out in the same manner. They all managed their businesses the same way, taking a percentage of the women's earnings and charging extra for minders, advertising and housekeeping. Neighbours or businesspeople who complained, non-compliant landlords and the Gardaí were all occupational hazards.

If a brothel had to close down, it opened up again very quickly in a new location. Continuity of earnings was ensured. In March 2001 the Criminal Assets Bureau carried out a forensic analysis on the finances of eight brothel-keepers. It found they were all earning, at the very least, between £1,500 and £5,500 in cash a week. They ignored the law that said they couldn't and shouldn't operate. Experience had shown them they were right to do so.

Operation Gladiator was the first time a dedicated vice squad had ever been set up in this country to target those profiting from organised prostitution. It was one of the most successful Garda operations ever — while it lasted. In less than a year it had identified, arrested and built cases against the major brothel-keepers in Dublin. Of the eighteen individuals it went after, fourteen were convicted, two others fled the country and the remaining two got away. They're still operating. The last target was sentenced more than three years after the operation began.

Gladiator was supposed to be a national operation but it never carried out any investigation outside the capital. The brothels in Cork, Limerick, Waterford and Galway, some of which were run by the main Dublin players, continued to operate at will. Gladiator proved that focused, specialist and determined police work could bring those at the top of the vice trade in Ireland to justice.

The Gladiator team was never disbanded. It was allowed to dissolve as one by one the detectives went back to their units in Dublin. There is still a lucrative and active vice industry in this country but there is no dedicated vice squad in the Garda Síochána to tackle it. The success of Gladiator presents compelling evidence for the establishment of one.

Operation Gladiator has changed the way the illegal sex industry works. Hundreds of brothels are still operating all over the country and prostitutes are readily available to anyone who wants one. But the brothels are no longer as easily identifiable and are no longer at street level. The investigation has driven them underground and behind closed doors. In many ways, Gladiator has 'smashed the glass into a thousand pieces'. The majority of brothels now operate on a smaller scale with a smaller number of women, in some cases as few as one or two. The days of employing up to twenty women at a time are gone.

The tactic of surveillance followed by statement followed by warrant followed by raid may prove redundant in future prostitution investigations. The brothel-keepers all know how the Gardaí operate and what they can do to stay out of jail. Towards the end of Gladiator, at least one brothel-keeper was able to circumvent the investigation and avoid prosecution. It is unlikely that any such similar investigations will ever be as successful again.

Experienced drug dealers tend not to get caught with large quantities of heroin. Experienced brothel-keepers are learning to distance themselves from their operations.

The mobile numbers are still operating but they are no longer advertised in the newspapers or mainstream press. The illegal sex industry has moved its advertising on to the Internet. This makes the crime of advertising prostitution much more difficult to prosecute. The individual has to be caught loading the advertisement on to a computer. It also has to be proven that the offence took place in this country. With lap-tops and the Internet, it can be done anywhere. Advertising prostitution has come a long way since *In Dublin* and is now a far more difficult crime to detect. And with websites like Dublinprostitutes.com offering prostitutes, lists of brothels and a definitive guide to Dublin's red-light districts, finding an 'escort' in Dublin remains relatively easy.

The brothel-keepers and prostitutes no longer carry incriminating evidence like business cards blatantly advertising their services. One Dublin prostitute's card consists of a picture of two cars with 'auto repair' written beside them and the catchphrase 'repairs for all *foreign* parts!' Her landline and phone number along with a false address on the Naas Road are also on the card. Unless a Garda knew what was going on, he would never suspect the card was for a brothel — not a mechanic – and, even if he did, it would be impossible to prove in court.

Gladiator educated criminals not just to the investigation methods used by the Gardaí but also to the vagaries of the law. The 1993 Criminal Law (Sexual Offences) Act was primarily introduced to decriminalise homosexuality. It also made soliciting and kerb-crawling offences and was therefore proclaimed as a step forward that would lead to the prosecution of more clients. However, in its first year and a half, ten times more women were prosecuted than men.

It's a trend that continues. The Gardaí may be reluctant to prosecute the prostitutes but it is the men who solicit them who are more likely to go free. The Gardaí taking statements during Operation Gladiator were obliged to first tell each man he hadn't committed an offence. It's a wonder they got so many to talk to them at all. They provided essential evidence without which there would have been no prosecutions.

Prostitution cannot survive without the men who are prepared to pay for sex. They are the bedrock of the vice industry and yet they are rarely prosecuted. It is illegal for either a man or a woman to solicit but it is not illegal for a man to walk into a brothel and pay for sex or a woman to take the money and have sex with him. A woman is a prostitute in the eyes of the law only if she's on the street.

The law, therefore, makes it extremely difficult for the Gardaí to tackle the vice industry. Brothel-keeping is illegal but the men and women in the brothels are not doing anything illegal. The only person committing an offence in a brothel is the owner or manager. In the aftermath of Gladiator, no smart brothel-keeper is going to be caught in his or her brothel.

The loopholes in the legislation are perhaps a reflection of Irish society's attitude towards prostitution and the question of whether or not it should be illegal. Politicians, judges and the Gardaí are not sure how to deal with it. The absence of a dedicated vice squad means investigations are left to individual detective units in each division. This can mean the approach of the force is different in different areas. The enthusiasm with which Gardaí can pursue criminals is often determined by factors such as priorities and resources.

In comparison to murder or violent crime, prostitution is not very high up the priority list. If brothel-keepers keep their heads down, don't cause any trouble and move on when they're discovered, chances are they can operate with little disruption. Besides, prostitutes and those who work in the sex industry are good sources of information and tend to know what's happening on the streets. They will also co-operate with the Gardaí if they feel they are there to protect rather than persecute them.

The success of Gladiator has also highlighted serious shortcomings in the way brothel-keepers are processed and dealt with by the courts. If they are charged, they have in reality little to fear from a conviction. The fines are meagre in comparison to the money they make and very few are sent to jail. The judiciary tends to take a sympathetic approach particularly towards female brothel-keepers. Only two of Gladiator's targets ended up in prison and they have since been released. The most serious cases took over three years to trundle through the criminal justice system. Justice delayed is justice denied.

The real scandal is, however, the fact that at least five of Gladiator's targets were granted free legal aid while they were being prosecuted in spite of the fact that they earned vast amounts of money and owed millions in tax. The State handed over nearly £30,000 to pay solicitors, barristers and senior counsel to defend Thomas McDonnell, Marie Bridgeman, Karen Leahy, Samantha Blandford Hutton, and her brother Stephen Reginald Hutton.

Top of the brothel-keeper's payout list was Tom McDonnell who owed nearly £1.9m to the Revenue Commissioners. The tax-payer paid his lawyers over £11,800. Karen Leahy's legal expenses of more than £10,300 were also covered as were £4,300 for Reggie Hutton, £2,200 for Marie Bridgeman and £592 for Samantha Blandford Hutton. Legal aid is a discretionary matter for the courts. Surely judges have a responsibility to scrutinise such applications a lot more closely.

Ambivalence towards the prostitution business in Ireland goes right to the heart of government. Politicians could certainly put a severe dent in the multi-million euro earnings of brothel-keepers by tackling the demand as opposed to the supply. It would dramatically reduce the numbers involved in the sex trade by making it an offence, as it is in Sweden, for a man to procure a woman.

A change in telecommunications legislation or regulation would also seriously damage the industry. Mobile phones are the lifeblood of the vice trade through which all communication is channelled. Phone companies could be required to disconnect phone numbers if they had evidence they were being used to promote prostitution. Phone companies could be made responsible for taking reasonable steps to ensure individuals do not use their products to build lucrative criminal enterprises. It's clear from a glance at the numbers on the Internet which ones are advertising prostitutes and brothels.

There are, of course, dangers inherent in being ambivalent towards this criminal activity. The absence of a coherent policy to deal with all aspects of the vice industry has implications for society as a whole. It may be perceived as a less serious form of crime but such crime unchecked can lead to more serious organised crime involving violence, sexual assault, drug abuse and in some cases murder.

There are also the health implications. The dangers of spreading HIV and other sexually transmitted diseases (STDs) go with the territory. Prostitution is one factor along with an increase in sexual activity and unsafe sex practices, which has contributed to an annual 10 per cent increase in STDs in Ireland for the past two years. It is usually the women in vice who are blamed for this but who checks the health of the men who use prostitutes?

The clubs describe it as adult entertainment, titillation and harmless fun but there is also some evidence here of links between lap-dancing and prostitution. In October 2002 *Sunday World* reporters were offered lap-dancers as prostitutes at a Dublin club for €300 an hour. A video taken from the safe of another lap-dancing club in Dublin showed women having sex with the customers. The Gardaí couldn't prosecute as the pictures were over six months old so the offences were statute-barred. In brothel-keeping cases the investigation must be complete and a file submitted to the DPP within six months of the incident taking place — another questionable legislative condition. The Gardaí have closed down at least three lap-dancing clubs in Dublin.

The Dublin District Court also revoked the licence of one of city's plushest and most exclusive lap-dancing clubs in March 2003. Judge Michael Connellan found an illegal sex act had taken place at the Barclay Club in South William Street. When the Gardaí visited it, they found a man groping a woman and asked the manager if he was running a brothel. The club appealed the decision to the Circuit Court, but on Monday 28 April 2003 it was permanently put out of business. 'There was inadequate control of the dancing girls once in private sessions,' Judge Bryan McMahon said, 'I'm convinced that whatever was going on at this club was not the kind of dancing envisaged by the Public Dancing Act.'

A former Swedish lap-dancer told a conference in Dublin that lap-dancing clubs foster prostitution. Louise Eek was paid to dance but she made the real money selling her body. 'It is about men using money to exploit women for exploitation's sake,' she said. 'It's an industry created by men for other men.' The Government has now stopped issuing work permits to foreign women who want to come here to work as lap-dancers. Dr Pauline Conroy, a social policy analyst who conducted research on migrant workers for the Equality Authority, said that work permits should not be issued to support the sex industry.

But surely questions need to be asked about an industry whose fundamental business premise is based on sexually arousing and exciting males, most of whom have had a few drinks, while at the same time evicting and punishing them for acting on their natural impulses. Is it right that foreign women are brought into this country by an employer who controls their accommodation, work and the people they associate with? They live in a bubble whereby they are taken to and from work and have minders watching what they do in the houses they live in. In the Barclay Club the women were fined for 'fraternising' with the customers. In other words they were punished for meeting other people during one of the few opportunities they may have had to do so.

In April 2003, Gardaí set up an investigation into allegations of people-trafficking, prostitution and other criminal activity within the lap-dancing industry. Led by Assistant Commissioner Kevin Carty, 'Operation Quest' involved detectives from units all over the country and specialists from the National Bureau of Criminal Investigation, the Garda National Bureau of Immigration, the Criminal Assets Bureau and the Special Detective Unit which deals with subversive crime. A former officer commanding the Provisional IRA in Dublin, as well as members of dissident republican groups such as the Continuity IRA and ex-INLA men, were suspected of being involved in running lap-dancing clubs.

In the early hours of Friday 6 June, almost 300 Gardaí raided ten lap-dancing clubs in Dublin, Cork, Galway, Dundalk and Limerick. One-hundred-and-one people, most of them women, were detained. They came from Estonia, Latvia, Lithuania, Russia, Bulgaria, Mongolia, Liberia, the US, Canada and Britain. Seventy-one were found to be working illegally. A small quantity of drugs — cocaine and cannabis — was seized, along with financial records, documentation on the clubs and their employees, over €100,000 in cash and a shotgun.

Operation Quest has also highlighted the fact that there is a more sinister side of the prostitution business. It is already well established in Europe and is believed to be in its infancy here. Immigrant women, mainly from Eastern Europe, are trafficked, abducted, held captive, trapped and made to work as prostitutes in countries like Spain and Italy. There is no reason to believe this will not happen here. There is anecdotal evidence that it already is. Outreach workers are hearing stories from foreign women who say they've been trafficked here. Organised East European criminal gangs from countries like Russia, Albania and the Balkans are already beginning to emerge. Chinese triads already operate brothels here with Chinese prostitutes for Chinese people.

The Gardaí accept that trafficking in women for prostitution could become a serious problem here. They have been able to deal successfully with Irish brothel owners. But there are different attitudes to women and levels of violence associated with foreign criminals. With language, cultural and residency problems, it is an aspect of the criminal underworld which is far more difficult to penetrate. There is no doubt but that it will become more prominent in the future.

Prostitution is a lucrative and thriving area of criminal activity in this country. Enterprising criminals are still running the business but with the arrival of foreign operators the business is changing. This is clearly an area which will need to be watched closely. It requires further investigation. But as long as there is a market for prostitution in Ireland, the vice industry here will continue to thrive.